3D and 4D Cartography of Archaeological Stratigraphy

A case study at the Western Forum in Ostia Antica

Undine Lieberwirth

BAR INTERNATIONAL SERIES 3040 | 2021

BAR
PUBLISHING

Published in 2021 by
BAR Publishing, Oxford

BAR International Series 3040

3D and 4D Cartography of Archaeological Stratigraphy

ISBN 978 1 4073 5786 7 paperback
ISBN 978 1 4073 5787 4 e-format

DOI https://doi.org/10.30861/9781407357867

A catalogue record for this book is available from the British Library

COVER IMAGE *West Porticus of the Main Forum in Ostia Antica with 3D model of trench 1'. Photograph taken by the author, model created by the author*

BAR
PUBLISHING

BAR titles are available from:

BAR Publishing
122 Banbury Rd, Oxford, OX2 7BP, UK
EMAIL info@barpublishing.com
PHONE +44 (0)1865 310431
FAX +44 (0)1865 316916
www.barpublishing.com

Of Related Interest

Acknowledgements

This journey would not have been possible without the support of my family, professors and mentors, and friends. To my family, thank you for encouraging me in all of my pursuits and inspiring me to follow my dreams. I am especially grateful to my husband Dr. Holger Remde, who has supported me emotionally over all these years while I have tried the balancing act to bring family, career and research under one roof, and my son Karlson Fridtjof Lieberwirth for stimulating discussions about mathematical algebra.

The study would not have been possible without the funding and support by the Excellence Cluster Topoi (http:// www.topoi.org/), under the leadership and supervision of Prof. Dr. Michael Meyer, who supported the idea and has tirelessly accompanied the study throughout. I also thank the Excellence Cluster Topoi which supported Project A-III-6 financially. The project belonged to Excellence Cluster Topoi research area A which dealt with landscape archaeology in general and was affiliated with Subproject A-III which focused on methodological research in terms of landscape and fundamental research. Under the headline of Project A-III-6 several workshops, conferences and excavations were organised by myself including the 'Topoi Summer School 2009 at Hornsburg, Austria'. Many thanks for the inspiring cooperation of the excavation team under the supervision of the University of Vienna by Prof. Dr. Wolfgang Neubauer and Prof. Dr. Michael Doneus where we shared experiences and discussed workflows with digital excavation technology.

The latter was a kind of rehearsal for a digital excavation at *Ostia Antica*/Italy during the summer term 2011. The *Ostia Antica* excavation is described in detail in this monograph. The site served as a test field for the 'digital excavation', its data for the prototype development in the 'digital reconstruction'. This successful cooperation between the Excellence Cluster Topoi A-III-6 project and the BKO Berlin-Kent-Ostia Excavations under the auspices of the *Soprintendenza Archeologica di Ostia Antica* and with the help of 10 students from the seminar '*Lehrgrabung Ostia Antica – Topoi Summer School 2011*' enabled an excavation exactly to the requirements of the study (http:// ostiaforumproject.com). I thank, firstly, Prof. Dr. Stefan Schmid, who established the connection, Prof. Dr. Axel Gering, who was the archaeological excavation director at our site, and our students.

The idea of this study was to include also data from side subjects like geophysics. Hence, I deeply thank the Berliner geophysical company Eastern Atlas®. Without their innovative ideas and willing to experiment with new equipment, this study would not have been possible in this quality.

Similar thanks go to Dr. Philipp Hoelzmann, director of the Institute for Physical Geography, Free University Berlin, and his team for the pedological analysis.

I thank Dr. Markus Neteler and Dr. Sören Gebbert for encouraging discussions from the GRASS GIS community during the modelling and analysis phase of this study. My infinite gratitude goes to Dipl.-Math. Irmela Herzog. After 12 months with no progress, she provided the decisive hint as to why the VTK-data could not be displayed (see section 5.3.7 RQ iv).

The work and funding of the Excellence Cluster Topoi also gave me the opportunity to join regularly CAA conferences (https://ocs.caaconference.org) where I could meet and discuss my first results with the computer application and GIS community in archaeology – a worldwide network of computer 'nerds' in archaeology.

My final thanks goes to the person who initiated the idea, Prof. Dr. Andrew Bevan, who was my first teacher in 'GIS in archaeology' and laid the foundation for all of my subsequent research in this area.

I thank all the people who worked on this book and the editors for their innovative idea to publish videos instead of pictures.

I would especially like to thank Charles Lauder for the excellent proofreading and the Ernst-Reuter-Gesellschaft e.V. of the Free University Berlin of covering these costs. I thank the Managing Director of the 'British Archaeological Reports' and 'BAR Publishing', Birgit Thaller, for the admission of this book to the 'BAR International Series'. The supervision by Jacqueline Senior, Ruth Fisher and Lisa Eaton on the part of the publisher was extremely professional.

Contents

List of Figures

List of Tables

Foreword

This volume shows the digital reconstruction of an archaeological site as a solid 3D model for further spatial analysis. It represents my PhD thesis which has been a research work of the past 8 years. It is based on former studies of mine which have been revived by the scientific research project 'Methodological Basic Research in Archaeoinformatics: Is archaeological stratigraphy measurable?' – a project funded and supported by the Excellence Cluster Topoi, Free University Berlin from 2009 to 2012. The aim of this project was the improvement and further development of solid 3D GIS models of archaeological stratigraphy based on my masters thesis from 2007 with a focus on spatial analysis.

After first presenting of the model to the archaeological GIS communities (Lieberwirth, 2008a), I was encouraged to dive deeper into this topic. The model had the potential to solve a general problem of archaeological documentation: the dilemma between the excavation of solid 3D objects and their documentation in 2D or 2.5D.

Archaeologists always have to cope with different documentation media during excavations to bring all acquired information together into one system. Furthermore, the 3D site often has to be squeezed into a 2D documentation space. In general, a complete 3D reconstruction exists only in the mind of the researcher.

This work is an attempt to overcome this dilemma by converting the researcher's mental map into a digital one.

Because of general advances in digital technology it is now possible, in comparison to 2007, to develop complex digital models from different data types in high resolution in one solid 3D system. Hence, I thought it might be the right time to start a proof-of-concept study with real excavation data and new technologies.

In comparison to the first model, made of 50-year-old excavation paper drawings, the first aim of this study was to find an efficient workflow to generate a complete digital 3D documentation of an excavation site for the subsequent reconstruction. Secondly, to develop a digital 3D model incorporating all acquired data into a GIS environment for further spatial analysis. Furthermore, the new workflow should reduce documentation time and post-processing working steps while maintaining high precision.

Fortunately, the project was equipped with state-of-the-art measurement hardware. And we had the opportunity to use high-performance computer workstations for post-processing, model building and analysis at the project's GIS laboratory.

The main target group for this application is archaeologists but there might be other disciplines like geography, geology, hydrology, climatology, meteorology and cartography that are working with 3D data. The list of uses and users is virtually endless as long as their data have a 3D or geographic reference.

This work has its focuses on digital 3D solids, which, in addition to their 2.5D (draped) surface, also provide full-body inside (volume) information which is best known from medicine MRI (Magnetic Resonance Imaging). In comparison to them, archaeological data have geographic reference. Hence, these models can be called solid 3D volume maps.

In this thesis, I show a way how 3D volume maps can be created, visualised and analysed in an interactive 3D environment out of archaeological, geophysical and pedological data simultaneously.

1

Introduction

This work is an attempt to develop an interactive 3D volume map of an archaeological excavation site in a georeferenced 3D space.

The aim is to narrow the gap between two-dimensional representation and three-dimensional measured values in space. Digital 3D volume maps connect digital 3D models with the measurable, cartographic space and thus achieve an enormous boost towards reality. Besides the representation of 3D objects in 3D space, they allow an insight into 3D volume structures like archaeological layers or deposits. Hence, compact information above and below the Earth's surface becomes visible and measurable and can be crosslinked and analysed together. Furthermore, the resulting 3D volume maps can fill the empty space between measured information with continuous probability values in space. Archaeologists thus can be provided with an epistemic tool for better understanding the interactions and relationships of objects in a geodetic 3D spatio-temporal environment.

The study focuses on archaeological stratigraphy. It tries to overcome the so-called 'intra-site GIS-crisis' (Merlo 2016, p. 2) by applying FOSS 3D GIS-modelling and analysis on a micro-scale. Taking into consideration, publications about similar applications in archaeology over the past 10 years, many discussions in this field have occurred (Merlo 2004) but nothing of this kind has been published between my last publication on this topic (2008a) and Merlo's dissertation (2016). Case studies of 'true' (geodetic) 3D mapping from Nigro (2002), Green (2003), Bezzi et al. (2006) and Katsianis (2008), where a full 3D volume object within a 3D coordinate system is created, are discussed in my master's thesis (Lieberwirth 2008b).

Reasons for the 'crisis' might lie in:

– a still small GIS community in 'Digital Archaeology' (DA) which might be deterred from using the non-straightforward application,
– high-performance demands of computer's memory space and graphics cards for solid 3D volumes,
– a focus on large-scale landscape analysis in archaeology, and
– the introduction of 'Virtual Reality' (VR) in archaeology with a focus on architecture in 3D space (Reindel et al., 2016).

The first and second obstacles will be resolved on their own due to general technical developments. The third might be a trend that can change quickly, especially considering the technical advances in the documentation of archaeological excavations. 'Digital excavation' techniques have been improved worldwide not only because high-precision documentation techniques are more available in general but also because of low-price documentation software specially tailored for archaeology (e.g. ArchäoCAD®, TachyCAD Archaeology®).

This study takes up the technical level of my prototype from 2008 (fig. 1.4) for further improvements and a practical test.

The prototype was built from 50-year-old excavation paper drawings of plans and sections of a local (not geodetic) excavation coordinate system. The model can represent solid spatio-temporal phenomena, e.g. the sequences of layer deposition. Archaeological stratigraphy and architecture are represented as voxel geometry volumes which can be clipped in any direction to create digital sections and plans at any place (horizontal, vertical, diagonal). By switching the volumes and layers on and off, a time series of deposition sequences can be animated. Vector, raster and voxel geometry can be depicted at the same time. All vector data can be classified and labelled according to their attributes, e.g. layer number or dating. Raster data can be displayed either with full-scale information or by adjusting thresholds for continuous values (Lieberwirth, 2008a, 2008b).

In contrast to the prototype, this work tries to improve the model in three main parts:

– the model should become a true 3D map by fulfilling all requirements of a cartographic representation (no local coordinate system = research question RQ i),
– the model should be generated from acquired digital excavation data (RQ ii) and
– the 3D environment should provide the same spatio-temporal analysis options as in common 2D GIS (Conolly & Lake, 2006, chap. 8) (RQ iii).

The result should be an analytical 3D volume map in a FOSS GIS-environment. FOSS is chosen to enable further applications and developments of the software in this field.

To solve this task, a conceptual design and operational framework has been developed to serve as the theoretical scope for implementing the working hypotheses concerning data acquisition (chap. 2) and model building (chap. 3).

1.1 3D cartography in archaeology

Cartography deals with areas on the Earth's surface which are described with exact position information (x and y coordinates). Already in the 1970s it became obvious that the definition has to be extended not only contextually but also dimensionally:

> *'The term Cartography is the art, science, and technology of making maps, together with their study as scientific documents and works of art.' (Meynen, 1984). 'In this context, we may regard all types of maps including all plans, charts, and sections, three-dimensional models and globes representing the earth or any celestial body at any scale.' (ICA, 1992).*

This definition includes 2.5D surface maps where the third dimension is expressed via attribute as well as 'true' 3D volume maps. In contrast to 2.5D, 3D maps are represented in 3D coordinate systems with x, y, z-axes which frees up the attribute for other factual information, e.g. non-spatial information like geochemical values or time (Merlo, 2016, p. 12 fig. 2.1.). Technically, an interpolation of these attribute values in 3D space results in a raster volume. As long as such a volume fulfils all requirements of a geographic map, the result can be sorted into the category of 3D cartography (fig. 1.1).

In the context of this work, 3D cartography is meant to model archaeological stratigraphy, deposits, finds and features in a 3D geodetic environment. Since these objects have a three-dimensional volume in reality they are best described as digital volumes in 3D space.

The term '3D map' is mainly used in the context of historical city landscapes and architecture (Picolli, 2018; Reindel et al., 2016). It has often a reference to real geographic positions, e.g. Google Earth© (Google, 2021). However, due to the missing height-axis the third dimension is not measurable in these maps and hence

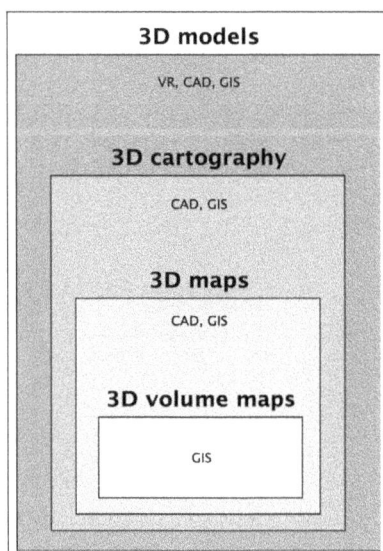

Figure 1.1. Venn diagram of applied DA *termini* in this study.

cannot be considered in analysis. From a technical point of view, these models are reconstructions in 3D space. They are hollow objects made of meshes with exact location and a height expressed as attribute placed onto a 2.5D elevation map. The 3D space between and inside these objects is 'empty'. Filling this 'empty' space with information results in a solid volume above or underneath a continuous elevation surface. As long as such a volume has geodetic coordinates, one can call it a 3D volume map (fig. 1.1).

The most common digital 3D systems in archaeology are CAD-programs and GIS. The first is mainly used for technical vector drawings and drafting in local 2D and 3D coordinate systems. Initially, it was designed for object drawing, replacing technical drawing boards. Recent applications in landscape architecture and urban planning (Akahoshi et al., 2020; Kaden et al., 2020) require the incorporation of geodetic coordinate systems and even limited raster representation (AutoCAD Civil 3D® 2019), but its main emphasis still rests on visualisation and measurement.

In contrast, the focus of GIS is on geodetic coordinate systems with raster calculation, surface visualisation and spatial analysis. Although GIS can also cope with vectors, its main difference to CAD is its analysis function which can combine both raster and vector geometry with geospatial database information. Some can visualise 2.5D raster surfaces by incorporating elevation information in a pseudo 3D space, e.g. ArcGIS 3D Analyst® 2018 and QGIS© 3D Pointscene 2018. At the moment, the only FOSS GIS which provides a complete 3D coordinate system with x, y, z – axes is GRASS 2018a. Therefore, this software is chosen for the modelling and analysis in this study. Further supportive arguments are:

– it belongs to the FOSS community and therefore offers the possibility of repetition, further development and improvement,
– it can handle large data sets (GRASS, 2018a) and
– it can calculate solid volumes as 3D raster cells (voxel-geometry (GRASS, 2018b; Lieberwirth, 2008a, p. 80–81)) in different ways.

Why do archaeologists create maps? *'Maps are graphic representations that facilitate a spatial understanding of things, concepts, conditions, processes, or events in the human world.'* (Harley & Woodward, 1987, p. xvi). A map creates a spatial link between an archaeological structure and its environment by the use of spatial landmarks. This is even true for sketches which were historically the first steps of map creation (e.g. fig. 2.3). The scientific work of an archaeologist as excavator depends on spatial facts explored at archaeological excavations sites or surveys. These facts are the so-called 'first source data' (Conolly & Lake, 2006, p. 61) which has not been altered, edited or undergone a creative filtering or interpretation like written sources or iconography. Hence, archaeologists have used maps to place these archaeological facts as structures in a wider spatial context.

Simultaneously with the development of measurement technology, archaeological equipment has been developed too and is nowadays able to create technical CAD-maps with an accuracy of within a millimetre. CAD-software for documentation is nowadays common on excavation sites worldwide. A major reason for its popularity is its true 3D coordinate environment. Excavators can thus easily discover errors and draw conclusions by switching between various perspectives (from topview to section view and vice versa). CAD describes the real world by using mathematics (vector geometry and linear algebra). With three simple geometric formats (point, line, polygon) former paper-based technical drawings are upgraded by providing:

- interactive access to different kinds of views,
- interactive scaling (zoom in and out),
- precise measurement in true 3D space of the first source data,
- connected attribute information, e.g. via CAD plug-in MonuMap® and TachyCAD Archaeology® or ArchäoCAD®,
- orthophotos, e.g. via CAD plug-in PhoToPlan® and with ArchäoCAD® and
- 3D point cloud objects, e.g. via CAD plug-in PointSense® (PointSense, 2015) or ArchäoCAD®.

The latter can be converted into a continuous mesh surface.

CAD-users can thus get a 3D model of all acquired excavation information. CAD-plans are hence a good basis for 3D modelling in a VR environment. The main application of CAD in archaeology, however, is the creation of technical sections and plans as digital advancement for paper drawings.

To create a map out of these technical drawings is to use a GIS. The interface between both programs and common exchange formats (e.g. via DXF or SHP via TachyCAD®) make a perfect symbiosis. Furthermore GIS offers:

- the combination of maps and drawings from different excavation campaigns in the same area and in a geodetic coordinate system,
- the combination of old paper drawings and modern photographs as long as they have the same coordinates,
- the combination of maps and information from side subjects like environmental science, hydrology, geology etc. and
- the combination of numeric, non-numeric attributes and database content with spatial archaeological information (e.g. non-spatial text descriptions usually handwritten in an excavation notebook).

An additional value is the common GIS-analysis of all data combined together in one system.

Cartography in archaeology can be summarised as the creation of a georeferenced map with archaeological content. Georeferencing in this context means that maps contain position coordinates of a known local, national or world coordinate system. Additional to the archaeological

content, these maps are enriched with information from other areas like topography to bring the main topic into a spatial and environmental context. These thematic maps help to understand the wider spatial context of the archaeological structures. In Landscape Archaeology, which deals with the environment around past societies, several spatial analysis methods have been established, e.g. pattern detection (Conolly & Lake, 2006), least-cost path reconstructions (Herzog & Yépez, 2015) and network mapping (Verhagen, 2017) which work fine on large scales (inter-site analysis). In contrast, intra-site analysis works on an excavation scale and therefore addresses other questions (Bevan & Lake, 2013; Blankholm, 1991; Hietala & Larson, 1984; Konsa, 2013). Nevertheless, intra-site analysis can use the same digital environment (GIS) with the same spatial analysis tools (based on descriptive and spatial exploratory analysis) in order to generate fully functional interactive 'archaeological excavation maps' in 2D, 2.5D and 3D.

1.1.1 GIS & space in archaeology

Space in archaeology has always been described with the tools the researcher has at hand. Before the introduction of GIS, archaeologists used cartography or even artificial pictures to demonstrate the spatial relationships of features. Regardless of which method is applied, studying space in archaeology first requires a concept of space.

Archaeologists generally refer to two concepts in this regard (Conolly & Lake, 2006, p. 5).

The first concept deals with measurable information, following the concept of absolute space which requires units of measurement to describe space and was first mentioned by the a Greek mathematician Euclid. Known as Euclid's theorem, it is a basic concept for measurements in 2D and 3D space that remains in use today. The subject was further developed by atomist philosophers in antiquity. Finally, in the seventeenth century, Descartes (1637, p. 297–413) invented the Cartesian coordinate system based on Ptolemy's idea of a grid spanning the globe. This scheme led to the development of accurate 2D and 3D projection systems that remain the basis of cartography today. Finally, Newton's laws of motion, first described in his *Philosophiae Naturalis Principia Mathematica* (Newton, 1687), require an absolute and measurable space as a container for objects within space and time, because – as Newton sees it – objects cannot exist without a spatial relation (an idea that might have its origins in the Greek natural philosophers). This concept is still in use in cartography but not in physics where it was displaced by Einstein's general theory of relativity (Einstein, 1917).

The second concept of relative space (and time) deals with the description of data from a topological perspective. It focuses on the relationships of entities within space, ideas like 'nearby', 'in the direction of', 'between' or 'similar', by using a spatial reference that may differ from a measurable coordinate like travel costs (Barceló & Pallarés, 1998). The concept has been described by philosophers and physicists starting with Galilei, who mentioned a spatial reference or scope for describing the location and movement of objects (Galilei, 1632). Einstein's general theory of relativity continues to provide the basis for describing relative locations (where objects and entities are described according to their spatial relationship to one another).

In addition to their use in GIS, relative space concepts in archaeology are also implemented in the Harris Matrix system (Harris, 1989), for example where the vertical sequence of stratigraphical layers is arranged spatially relative to one another (i.e. 'above', 'underneath') while supporting the temporal interpretation ('simultaneously', 'older', 'younger' etc.).

The two concepts of space are universally applicable in archaeology regardless of periods and places. They are applied in 2D sketches (Nibby, 1819), maps (2.2) and GIS.

An archaeological model tries to reconstruct this sensory environment to test hypotheses of different cognitive perceptions. The challenge of the model is to incorporate all relevant information (Lock, 2003, p. 7 fig. 1.1). But what kind of information is relevant? How do we deal with the incomplete, fuzzy, and subjectively perceived information that is typical of archaeological data?

Perceptions can be distinguished using absolute locations (simply measuring distance and direction) or relative spatial relationships. These scopes can be either spatially explicit where absolute spatial location is essential or implicit, where it is not). Implicit space requires a reference, such as the description of a spatial relationship, whereas explicit implies an exact location. Dealing with space as an attribute is a much more flexible concept for model-building. Relationships can be structured according to their connections, such as a 'one-to-one relationship' or a 'one-to-many relationship' (Stanilov, 2012, p. 255). These relations can be quantitative or qualitative (Gatrell, 1983, chap. 2). The implicit concept is congruent with database design, where both types of relationships can be modelled with identifiers as connectors. This explains why the incorporation of the theoretical concept into a geodatabase is implemented in Geographic Information Systems (Parker et al., 2003). Furthermore, we can choose between isotropic (directional independency) and anisotropic (directional dependency) approaches in GIS. These are mainly incorporated and used in such procedures as cost-surface analysis (Conolly & Lake, 2006, p. 215), where archaeologists can analyse economic routes from A to B or investigate easily accessible areas around a central point. Perceptions are generally scale-dependent. The impression of an area or environment might differ strongly with the change of scale: it matters greatly if an area is perceived either from a bird's-eye view or on foot, for example, or by a static watchman or a dynamic horseman, since the scale for the latter might change over time.

The perspective of a researcher working with cartographic material might give a useful overview, but this is generally not the way that past societies viewed their environments. The representation of scale must be acknowledged from two perspectives: the past community's view and the analyst's view. The applied analysis should therefore be executed as a multi-scale analysis. The applied scale also has an impact on the resolution of the model (its level of detail), however, and should therefore be acknowledged during the model-building process (Romanowska, 2015, p. 10 fig. 2). The next steps require a transformation of the scope descriptors into the language of the GIS-system to obtain an analytical unit. As long as such descriptors have a location and can be expressed quantitatively, they can be incorporated into GIS.

The purpose of Geographic Information Systems for archaeology is to capture, store, compute, analyse, and present spatial data and their relationships. These functions can be assembled in five processes: data acquisition, spatial data management, database management, data visualization, and spatial analysis (Conolly & Lake, 2006, p. 11). Depending on the intended use, the result can be a map, model, table, or statistical value. GIS needs location information to describe the objects under examination, as well as an attribute for those objects. For the graphical description, GIS uses two data formats: the vector format and the raster format. The first works based on analytical geometry to describe objects like points, lines, and polygons in a defined space. The raster format is used for continuous data (a detailed description of GIS-data models can be found in any GIS-handbook). The voxel format used in this study can be understood as an extended raster in the third dimension by keeping the same properties. The first type can be attached with attributes from a table or a database system. This connection – the combination of spatial information with attributes, called a geodatabase – is what makes GIS so powerful. Attributes without an explicit location, on the other hand, can be depicted with the second format type, the raster format. This format type can hold only one attribute spread over a defined, square-shaped space (Conolly & Lake, 2006, chap. 2.4.2). The size of the square, pixel or voxel can vary between the layers, which makes it possible to adjust the resolution of the model according to the background knowledge and level of detail one would like to reach. The latter is more of a conceptual than a technical issue. From a technical point of view, there is no limitation on detail (a topic that refers to fractal geometry, Mandelbrot 1982, chap. II). Nevertheless, what kind of detail is necessary depends on the concept and research question and gives the user opportunities for modelling fuzzy information where location is only described as a spatial reference. Both types (raster and vector formats) consist of a unique location within a defined space so they can provide absolute distances according to either Euclidean geometry or surface distances and topological information. With these possibilities at hand, archaeological GIS users are able to create a digital model of the real world (Conolly & Lake, 2006, p. 4). Furthermore, three data formats allow the flexible application of the two concepts of space (1.1). GIS might not be a high-end technology from a technical perspective but it gives the archaeologist opportunities to create a meaningful, analysable model of an archaeological site (Wheatley, 2004, p. 3).

1.1.2 3D models in 3D space

According to Stachowiak, a model is characterized by at least three features:

1. *A model is always a model of something – a reflection or representation of a natural or an artificial original, and this original itself can be a model in turn.*
2. *A model generally does not capture all the attributes of the original, but only those that appear relevant to the model creator or model user.*
3. *Models are not clearly assigned to their originals. They fulfil their replacement function*
   a) *for certain subjects (for whom),*
   b) *within certain time intervals (when) and*
   c) *they are restricted to certain mental or actual operations (for what).* (Stachowiak, 1973, p. 131–133).

The best case scenario would be that the extension, realm, distortion and quality of a model is outlined. The crucial point in archaeological model building is its verification. Archaeological documentation is based on a 'macroscopic anatomy' of the excavated objects. In other words, we can only document what we see. This is also described as 'human conceptualisation of reality' (Peuquet, 1984, p. 67). However, optical conditions change even during one day. What we have seen in the morning might have vanished by the afternoon. Hence, there will always be an open question as to whether everything vital was seen, recognised, identified and finally documented. Furthermore, we never know how much we missed.

Models are a simplification of the real world (Orton, 1980) and always imperfect (Ervin & Hasbrouck, 2001, p. 4). So why model if we never meet reality?

The creation of a model gives us the opportunity to focus on certain aspects of a complex system. An abstraction can make complex relationships more coherent. Models are the basis for further analysis in mathematics, statistics (Orton, 1980), diagrammatic reasoning, etc. (Romanowska, 2015, p. 27). In other words, a model can act as a link between theory and the real world (Orton, 2000).

The first step in working with GIS is to create a model, a process through which real-world information is transformed into a digital, quantitative GIS-environment. This quantification of archaeological facts in general is not new. Since the beginning of archaeology, tables and catalogues have been used to structure and categorize high amounts of data (Petrie 1899, Foucault 1966, p. 143). These structures now form the basis for databases and further

analysis (Orton, 1980). Today GIS offers the opportunity to bring together all spatial, quantified information in one system with the option of further analysis even in 3D cartography.

As in statistics, one of the first steps during the conceptual phase (Romanowska, 2015, p. 10 fig. 2 'the model development sequence, step 3') is to make decisions about the selection of data that will be used for model-building. The model ultimately represents the sample population. It is the general pool of data for further analysis. Hence, what kind of data we choose and how we depict them in GIS is a sensitive point in GIS-analysis because all further work refers back to this data selection.

In archaeology, the very first selection of data is made during excavation, when one decides what kind of data is to be documented and in what resolution. The choices made here depend on archaeological expertise, applied measurement methods, and survey devices. This data pool should be used for a second selection that considers the research question and the suitability of the data to be included into the GIS-system. Transformation and calculation processes for model-building might incorporate further data transformation, smoothing, oversimplification or alteration of the legacy data by interpolation or extrapolation algorithms to generate probability values at places where no legacy data exist. The vectorization of raster data sets (like photographs or scanned excavation plans) can create precise borders that were originally fuzzy and vice versa. Since the aim of the process is to create a meaningful model, however, these processes might be acknowledged as formation processes for obtaining a suitable basis for analysis, experiments, and scenarios. As Lock points out, creating a model is often the only way of dealing with archaeological data that have been subjected to similar site formation processes (Lock, 2003, p. 147).

In each case, the excavated archaeological material must be transformed into a document readable by either human or machine. By this point decisions have already been made about the clearness of borders, middle points of objects, transition areas, etc. As mentioned above, it is possible to incorporate these interpretations in the GIS because the transformation has been already done in the scientist's mind. The potential of GIS means that it can combine different information in one system to facilitate new views of the data. This perspective may be more complex than that at the excavation or survey itself. The changed perception begins at the moment of data collection, which is already selective.

How accurate is the model? The application of statistical and quantitative methods to archaeology proved reliable even before the introduction of GIS (Baxter 2003, Orton 2000). If the aforementioned considerations about statistical bias are kept in mind, GIS remains a useful analysis tool and makes it possible to use statistical verification methods, significance testing, and hypothesis testing.

Verification is a guarantee of quality. This step comes right after the creation of the model and has to be included in the methodological circle (Romanowska 2015, p. 10 fig. 2, Breitenecker et al. 2015, Brughmans et al. 2014, p. 445).

Most common statistical verification methods nowadays comprise an integral part of certain types of GIS-software packages like significance testing of parameters with parametric or non-parametric tests for large or small sample sizes, robustness tests performed on models using hypothesis testing such as the chi-square test and the *Mann-Whitney U test*, and inferential statistics for investigating the relationship between two or more variables (Hodder 1986, p. 14, Lock 2003, p. 2,118,125 infobox 5, Lieberwirth et al. 2015).

But how do we verify an incomplete model? One possible solution might come from other subjects and applications in archaeology which deal with discrepancies by keeping models as simple and as abstract as possible and focusing only on certain aspects (Brughmans et al. 2014, p. 446, Romanowska 2015, p. 25, Lock 2003, p. 148). If a model theory can be tested under controlled conditions, there are more facts than hypotheses (Heppenstall et al., 2012, p. 740).

Translated into a more abstract model of mathematical set theory, where M_r represents the summary of all real world data (M stands for amount, r for reality) and M_m represents the amount of modelled data (m stands for model, a subset of all real data), one could say:

$$M_r = \{A \subseteq M_r, B \subseteq M_r, C \subseteq M_r, D \subseteq M_r, \infty \subseteq M_r,$$

$$E = M_r \subseteq M_m\}, E > 0 \qquad (1.1)$$

where

$$M_m = \{A \subseteq M_r, B \subseteq M_r, C \subseteq M_r, D \subseteq M_r\} \qquad (1.2)$$

and

$$M_m = M_r \setminus E = \{x \mid x \in M_r \wedge x \notin E\}$$

see fig. 1.2.

The amount of the unknown E, the missing information of a model M_m, will never be *zero* but we can try to come as close as possible. This exactly is the aim of this study – to minimise E with the hybrid approach of combining information from different subjects to model the same object.

The conceptual design considers three perspectives:

– a content perspective,
– an external design requirements perspective and
– a structural perspective.

In contrast to Merlo (2016, p. 70 fig. 5.1) the content perspective in this study aims to acquire as much data as possible, disregarding the current research question. The idea behind this is on, one hand, to minimise E, while

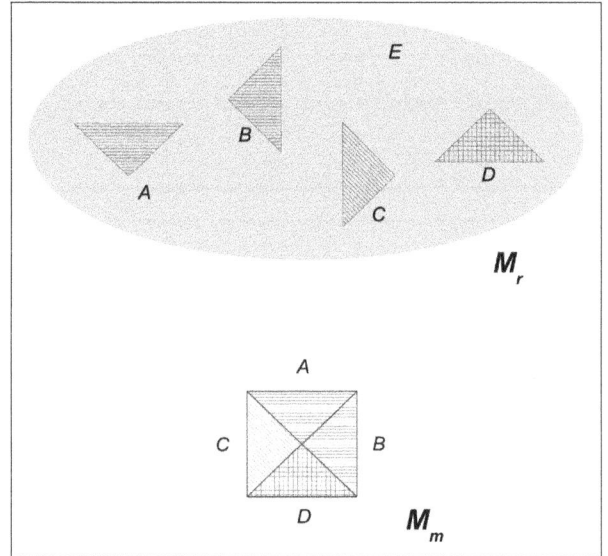

Figure 1.2. Graphical representation of formulas 1.1 and 1.2.

on the other hand to be aware of as much information as possible from a process which can never be repeated. The challenge in modelling is to find an optimal way to transcribe the perceived and measured information into something readable and storable.

Filter 1, displayed by A, B, C, D in the formula (fig. 1.2), represents the process of documenting at a site. With different measurement techniques and sensors it is possible to reduce the unknown amount of E within the total amount of M_r.

In the modelling process, the second step (filter 2) one has to find an ideal reconstruction environment that will not minimise the already reduced amount of M_m left after the first operation (fig. 1.3).

The third step includes the structural perspective. Its aim is to find an optimal environment for managing, storing and analysing the model's information to produce the best possible harvest from the legacy data. The challenge here is to find the most suitable model from all the acquired data relevant to the analysis (Stachowiak, 1973, category 2).

A solution can be found by the computational perspective which takes into account these external design requirements. This approach can be seen as a combination of the two perspectives described above.

Besides concrete and mathematical models, computational models form a separate class of models for simulations. Weisberg (2013) describes the computational environment like a laboratory, a sterilised space that helps to focus on the object of interest.

This perspective includes already the acceptance of simplification which has been discussed in recent studies as one of the most feasible solution for simulating complex societies. According to Stachowiak's category 3 (1973), Romanowska (2015) and Deng (2001), this concept of

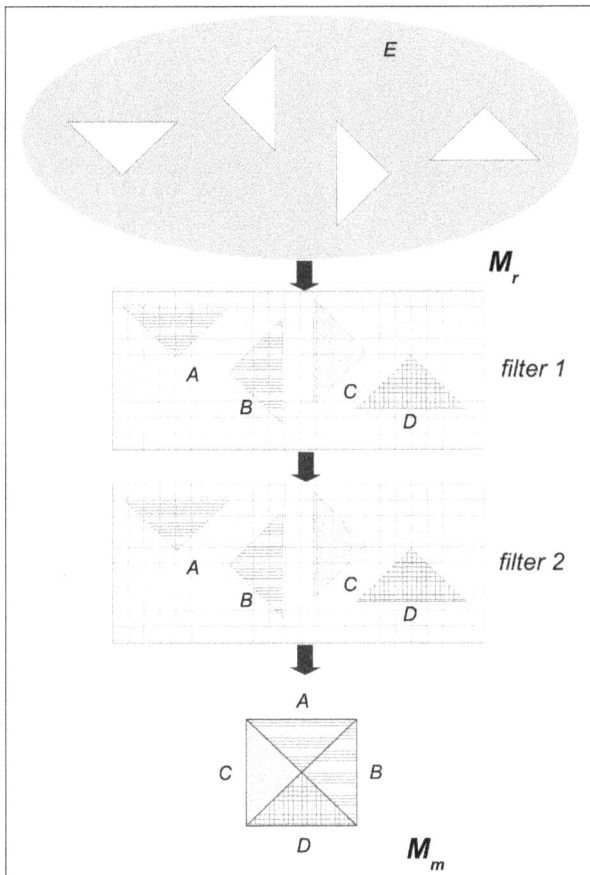

Figure 1.3. Graphical representation of formulas 1.1 and 1.2 with filters.

'constraint data models' helps to focus on certain aspects better than trying the impossible task of creating a second real world (Kowarik et al., 2015).

Archaeological 3D models (fig. 1.1) have their origins either in CAD with a defined coordinate system or in a graphical VR environment with a local (inherent in the system) coordinate system (Landeschi et al. 2015, Paliou 2013, fig. 5.6b, Soler et al. 2017). All three systems, GIS, CAD and VR, have their similarities and overlaps but can be distinguished on the basis of their priorities:

– spatial analysis for GIS,
– focus on measurement in CAD and
– reconstruction in VR.

According to the aims of this study, the resulting 3D model has to be available for spatial intra-site analysis. Hence, GIS as the 'system of choice' seems to be the best environment for the task in this study.

The most complex 3D format of a 3D model in a digital 3D space is the 3D volume map – 'the format of choice' for this study. It fulfils all requirements of a 3D model, can be displayed as VR but can be also be calculated in GIS (1.1). The main distinctions between VR and GIS models are:

– VR does not necessarily have a reference to a geographic location,

– VR cannot handle solid volume information underneath a 2.5D map for a quantified exploration and
– only GIS has (so far) the possibility of spatial analysis.

CAD environments are, according to their functionality, much closer to GIS than VR. The two main distinctions between CAD- and GIS-models are:

– CAD cannot handle the solid volume information and
– CAD has limited spatial analysis functionality.

To summarise, a 3D GIS-volume map can be a VR model in a 3D space (1.1) but a 3D VR model cannot be a 3D map because it might lack geographic information. A CAD-system cannot (yet) depict a 3D GIS-volume map (fig. 1.1).

All three 3D models systems, GIS, CAD and VR, are acting in 3D space and are a simplified reflection of reality. CAD and VR follow the concept of a so-called 'spaghetti model' (wire-frame model) (Laurini & Thompson, 1992, p. 399–425). GIS, on the other hand, can also include the concept of the 'pizza model' (concept for areas and volumes) (Laurini & Thompson, 1992, p. 426–443). Since this study focuses on archaeological excavation models, simplification is not the first aim of archaeological modelling here – rather the opposite. In general, an archaeological record is rare and therefore precious to archaeologists who try to collect and document as much as they can, because after the excavation the whole structure is vanished and the process cannot be repeated. The scientific model building in this study follows a similar strategy best described as the concept of 'constraint data modelling' (Deng & Revesz, 2001). At first, a model will be built from all available information of the site. Only in a second step will the model be reduced according to the research question under analysis. The best situation for this deliberate model reduction would be to know what and how much is left out.

1.2 Conceptual design & operational framework

The prototype from my master's thesis (2008, fig. 1.4) serves as a starting point for further development.

In contrast to the previous model, the result of this study should be further developed towards an interactive, archaeological, digital 3D volume map (RQ iv). To meet this goal, a conceptional design has been developed and implemented into the operational framework of this study.

From a methodological standpoint, the three main working steps of data acquisition (excavation), data modelling and data analysis have to be carried out (fig. 1.5). However, one must bear in mind that the requirements of the analysis software influence the previous working steps in terms of data format, respectively hardware and software. Therefore, the conceptual design process must follow the working step process vice versa.

In order to approach the research aims of this study, demonstrations in section 1.1 show what kind of concepts

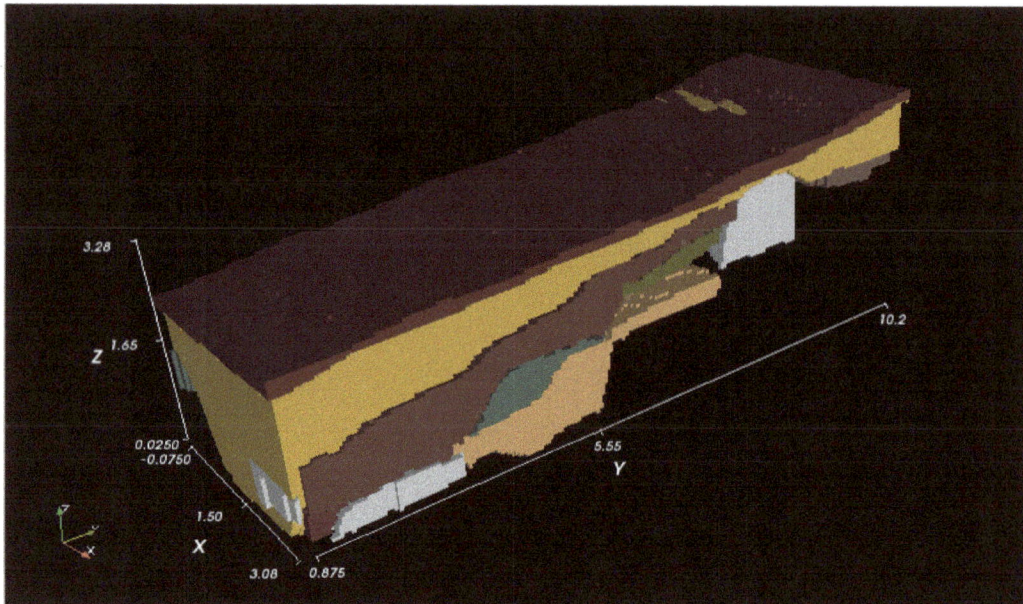

Figure 1.4. Prototype, reconstruction of excavation trench ix at the site of Akroterion at Kastri in Kythera/Greece (Reproduced of U. Lieberwirth, 2008a, fig. 14).

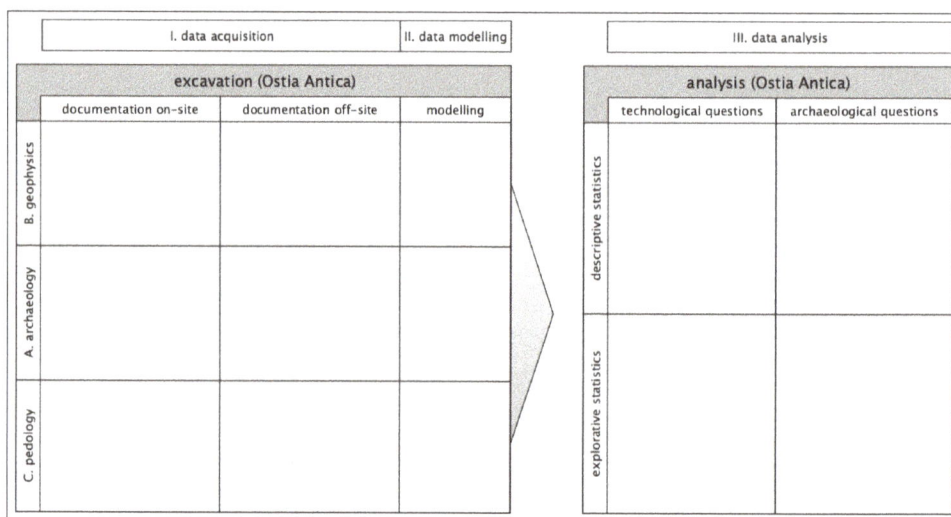

Figure 1.5. Process chain of conceptual design.

might be most suitable. It is preferable to minimise platform and system changes in order to save time and money and to avoid data exchange errors (RQ v). Finally, the needs and requirements of the platform will specify the operational framework for the data documentation. The detailed description of the methodological concept of this study is outlined in subsections 1.2.1, 1.2.2, 1.2.3.

Concerning the research aims, which include low costs and open code for the applied software, the only Free and Open Source Software (FOSS) which can calculate and manage 3D volumes in a true 3D coordinate system is GRASS. It was used successfully to develop the prototype (fig. 1.4), and, with no alternative software available, is ideal for this study. Additionally, this software meets the methodological requirements.

The concept of this study is to overcome the discrepancy between reality and model by minimising E (fig. 1.2).

One part of the solution was to integrate 3D geophysical measurements. Geophysics is generally used before an excavation starts in order to select the most interesting archaeological spots (visible as geophysical anomalies) as a kind of prediction. However, the results can also serve as a verification system in the post-excavation process.

Hitherto, geophysical results are used as two-dimensional pictures. They generally come as georeferenced images, so-called 'time slices' of different depths. GPR wavelengths are recorded in 3D space (Biel & Klonk, 1994, chap. 27.1.8) and therefore are available for the whole excavation trench volume. Hence, in this study the question arose: why not reconstruct this record completely as a 3D volume structure?

The same method could be applied by using geochemical information from an archaeological trench. Soil samples are usually taken on top of an archaeological stratum, e.g.

to differentiate working and living zones inside a building or area (Biel and Klonk 1994, chap. 7.1, Brandt et al. 1992, Lloyd and Atkinson 2004, Salisbury 2013). We took soil samples of the whole trench as punctual information, disregarding strata borders. In this study, I wanted to go a step further and extend these distribution maps into the third dimension. The aim were to visualise geochemical volumes in order to find new strata (from a geochemical perspective), to confirm archaeological layer borders in 3D and finally to minimize *E*.

1.2.1 Data analysis – a methodological & archaeological approach

GRASS, the chosen modelling software, calculates solid volumes inside a geodetic 3D coordinate system. Alternative FOSS GIS-software programs like QGIS (2018) and gvSIG (2018) are currently only able to deal with 2.5D raster surfaces and vector data. The GRASS GUI (graphical user interface) accelerates the calculation process, which is one reason for the flexible management of large data sets like 3D point clouds, the main format in this study. This effect is supported by the software's module structure with, for example, a separate viewer window which can be switched off during RAM-consuming processes for calculating volumes. The same is true for the 3D analysis processes. They were executed either in GRASS or via FOSS ParaView© (2016). The latter is a scientific graphical viewer enriched with analysis functions and filters in 3D. It is recommended by the GRASS community when it comes to its visualisation limits. As well the viewer offers several 3D analysis tools and filters (Ayachit 2018, chap. 3–6, Lieberwirth 2008a).

From an archaeological perspective, this study aims to incorporate all documented information (including the geophysical and geochemical) from the excavation site into GRASS, respectively, ParaView© for analysing. The study tries to prove that an accurate 3D model of an archaeological excavation site cannot only include all data but can also be used as a basis for spatial 3D analysis. With the combination of different parameters and the application of statistical tools it should be possible to calculate and export new data out of the imported. The aim is to create a digital 3D GIS-model of the excavation trench. It should not only visualise surfaces, features and finds but also archaeological stratigraphy as solid 3D volume objects (RQ vi).

From an archaeological point-of-view, the following questions should be answered by this study (RQ vii):

- Is it possible to extract archaeological stratigraphical borders out of the geophysical record?
- Is it possible to extract archaeological stratigraphical borders out of laser scan RGB-values?
- Is it possible to extract archaeological stratigraphical borders out of the geochemical (pedological) record?
- Are the 3D borders of archaeological strata, geophysical strata and geochemical strata congruent?

- Are the concentration centres of archaeological, geophysical and geochemical anomalies and their statistical outliers congruent?

Finally, with the combination of data from these three subjects (geophysics, pedology and archaeology) the following questions arise:

- Can we recognise the same structures with different methods?
- Can different methods act as verification for each other? and
- Does this mean we can get reasonable results with just one method?

From a methodological point-of-view, the analysis of the 3D volume model should enable the user to (RQ viii) include all quantified information and combine them to thematic multi-scale 3D maps, which:

- can be statistically analysed in 3D space,
- are as precise as the documentation data and
- extend the analysis into the fourth dimension.

1.2.2 Data modelling – a methodological approach

The 3D model and data should be as objective as possible to get a model as close as possible to the real world. The aim of the modelling working step is to reconstruct the site as it was at the time of the excavation as a basis for spatial analysis.

In comparison to the 2008 prototype (Lieberwirth, 2008a), this model will be enriched with data from the side subjects geophysics and pedology. For this aim, these data need to be in a numeric format, in the same coordinate system and with the same resolution as the archaeological record.

The chosen GIS-environment for modelling offers the data format voxel (volume pixel) for solid volume calculation. This format was successfully tested with the first prototype to calculate archaeological deposits (Lieberwirth, 2008a). According to the conceptual framework conditions of this study I am limited to the available solid modelling concepts of GRASS although there are alternative technical solutions available (Merlo, 2016, p. 44 tab.3.2). At the moment, there are five modules for voxel generation available (https://grass.osgeo.org/grass74/manuals/raster3dintro.html):

i) *v.to.rast3* (detailed description: https://grass.osgeo.org/grass74/manuals/v.to.rast3.html), which generates just one voxel around the original 3D point,

ii) *r.to.rast3elev* (detailed description: https://grass.osgeo.org/grass74/manuals/r.to.rast3elev.html), which generates a cube or cuboid of the defined 3D region out of raster surfaces via extrusion,

iii) *r.to.rast3* (detailed description: https://grass.osgeo.org/grass74/manuals/r.to.rast3.html), which performs just like r.to.rast3elev,

iv) *v.vol.rst* (detailed description: https://grass.osgeo.org/grass74/manuals/v.vol.rst.html), which provides the only interpolation algorithm in 3D space and

v) *r.vol.dem* (detailed description: https://grass.osgeo.org/grass74/manuals/addons/r.vol.dem.html), which uses extrusion of raster data between two raster surfaces.

According to the requirements and outputs of the modules, only options iv) and v) are useful in this study because v.vol.rst uses only probability statistics and r.vol.dem can outline the calculated result with reasonable borders in 3D space.

For iv) the input data need to be a 3D vector point cloud. The algorithm is a 3D interpolation of a so-called *w-value*. This value has to be a numeric attribute which can be any kind of quantitative information like geochemical or geophysical values. The *z-value* needs to be a real coordinate. Voxel creation via interpolation can be understood like the creation of continuous raster surfaces in 3D. The result is a continuous volume with fuzzy borders of adjustable threshold intervals. This calculation process is hence very suitable for measured values in 3D space.

Geophysical and geochemical information is, in comparison to archaeological, measurable information. This is seen as a great advantage against archaeological deposits in this study because the course of archaeological structures is determined by the excavator's decision only. The archaeological question here is, whether the geophysical or geochemical information shows the same course and borders as the archaeological. If this question can be answered positively, there might be a way to predict archaeological remains without excavating by using geophysics and geochemistry (RQ ix).

For v) raster surfaces need to be extruded in an up or down direction.

This GRASS module is chosen for calculating non-numerical archaeological volumes. The challenge in building a digital model out of the archaeological record is the transformation of archaeological interpretations into numerical data.

1.2.3 Data acquistion – an archaeological & methodological approach

Archaeological excavation documentation depends on measurement. To describe objects and their place of discovery, we need to assign their precise location in all three dimensions. The archaeological challenge of this working step in this study is transforming real objects (archaeological remains like finds, features and stratigraphy) into a computer readable format. The reality has been transformed into this frame. As demonstrated before, the analysis method dictates the data format for acquisition. The data documentation is the working step between physical excavation and modelling. Hence,

considerations have to be made before going into the field: what kind of documentation hardware and software should be applied and how can the objects be described in an efficient way at excavation and in a suitable way for later analysis, respectively. To avoid unnecessary working steps, the ideal documentation system should already generate the final data format (RQ xi).

Consequently, since the analysis software has already been chosen, the data acquisition has to be in a GIS-readable format. Hence, the use of digital devices which produce 3D vector data is preferred. The final concept for the operational framework of the digital excavation, which acts as a testing ground in this study, is described in detail in tables 1.1, 1.2, 1.3. In this study, the ideal data type for documentation would be a format readable by GRASS, or at least in a GIS in general. The same is true for documentation software solutions. The less programs are needed, the less working steps have to be executed. This helps to avoid data transformation and conversion which might produce errors and distortions (RQ xii). The integration of additional information from two side subjects is a further challenge.

Geophysical data and the pedological data should produce similar data types as preferred over the archaeological.

In summary, the excavator is confronted with the challenge of transforming the real world into a digital model. During acquisition a solution has to be found for:

- What kind of information we want to depict and how much of it to model,
- What vector type (point, line, polygone) to use and
- How the data are to be acquired?

Geophysical investigation in archaeology belongs to non-destructive excavation methods. Its integration into the excavation process allows for precise planning in horizontal space. In this study, the third dimension of these data should be integrated, unlike the common application of 2D picture output, making it possible to plan the excavation more precisely even in a vertical direction (Gaffney et al. 2013; Sarris et al. 2018).

In this study, we take advantage of recent developments in sensor devices. It is assumed that due to more precise non-destructive insight possibilities underneath the surface at a significant depth, it is possible to recognise stratigraphical differences. It is therefore hoped that it is possible to find stratigraphical borders with geophysical support in three dimensions.

The same experiment is planned with geochemical data. In pedology, soil strata can be differentiated by their chemical compounds (Salisbury, 2013; Sarris et al., 2018). The idea of this study is to measure the chemical soil composition in 3D space. The result should be a 3D volume model in the same coordinate system and resolution as

Table 1.1. Archaeological working hypothesis: documentation of archaeological information

A. archaeology

	i) Record Type	**ii) Data Format**	**iii) Hardware**	**Software**
archaeological surfaces	course of archaeological strata	- 3D point cloud (multipoint)	- TLS - total station	CAD
archaeological features	location & size of features, feature context	- 3D polyline (vector line)	- total station	CAD
archaeological finds	location & size of features, feature context	- 3D point (vector point)	- total station	CAD

Table 1.2. Geophysical working hypothesis: documentation of geophysical information

B. geophysics

	i) Record Type	**ii) Data Format**	**iii) Hardware**	**Software**
geophysical anomalies	course & depth of geophysical strata & features	- GPR wavelengths	- GPR	ParaView©

Table 1.3. Geochemical working hypothesis: documentation of pedological information

C. pedology

	i) Record Type	**ii) Data Format**	**iii) Hardware**	**Software**
geochemical anomalies	course & depth of geochemical strata & features	- 3D point (vector point)	- total station	CAD

the archaeological and the geophysical models for further comparison.

For this reason, a probabilistic soil sampling procedure is planned by using a three-dimensional regular grid inside the excavation trench in order to obtain unbiased 3D raster information (Orton, 2000).

The practical implementation of the operational framework described above is executed in *Ostia Antica* at the Main Forum's West Porticus' archaeological excavation with trench 1. An introduction into the archaeological site follows in section 2.1.1.

1.3 Structure of this book

This publication is divided into two parts, a text book and for the sake of the third dimension, supplemented animated images and video.

It starts with a theoretical introduction into the topic of 3D cartography in archaeology and its application in this study. The following three chapters deal with the practical implementations. They describe the data acquisition, the modelling process and finally the analysis process of the model.

The last chapter discusses and summarises the results of the practical tests compared to the theoretical conceptual framework. They close with an outlook for future studies.

1.3.1 Chapter 1: Introduction

The chapter introduces the reader into the scope and intention of the monograph. It is presumed that readers have a background knowledge of GIS-applications in archaeology. The introduction starts with cartographic work in archaeology in general with a focus on 3D modelling.

It follows the conceptual design of the three main working steps of this study: data acquisition (chap. 2), data modelling (chap. 3) and data analysis (chap. 4). The chapter introduces the test setup and the operational framework tailored for the purpose in this work. According to these working hypotheses research aims and questions RQs are formulated. The latter are structured with a Roman numeral system.

The road to these destinations including all side streets and dead ends is described in the following chapters.

1.3.2 Chapter 2: 3D data acquisition

After an introduction to the experimental site at *Ostia Antica* the chapter presents the practical implementation of the methodology concerning 3D data acquisition. It contains a detailed description of all data acquisition processes on-site categorised under the subjects geophysics, archaeology and pedology. Finally, it describes the data management structure after the excavation as a off-site process.

For a better overview, working step sequences (WS) follow a Roman numeral system which is used throughout the monograph and appears also in processing chain charts which are displayed in chronological order including the applied hardware and software. Detailed descriptions of each working step can be found in tables by using the same numerical system for cross-referencing.

1.3.3 Chapter 3: 3D data modelling

The modelling chapter starts with the import of all acquired data into the chosen GIS-environment and ends with the export into a ParaView©-readable format, the viewer of GRASS GIS.

In between, one can find detailed descriptions of the workflows for each data type for generating the final 3D GIS-model. Again, the working steps are summarised in process chain charts and described in detail in tables with the same numerical system used in chapter 2.

1.3.4 Chapter 4: 3D data analysis

The analysis chapter starts with the import of all data from chapter 3 into the main analysis software ParaView©. The chapter is subdivided into different analysis approaches which try to answer the research questions from chapter 1.

1.3.5 Chapter 5: Discussion & conclusion

The analysis results and working steps are discussed and summarised in this chapter by taking up the same structure and numbering as above. It consists of comments about advantages and disadvantages (discussion), final results (conclusion) and suggestions for future applications (outlook).

Finally, all research questions (RQs) from chapter 1 and 2 are taken up and answered.

3D Data Acquisition

Chapter 2 describes the data acquisition of all data subjects (geophysics, archaeology and pedology) on the experimental site at *Ostia Antica*. The chapter starts with an overview about the archaeological site and research question, the experimental setup and methodological workflow, followed by a detailed description of the implementation of the operational framework.

2.1 Experimental setup & workflow

2.1.1 Archaeological background

The case study took place at the archaeological site *Ostia Antica* in Italy – the antique harbour city of Rome. The data were taken during a 4-week campaign in August/September 2011 as part of the *Topoi Summer School 2011* (see Acknowledgements). We investigated three trenches (fig. 2.1 'MFW 2011') at the Western Porticus in the northern part of the *Main Forum* of *Ostia Antica* right of grid 7 and left of grid 8). The acquired data of trench number 1 (fig. 2.5, 2.9) were used for to develop the model in this study.

Ostia Antica is situated in the Latium region at the mouth of the Tiber River on the *Tyrrhenian Sea* approximately 30 km downstream of the capital Rome (fig. 2.2).

First structures of the city date back to the late 3rd century BC and belong to a so-called *Castrum*. The remains are a tufa stone foundation of rectangular shape of 195 × 125.7 m (Martin, 1996). Its location is assumed in the antique city centre, the area of the *Main Forum* of *Ostia Antica* today (DeLaine, 2008, p. 87 fig. 3) which still shows a rectangular structure in the street layout (fig. 2.1, DeLaine 2008, p. 101 and Mar 1991, p. 87 fig. 4,5,12).

During the Republican period the place turned from a military into a commercially oriented port town. *Ostia Antica* and the nearby harbour *Portus*, the latter still visible as an octagon shape 3 km northwest of *Ostia Antica* (fig. 2.2), became an important supply area for Rome and its surroundings. By the end of this period it had extended up to 70 ha (Stöger, 2011, p. iii).

The city had its heydays between the end of the 1st and the 3rd century AD (Heinzelmann 2002, p. 105 and Meiggs 1973, p. 84, 186) with approx. 100,000 citizens (Stöger, 2011, p. 11). At this time, the city's west gate was very close to the *Tyrrhenian Sea* shore. In contrast to its nowadays location which is about 2 km from the shore (compare

fig. 2.2 with DeLaine 2008, p. 101 or with Heinzelmann 2001, p. 374 fig. 1). Many public buildings date to this period, e.g. the Capitolium at 120 AD (Calza et al., 1953, p. 215) at the northern part of the *Main Forum* between the *Western* and *Eastern Porticuses* (fig. 2.1) which has still a hight of 17 m (fig. 2.6).

The following period between the 3rd and 5th centuries AD is not yet fully explored. It is assumed that the city decreased in size along with a simultaneous development of certain zones (mainly public) becoming more luxurious (Stöger 2011, p. iv and Gering 2011, p. 315).

After the 6th century AD, *Ostia Antica* was slowly abandoned and never revived.

Throughout all the time periods, the area struggled with river flooding and earthquakes. Both events are regularly evident in archaeological remains (Gering, 2011) until modern times (Mastrorillo et al., 2016). The late antiquity ruins of *Ostia Antica* were finally covered by several meters of sediment (Nibby, 1819, p. 295) and never built over until the first official excavations began in 1802–1804 by Petrini (Lauro, 1995). This campaign and all subsequent ones in the 19th and 20th centuries mainly focused on the exposure of antique ruins rather than digging underneath (Gering, 2011, p. 301).

This was the situation when we arrived at the site in summer 2011. Together with Axel Gering and an official representative from the *Soprintendenza* (Italian heritage management) we looked for where a number of stratigraphical layers could be expected (a methodological requirement for the test). Fortunately, it was agreed we would investigate the area underneath the *Western Porticus'* pavement at the *Main Forum* in the heart of the ancient city and, according to Mar (1991) and others (see above), probably the centre of the former *Castrum* (fig. 2.1). Hence, samples of archaeological stratigraphy over a time span of 800 years of settlement history could be expected.

Besides getting a better understanding of the settlement history inside the city centre from its origin until abandonment, the archaeological research questions we wanted to answer with the help of the new model were:

– Is there datable evidence of flooding and earthquakes? and
– Do these dates coincide with others from the site? (RQ xiii).

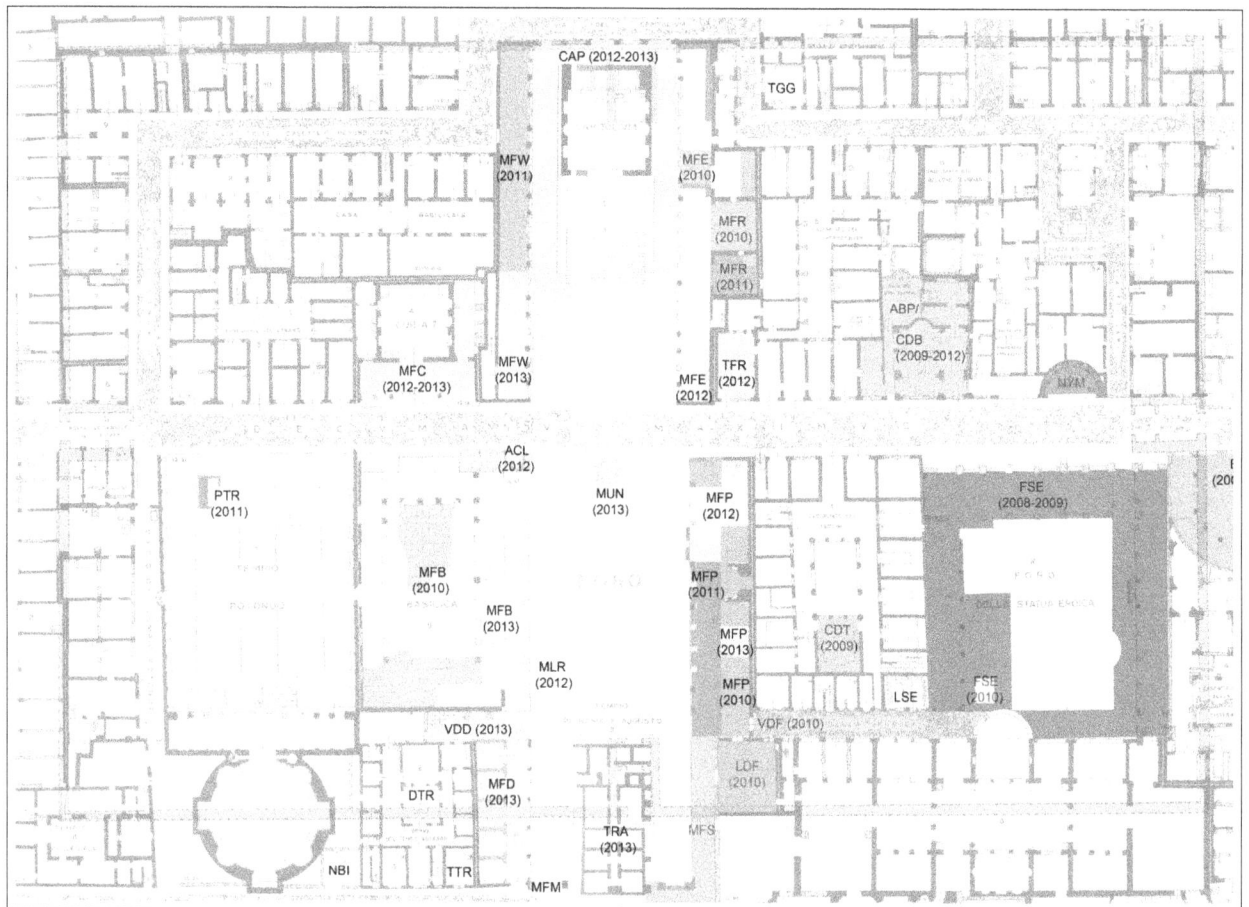

Figure 2.1. City center of *Ostia Antica* with excavation area MFW (2011). The red rectangle shows the location of the Castrum with four gates. Source: Reproduced with courtesy of A. Gering (2015).

2.1.2 Practical implementation

For data acquisition and excavation, the conceptual design and operational framework (sec. 1.2) had to be adjusted to the particular site's situation and by considering the regulations of the local heritage management *Soprintendenza* (1984). The implementation was inspired by experiences from a 'rehearsal' excavation two years earlier at the site of Hornsburg (Melichar & Neubauer, 2010), the guidelines of ARCHES (ARCHES, 2013) and the recommendations for the sustainable use of digital data in Classical Studies (IANUS, 2017).

In a first step the size and layout of documentation grids at the site (fig. 2.5) and the structure of the excavation database DB concerning entities and attributes (like architectural fragments, rubble and backfill as compensatory material with soil compositions in between) were defined (entity relationship diagram (ER), fig. 2.4).

Furthermore, the excavation method (table 1.1) was set up which had to be in a single-context-recording according to the conceptual framework.

The excavation site was separated into a system of seven grids (fig. 2.5) covering the western part of the

North Porticus of the Main Forum (fig. 2.1, 2.9). The size of the grids was defined by the distance of the Roman columns (fig. 2.5, 2.6, 2.7 – Roman columns are recognisable by Säulennummerierung starting with 'P'). Inside grid nos. 3, 4 and 5 we defined three trenches for excavation (fig. 2.5). Their location was chosen according to the archaeological and methodological questions by considering the geophysical results (sec. 2.2.1). For the model in this study only the data of trench 1 were chosen. In the following sections I will only focus on this trench.

The general workflow started with geophysics, followed by the archaeological excavation and documentation including the geochemical sampling (fig. 2.8).

2.2 Documentation on-site

The documentation process is the most sensitive in archaeological modelling. It requires unrepeatable decisions about what to document and how. These intellectual transformation and filter processes determine all subsequent working steps.

The challenge in this study was the transformation of all visible and non-visible objects from real world into

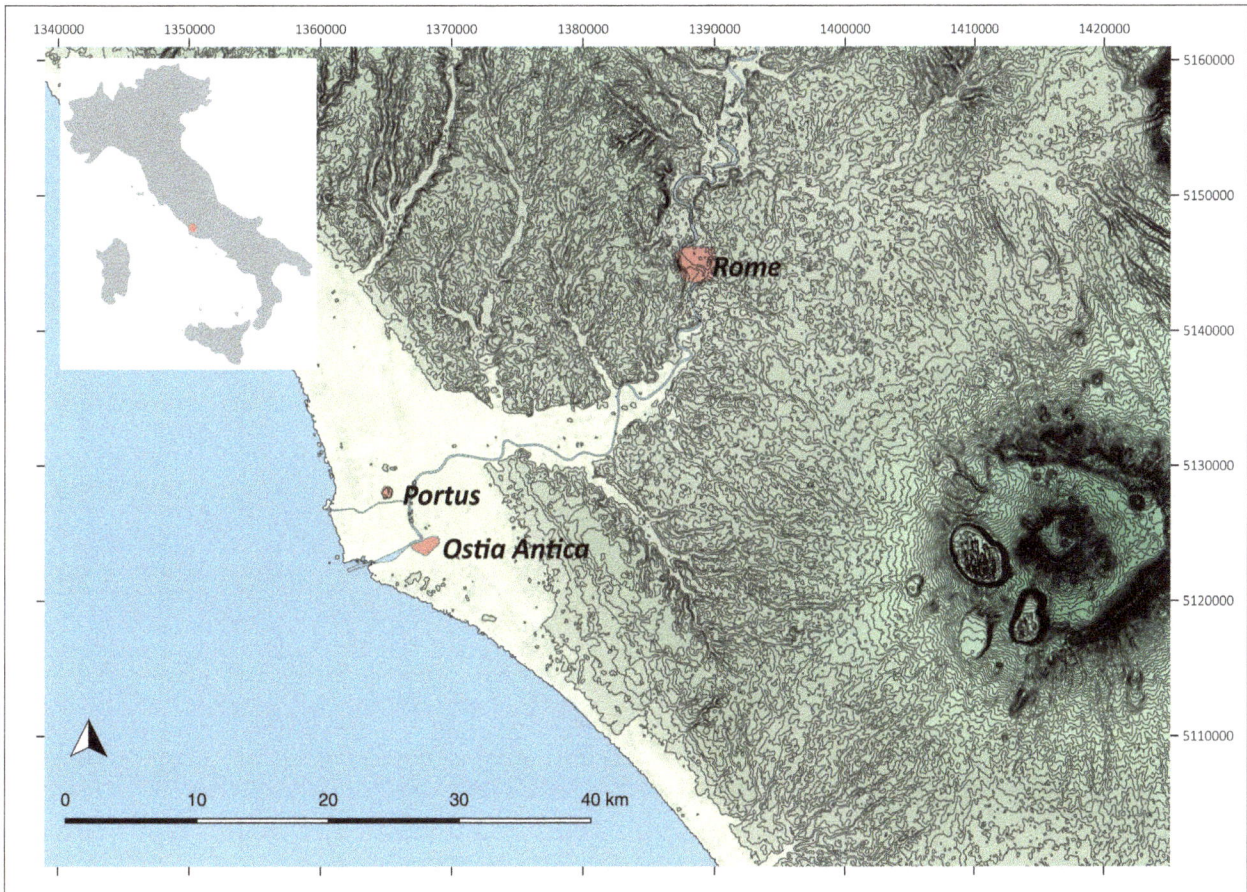

Figure 2.2. Modern location of *Ostia Antica* with antique towns and topography in its wider context.

the digital space. A further aim was to avoid intentional filtering in order to minimise *E* (sec. 1.1.2).

The chart figure 'process chain 1' (2.8) shows all working steps WS of the documentation workflow on-site. The Roman numbering is identical with the numbers in tables 2.2, 2.3 and 2.6 which contain detailed descriptions of each working step (WS). The sequence follows their practical execution. The chart should be read from top to bottom and from left to right. It also represents the transition processes from one system to another, including detailed information about the applied hardware and software.

2.2.1 Geophysical data acquisition

The geophysical prospection at the archaeological site in *Ostia Antica* was carried out using a GPR system by the company Eastern Atlas® Berlin (tables 2.1, 2.2).

After the first 'rough' investigation of the Western Porticus (column 2, fig. 2.11), two interesting areas for excavation were selected. They were investigated a second time by GPR ('Fläche A – Area A' and 'Fläche B – Area B' figs. 2.9, 2.10) with a higher resolution antenna and a lesser point distance of 0.01m and profile distance of 0.05 m (column 3, fig. 2.11).

These results were not communicated before the archaeological excavation started to avoid biased digging.

2.2.2 Archaeological data acquisition

The excavation started with the removal of the marble stone slab pavement of the West Porticus before the geophysical prospection (sec. 2.2.1, figs. 2.6, 2.7). After defining two excavation trenches two teams started by documenting the first surface which appeared underneath the marble pavement. They followed the tailored workflow according to the concept described for this excavation site in sec. 1.2, table 1.1 and the processes chain (fig. 2.8).

The chosen excavation method of 'stratigraphic recording' (Harris 1989, Biel and Klonk 1994) was applied to all layers (table 2.3 WS iii). After the removal of the first eight layers of trench 1 we reduced the trench's size to half the size in favour of greater depth (fig. 3.2).

In order to document continuous stratigraphy surfaces a TLS was applied. It creates 3D point clouds in a pre-defined resolution and area. The points get x, y, z – coordinates, including an RGB-value. The latter is taken from an intrinsic digital camera.

Figure 2.3. Early documentations of *Ostia Antica*. Source: (Reproduced of A. Nibby, 1819, p. 293).

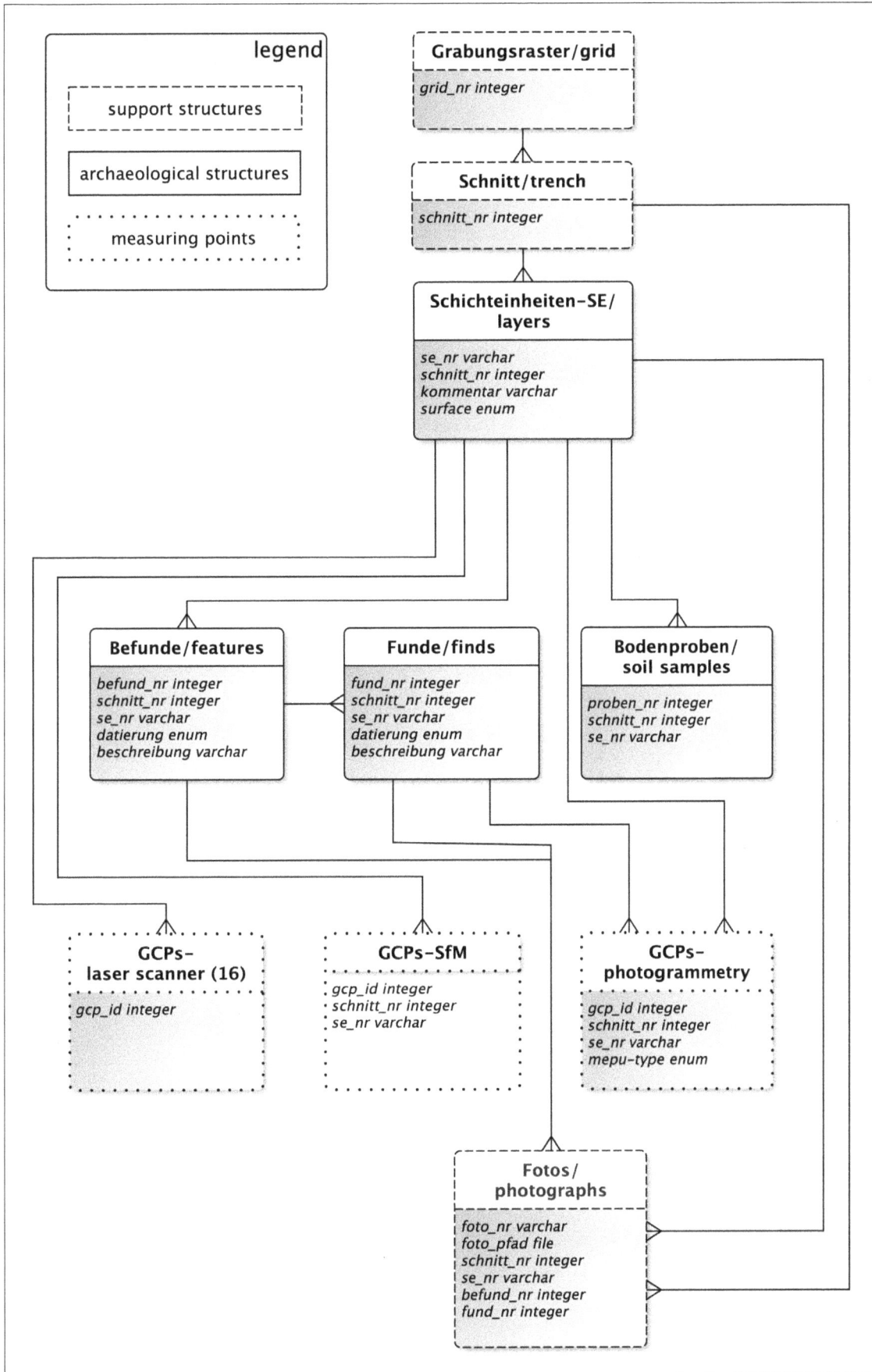

Figure 2.4. Entity relationship diagram of AutoCAD® plug-in TachyCAD Archaeology® with MonuMap®-DB, borders show the methodological topics.

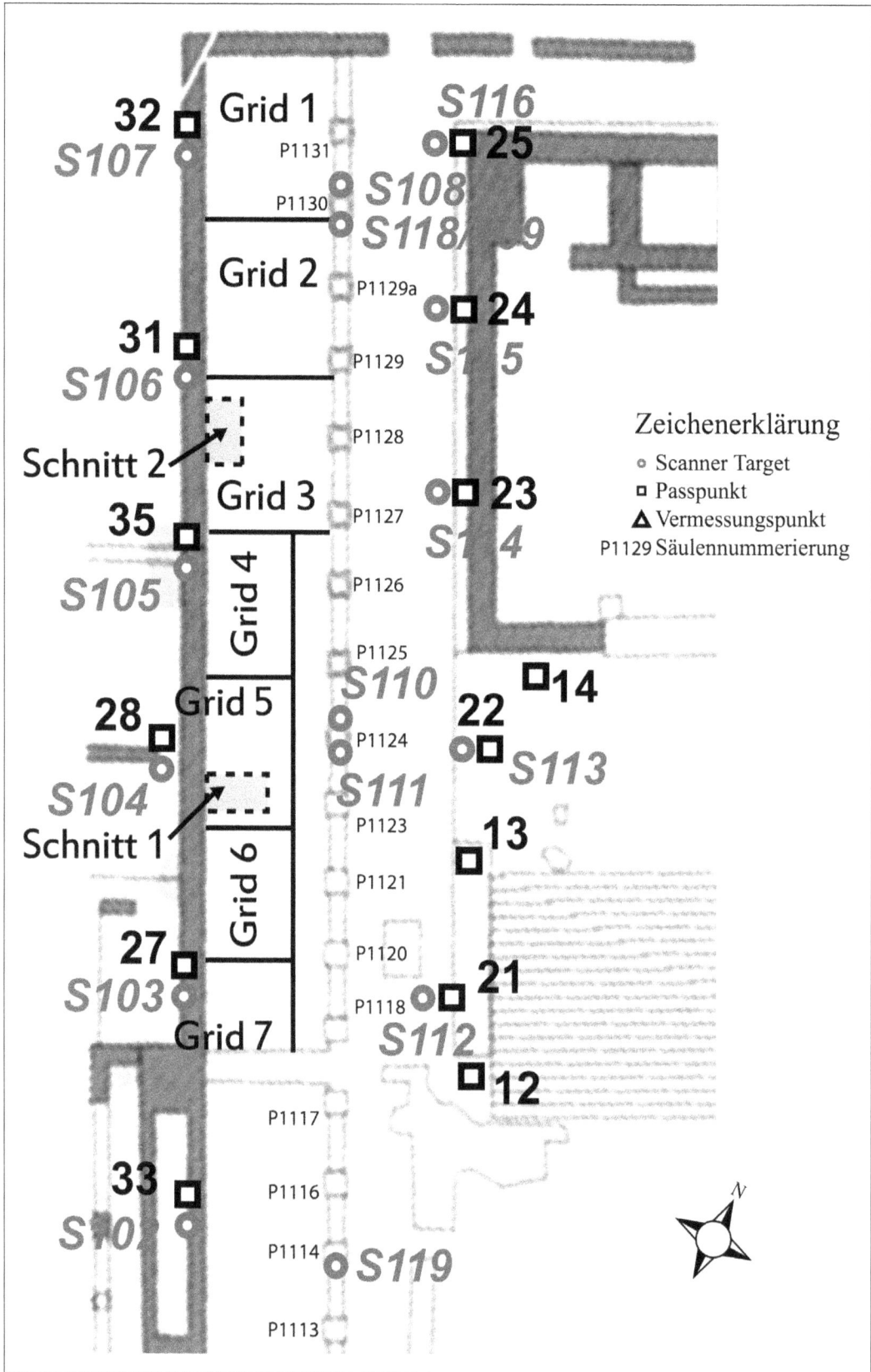

Figure 2.5. Map of excavation site, trench 1 = 'Schnitt 1'.

Figure 2.6. Overview of excavation area at West Porticus grid 1-7 with Capitolinum and Tiber River in the background, view from southeast to northwest. Reproduced with courtesy of Parco archaeologico di Ostia.

Figure 2.7. West Porticus area of grid 1-4, view from east to west. Reproduced with courtesy of Parco archaeologico di Ostia.

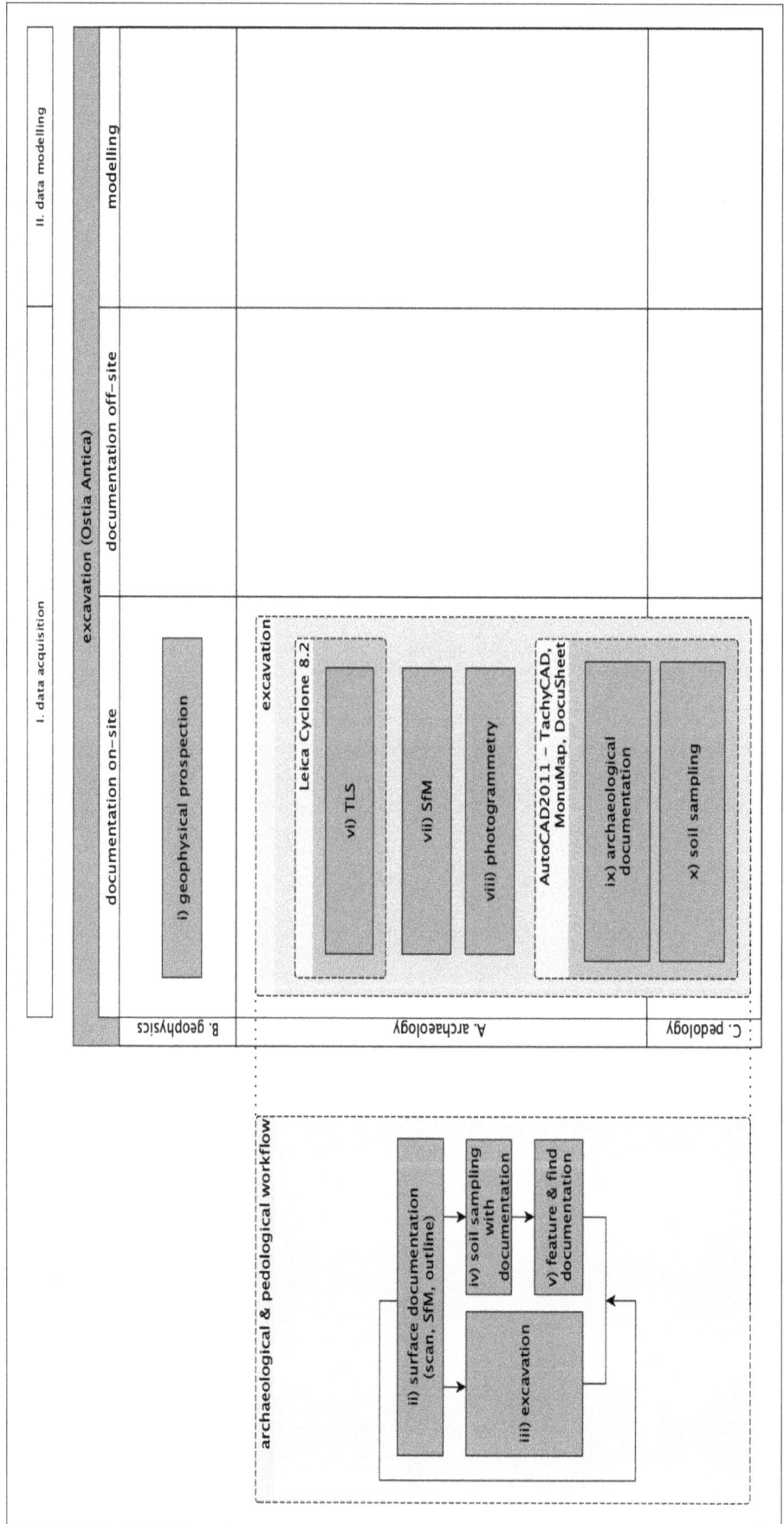

Figure 2.8. Process chain 1: workflow of data acquisition at *Ostia Antica*, part: 'documentation on-site'. With reference to the tables 2.2, 2.3 and 2.6.

Table 2.1. On-site documentation of geophysical information. Please compare with table 1.2

B. geophysics

	i) Record Type	**ii) Data Format**	**iii) Hardware**	**Software**
geophysical anomalies	course & depth of geophysical strata & features	- GPR wavelenghts	- GPR	- Reflexw® - ParaView©

Table 2.2. WS i

geophysical transformation processes, on-site documentation:

Process No.	Detailed Description with Hardware & Software
i)* **geophysical prospection**	# measuring GPR wavelengths # hardware: GPR device 'GSSI SIR-3000 900-MHz-Antenne' # software: Reflexw® (Sandmeier, 2017), ParaView©

*The process numbers are identical with the numbers (Roman numerals) in the workflow charts of process chain 1–4 (figs. 2.8, 2.16, 2.18, 3.1).

According to its vertical opening angle of 270° TLS reaches its limits by scanning deep pits. As a solution we used the *Structure from Motion* (SfM) method for the first time as an experiment (subsec. 4.3.2 and discussed in chap. 5).

The method of image-based modelling comes from the subject of computer vision. It needs overlapping photographs to create 3D structures out of moving pictures (see SfM and Lieberwirth and Herzog 2016, Lieberwirth and Bussilliat 2017, chap. 2.2). Like TLS it generates 3D

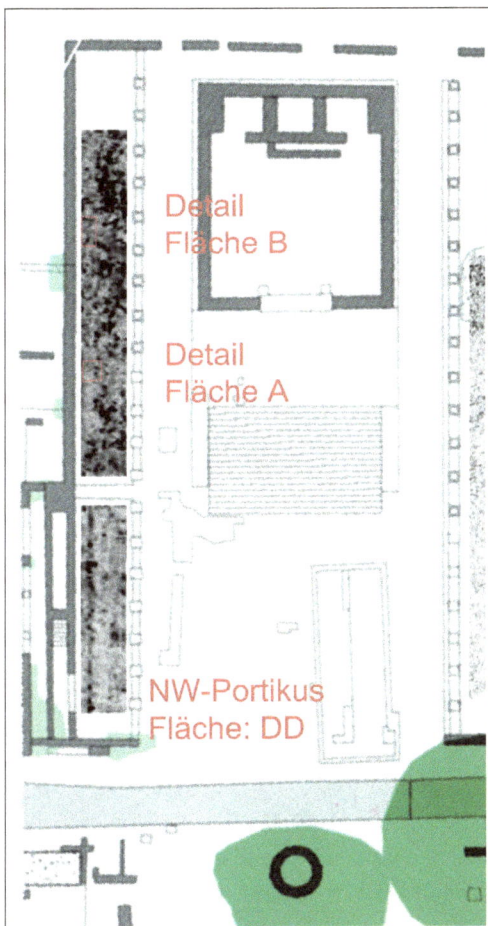

Figure 2.9. Geophysical investigation area, trench 1 = Fläche A. Source: Reproduced with courtesy of B. Ulrich, Eastern Atlas®.

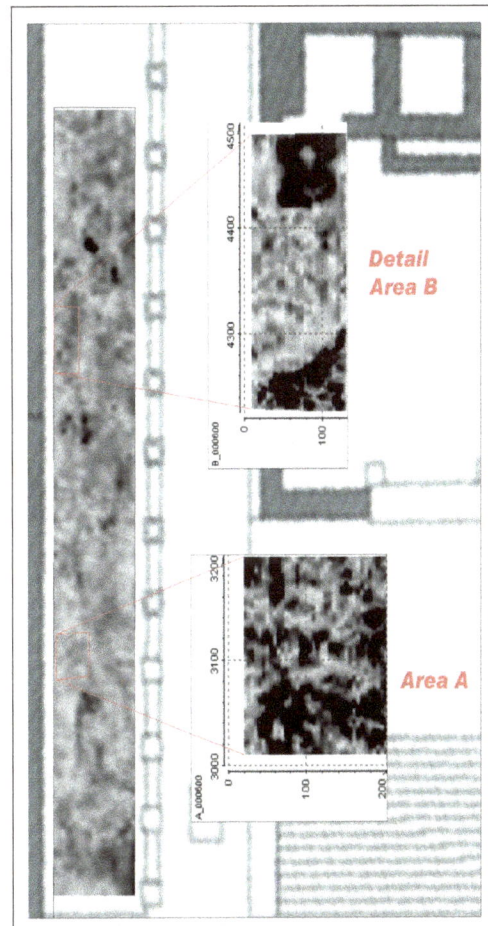

Figure 2.10. Detail of fig. 2.9, geophysical investigation area, detail trench 1 = Area A. Source: Reproduced with courtesy of B. Ulrich, Eastern Atlas®.

Teilprojekt	Vorerkundung Forum (A. Gering)	Detailerkundung (U. Lieberwirth)
System	Georadar GSSI SIR-3000	Georadar GSSI SIR-3000
Antenne	GSSI 270-MHz-Antenne / 900-MHz-Antenne	GSSI 900-MHz-Antenne
Messgrößen	Laufzeit und Amplitude, Registrierdauer 75 ns	Laufzeit und Amplitude, Registrierdauer 40 ns
Messflächen	Portikus Nordost, Fläche BB, 245 Profile Portikus Südost, Fläche CC, 202 Profile Portikus Nordwest, Fläche DD, 34 Profile	Portikus Nordwest, Fläche A: 37 Profile Portikus Nordwest, Fläche B: 25 Profile
Punktabstand	0,05 m (20 scans / m)	0,01 m (100 scans / m)
Profilabstand	0,25 m	0,05 m
Längenmessung	Odometer (Survey wheel)	Odometer (Survey wheel)
Datenformate	Rohdaten: DZT (Radan-Format), Prozessierte Daten: REFLEXW-Format, 2D-Visualisierung: Horizontalschnitte: jpg	Rohdaten: DZT (Radan-Format), Prozessierte Daten: REFLEXW-Format, 2D-Visualisierung: Horizontalschnitte: jpg 3D-Visualisierung: Modelle: vtk
Bildauflösung	5 cm x 5 cm (resampling)	2 cm x 2 cm (resampling)
Wellengeschwindigkeit	~ 0,08 m /ns	~ 0,10 m / ns
Datenprozessing und Filter	Background Removal, Energy Decay	Background Removal, Energy Decay

Figure 2.11. **Measurement and evaluation parameters of the GPR investigations for 'Vorerkundung Forum'-column 2 and 'Detailerkundung'-column 3. Source: Reproduced with courtesy of B. Ulrich, Eastern Atlas®.**

point clouds. For documentation only a digital camera is needed, which belongs to the archaeological equipment anyway. For georeferencing the photographs, special ground control points (GCPs, fig. 2.4) were placed around the surfaces (Lieberwirth et al., 2015).

The AutoCAD® plug-in TachyCAD Archaeology® 2011 served as an interface between the total station (hardware) and database (DB) MonuMap® as an archiving and management software (WS ii in table 2.3). The software provides a dynamic adaption to the site situation in three dimensions. The resulting technical drawing is interactively connected with the individually tailored DB for the site. It allows permanent verification of on-site measurements which leads to very few measuring errors. Only two geometry formats were necessary: 3D vector point and 3D polyline (fig. 2.12).

The combination of geometry and attributes has been proven very flexible because both can be adjusted on-the-fly to changing conditions in the field.

All hardware devices were operated by 10 students of the Lehrgrabung *Ostia Antica* 2011 (see Acknowledgements). They had been educated in a one-week workshop at the Free University Berlin.

At the site, they were provided with a detailed user manual. After one day of recapitulation, the students were able to operate the documentation equipment under my supervision and with the support of the manual. To guarantee that everyone got the chance to work with each device, they all got a specific task area for a period of time which were swapped about after a few days.

The manual is a compilation of selected pages from hardware and software handbooks, enriched with tailored comments and hints for the excavation site. It had been developed for the test excavation at Hornsburg in 2009 and was substantially modified in 2011.

The CAD-drawing and DB was checked regularly for completeness and redundancy, as well as for consistency of attributes and code names used in the docu-sheets and file names.

Each documentation sheet summarises all the information of one archaeological layer ('Schichteinheit' (SE)). They can be seen as an analogue summary of all collected data in order to combine all data types (3D point clouds, photographs, vector data, soil samples). With the sheets at hand, we were able to double-check lists and data of archaeological deposits, finds and photographs using them as a backup system. To meet the requirements of a digital excavation (see sec. 2.1), the form was created as follows (fig. 2.13):

Table 2.3. WS ii-iii, v-ix

archaeological transformation processes, on-site documentation:

Process No.	Detailed Description with Hardware & Software
ii, vi)* **surface documentation, soil sampling with documentation**	# scanning of top surfaces (Doneus & Neubauer, 2006, p. 193) as 3D point clouds (with a resolution of 1x1cm) via TLS after the trench outline was defined. Archaeological layers were outlined with a 3D polyline via total station. They got an ID number in the TachyCAD®-DB and documentation sheets with relation to the trench.
	# documentation of trench outline, top surface outlines/borders as 3D polylines via total station
	# documentation of scanner targets (scanner GCPs, fig. 2.4) as high resolution fine scan for georeferencing via TLS and via total station
	# hardware: TLS: Leica ScanStation 2®, total station: Leica TCR 405®
	# software: TLS: Cyclone® (Leica, 2011), total station: AutoCAD® plug-in TachyCAD® Archaeology
iii) **excavation**	# excavation of archaeological layers, features and finds in single-context-recording method
	# hardware: by shovel and trowel
v) **feature & find documentation**	# documentation of archaeological features and finds as 3D polylines or 3D points (find center) via total station
	# archaeological layers and finds were measured with at least 4 surrounding 3D vector points or 3D polylines to outline the size of the object via total station. They got an ID number in the TachyCAD®-DB and were related to the trench and/or layer (fig. 2.12 ER-diagram).
	# hardware: see ii,iv)
	# software: see ii,iv)
vii) **SfM**	# documentation of three top surfaces (se108, se112, se113) via digital camera
	# hardware: digital camera Canon D500
	# software: none
viii) **photogrammetry**	# documentation of archaeological layers (deposits and features were treated as layers) and finds *in situ* via photogrammetry. The photographs were taken as perpendicular as possible to the surface to avoid distortion (Kinne, 2009, p. 66). For later georeferencing it was important to include GCPs (fixed and flexible fig. 2.4 *'mepu-type'* in entity 'GCPs-photogrammetry') in the picture.
	# hardware: see vii)
	# software: none
ix) **archaeological documentation**	# documentation of archaeological layers, features and finds via total station including help lines: grid borders, trench borders, including help points: GCPs for photogrammetry and SfM (fig. 2.4 ER-diagram, 2.12)
	# documentation of archaeological layers on paper-based docu-sheets including all connected information about trench, features, finds, taken photographs, taken scans (fig. 2.13)
	# documentation of archaeological finds on paper-based lists
	# hardware: total station: see ii, iv; docu-sheets: paper-based
	# software: none

*The process numbers are identical with the numbers (Roman numerals) in the workflow charts of process chain 1-4 (figs.2.8, 2.16, 2.18, 3.1).

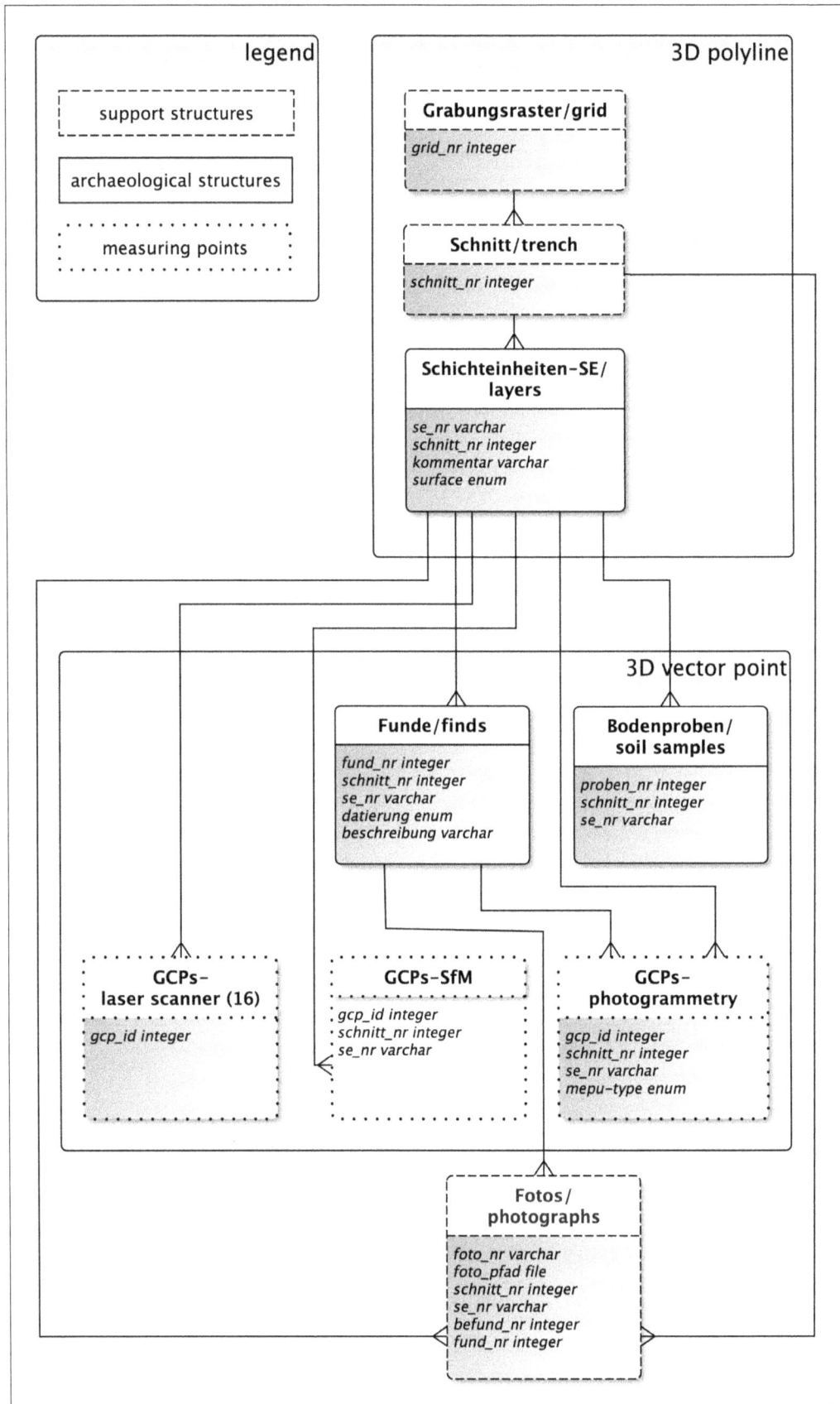

Figure 2.12. Copy of fig. 2.4 with vector data type for entities (without 'features' entity).

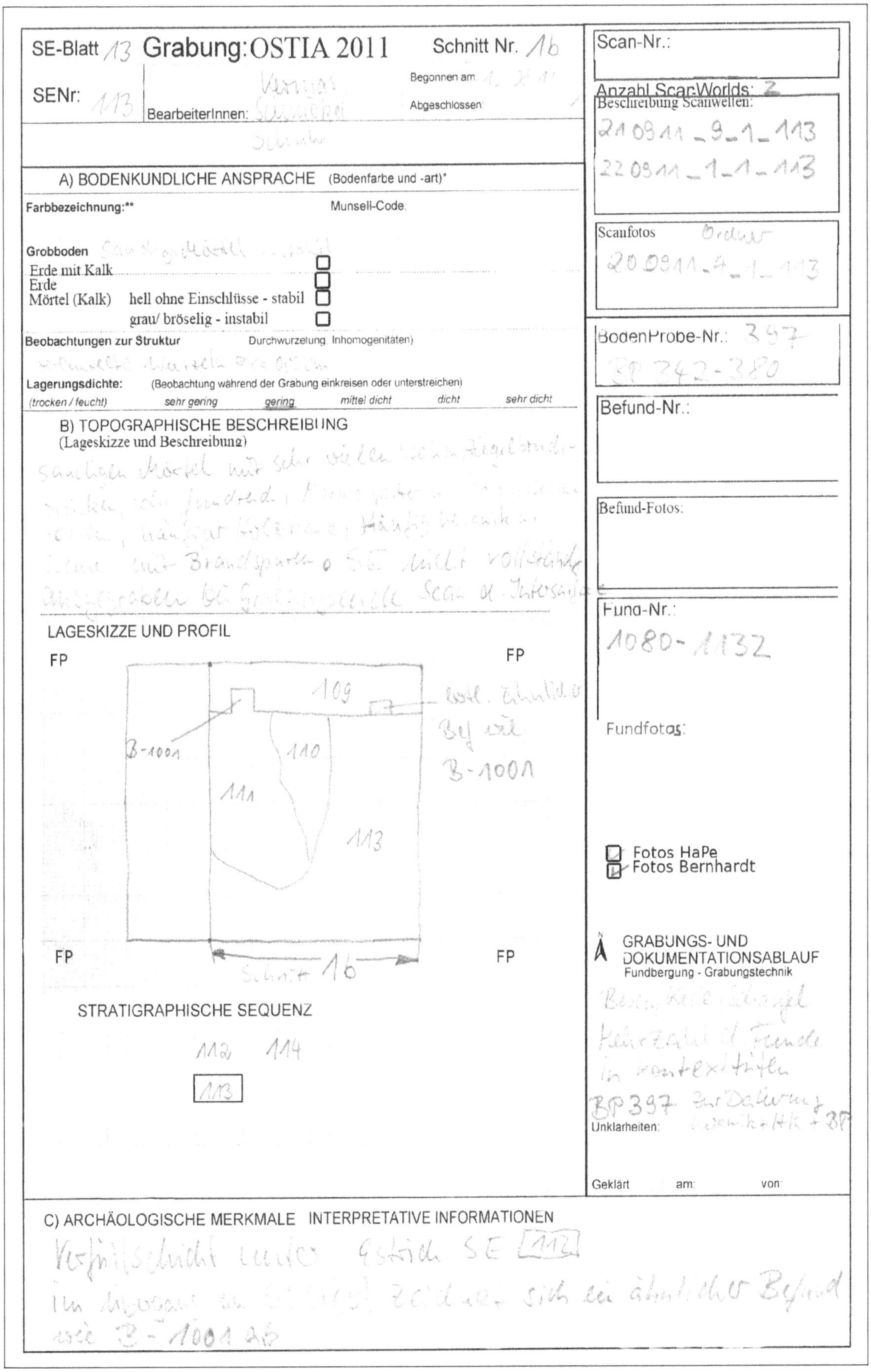

Figure 2.13. Documentation sheet for archaeological layers at *Ostia Antica* excavation with completion instructions.

The sheet's header contains:

- the number of the trench and
- the number of the stratigraphical layer (SE number),
- the excavation date and
- the names of the people who worked on it.

Part 1 contains

- a sketch of the layer's shape and horizontal position in the trench from a top view and
- a written description of the layer's shape and position inside the trench.

Part 2 contains

- a written description of the layer's soil composition and colour also as Munsell-code (Munsell 1975, Eckelmann et al. 2005, chap. 5.6.4).

Part 3 contains

- a written description of the layer's archaeological features and finds.

Part 4 contains

- a short text about the excavation process.

Part 6 contains

- questions and problems which came up during this process.

For describing the vertical position and spatial relationship of the archaeological layers in reference to its environment, an excerpt of the trench's Harris Matrix (HM) diagram was inserted in **part 5** (fig. 2.14).

Part 7–9 refers to the additional lists (excel sheets) of

- laser scans,
- archaeological finds,
- pedological samples and
- photographs.

The sheet's content was regularly updated and cross-referenced with all other documentation, the mentioned lists, technical drawings and the CAD-DB. All acquired vector data were sorted into categories (fig. 2.12).

A summary of the applied hardware and software can be found in table 2.4 and compared with the operational concept in table 1.1.

2.2.3 Pedological data acquisition

The sampling of geochemical data took place after the archaeological layer documentation (fig. 2.8) in a predefined 3D grid system (sec. 1.2.3 and fig. 4.7, 4.21). A detailed description of the sampling description can be found in table 2.6 and in tab. 2.5). The soil samples were stored in paper bags for drying and transportation to the laboratory (sec. 2.3.2). Each bag got a serial number as

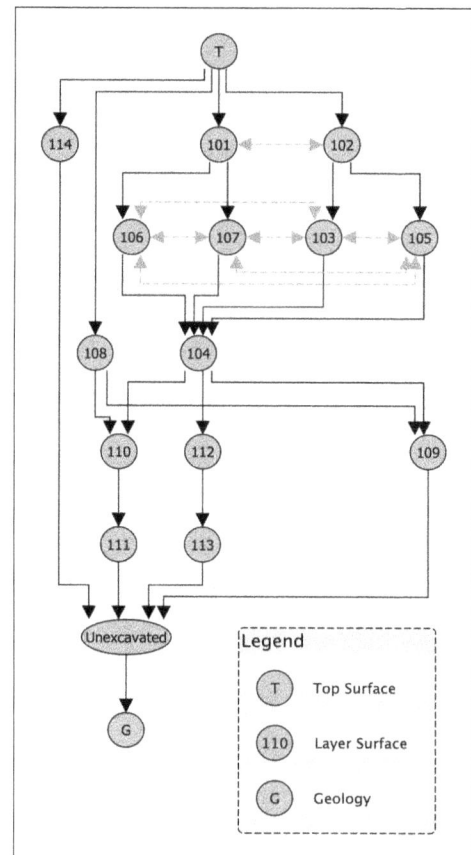

Figure 2.14. Harris Matrix of trench 1 created by the use of Harris Matrix Composer® software (LBI 2011, Traxler and Neubauer 2008, Harris 1989).

unique identifier (ID) for the DB to combine the geometry (vector point) with the laboratory results (sec. 3.3).

Since this excavation took place in an antique architecture environment, the deposits consisted mainly of occupation layers than soil. Therefore, it became partly difficult to take 100g/sample by shovel as advised.

2.3 Documentation off-site

2.3.1 Data management & storage

According to the conceptual design (sec. 1.2), the aim of the first part of the study, the excavation, was to summarise as much data as possible in one system. Fig. 2.15 shows the final result immediately after the end of the campaign at the site. Although most results are already digital, they occur in different data formats. Hence, the task of the off-site documentation was to complete the documentation in order to combine all digital data and make them ready for import into GIS.

To do so, the AutoCAD®-drawing served as the basis because of its complete 3D coordinate system. At first, all excavation data were transformed from the local coordinate system into the national coordinate system. Hence, all TLS data, SfM point clouds, photographs etc. could be imported into the final measurement system.

Table 2.4. Documentation of archaeological information on-site. Please compare with table 1.1

A. archaeology

	i) Record Type	ii) Data Format	iii) Hardware	iv) Software
archaeological surfaces	course of archaeological strata	- 3D point cloud	- TLS - total station - digital camera	- TachyCAD® - MonuMap® - TLS software - SfM software - docu-sheet
archaeological features	location & size of features, feature context	- 3D polyline (vector line)	- total station - digital camera	- TachyCAD® - MonuMap® - TLS software - SfM software - docu-sheet
archaeological finds	location & size of features, feature context	- 3D point (vector point)	- total station - digital camera	- TachyCAD® - MonuMap® - TLS software - SfM software - docu-sheet

Table 2.5. On-site documentation of pedological information. Please compare with table 1.3

C. pedology

	i) Record Type	ii) Data Format	iii) Hardware	iv) Software
geochemical anomalies	course & depth of geochemical strata & features	- 3D point (vector point)	- total station	CAD

Table 2.6. WS iv, x

pedological sample process, on-site documentation:

Process No.	Detailed Description with Hardware & Software
iv, x)* **soil sampling** **& documentation**	# soil samples of 100g/sample were taken in a regular 3D grid of 20 × 20 × 20 cm in horizontal and vertical directions
	# documentation of soil samples as 3D vector points via total station
	# hardware: manually by trowel, total station: see ii) in tab. 2.3
	# software: see ii) in tab. 2.3

*The process numbers are identical with the numbers (Roman numerals) in the workflow charts of process chain 1–4 (figs.2.8, 2.16, 2.18, 3.1).

The result was a CAD®-drawing containing all documented vector data, 3D point clouds and orthophotos in 'UTM-ED50' of trench 1 (table 2.7).

After a first short inspection, archaeological finds were left at the *Soprintendenza speciale per i beni archeologici di Roma* for separate analysis (first rough dating 2nd half of 5th century AD (Lieberwirth & Herzog, 2016)).

These off-site post-processions of the digital data took place in the winter term 2013/14 as the third part of the seminar 'Einführung in Digitale Dokumentationsmethoden – 3D Laserscanner und Vermessung mit der Totalstation' at the Free University Berlin, Institute of Prehistoric Archaeology (http://archiv.vv.fu-berlin.de/vorlesungsverzeichnis/ ss11/). All archaeological data were analysed at the GIS laboratory at the Free University Berlin, Topoihaus by using the following hardware: Win PC: Intel Xeon E5-1603 4@2,8GHz; 32GB DDR3; Nvidia Quadro 2000 1GB GDDR5 (fig. 2.16).

2.3.2 Pedological laboratory analysis

Simultaneous to the archaeological data post-processing, the soil samples of the campaign were analysed in terms of their chemical elements and element compositions in the Physical Geography Laboratory at the Free University Berlin. The result was a list containing the chemical element content for each sample. The list's ID numbers for each sample acted as the primary key between the vector geometry and the database (details in table 2.8).

All WSs of pedological data acquisition, as well as their storage and preparation for model building in GIS, are summarised in the chart figure 2.18.

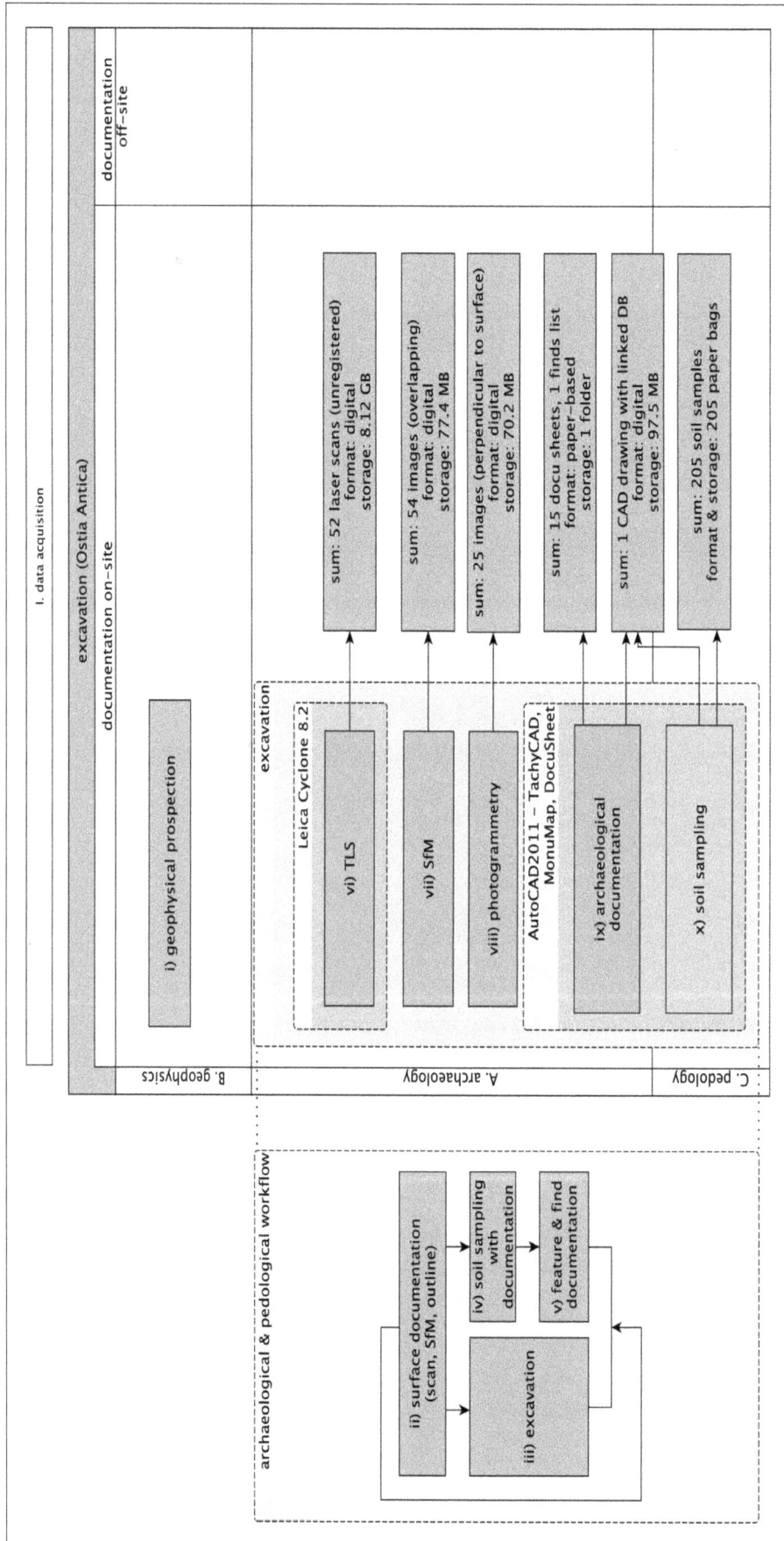

Figure 2.15. Process chain 1 – results: workflow of data acquisition at *Ostia Antica*, part: on–site documentation with results and statistics. With reference to the tables 2.2, 2.3 and 2.6.

Table 2.7. WS xi–xvii

archaeological & pedological transformation processes, off-site documentation:

Process No.	Detailed Description with Hardware & Software
xvi, xvii) **archaeological and pedological data processing**	# coordinate transformation For reference three GCPs of 'ED 50 PROIEZIONE UTM' (V8, V9, V10) were used. The transformation was executed by using the 'Advanced HELMERT transformation' (TachyCAD® 2017, p. 297ff.). detailed WSs:
xvi, xvii)	# creation of one main CAD-drawing with reference drawings Further drawings were categorised according to thematic data like 3D point clouds and photographs for efficient handling (fig. 2.17).
xi, xiii)* **3D point cloud processing**	# export of TLS-DB At first, the point clouds obtained by TLS had to be registered (combination of several scans belonging to one surface), georeferenced (adjusting geodetic coordinates, see table 2.3) and cleaned (removing all points outside the area of interest, as well as overshoots and undershoots). Export and import procedures were done by the software Leica Cyclone® and the AutoCAD® plug-in PointSense® using PTZ-file formats (WS xvi, xvii). Secondly, precise cutting of the 3D point clouds using the layer outlines (3D polylines) was done in the plug-in. The result was a georeferenced 3D point cloud describing each archaeological layer surface with a point resolution of 1 × 1cm and exported as multipoint shapefile (SHP-file).
xii) **3D point cloud creation**	# creation of 3D point clouds out of overlapping photographs The overlapping photographs of trench 1 layer 108, 112, 113 were processed because of the limits of TLS (sec. 2.2.2) and georeferenced in the propriatary software Agisoft PhotoScan® (Agisoft, 2014). Firstly, the photo series were sorted by selecting the most suitable photographs for further processing using *Structure from Motion* (SfM) method Referenz zur Introduction und (Lieberwirth & Bussilliat, 2017, chap. 2.2). Georeferencing in Agisoft PhotoScan® works in a similar way as in Cyclone® (WS xi, xiii). The more photographs are connected the more precise is the model. Therefore, the 3D resolution cannot be adjusted like in TLS. Automatic GCP detection is possible but should be evaluated (Lieberwirth & Bussilliat, 2017, chap. 3.2). The georeferenced point clouds were exported as 'colored point clouds', imported into AutoCAD® where they were processed like the TLS clouds (cutting by 3D layer borders) with the plug-in PointSense® and finally exported as multipoint SHP-file for GIS import.
xvi, xvii) **archaeological and pedological data processing**	detailed WSs:
	# post-processing of AutoCAD® MonuMap®-DB All geometry types (fig. 2.4, 2.12) were checked of their internal consistency.

*The process numbers are identical with the numbers (Roman numerals) in the workflow charts of process chain 1–4 (figs.2.8, 2.16, 2.18, 3.1). The graphical workflows in the tables show always only one typical example of each data type.

3D and 4D Cartography of Archaeological Stratigraphy

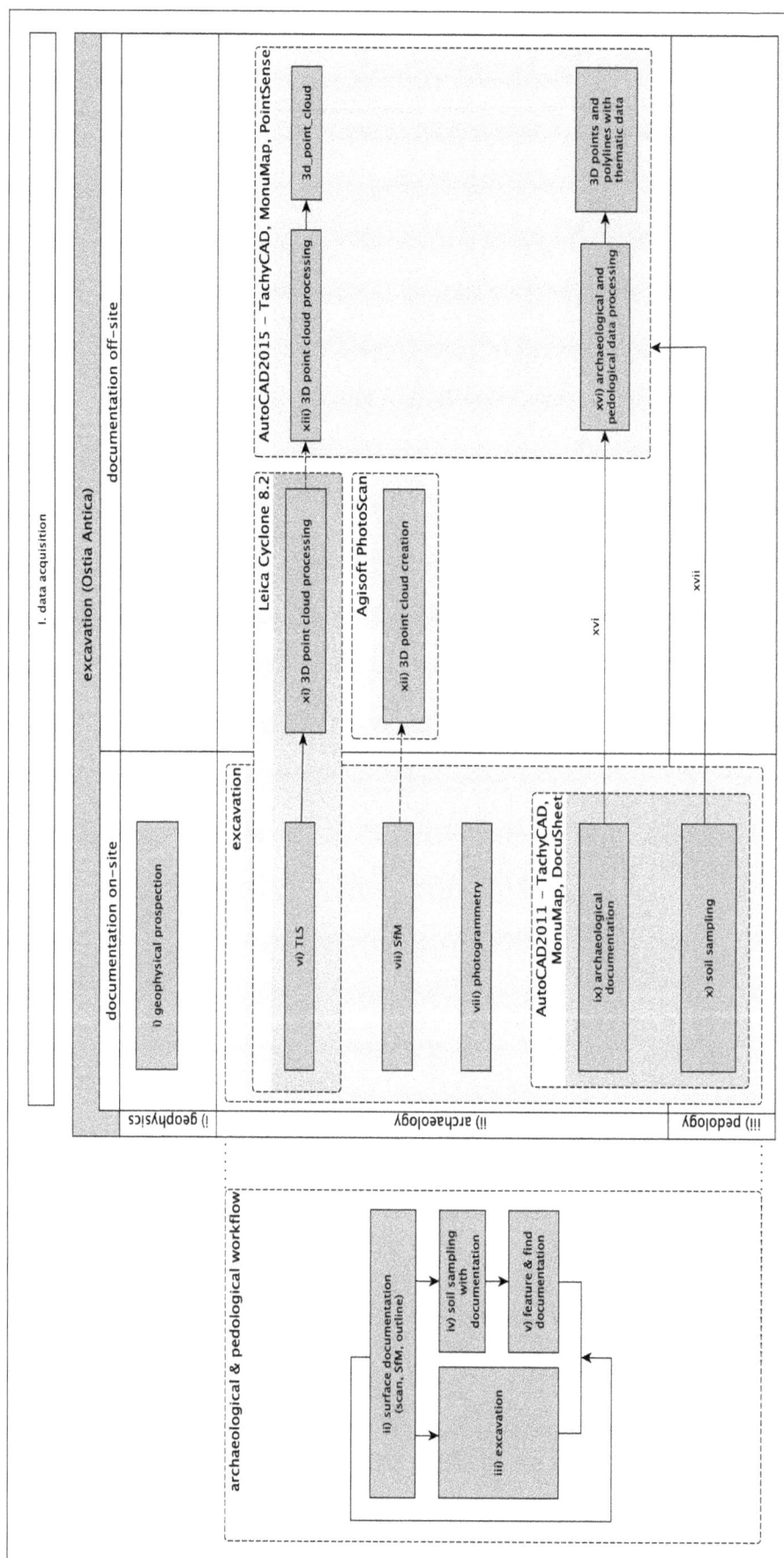

Figure 2.16. Process chain 2: general workflow of on-site data acquisition at *Ostia Antica*, part: off-site documentation. With reference to the tables 2.2, 2.3, 2.6 and 2.7.

30

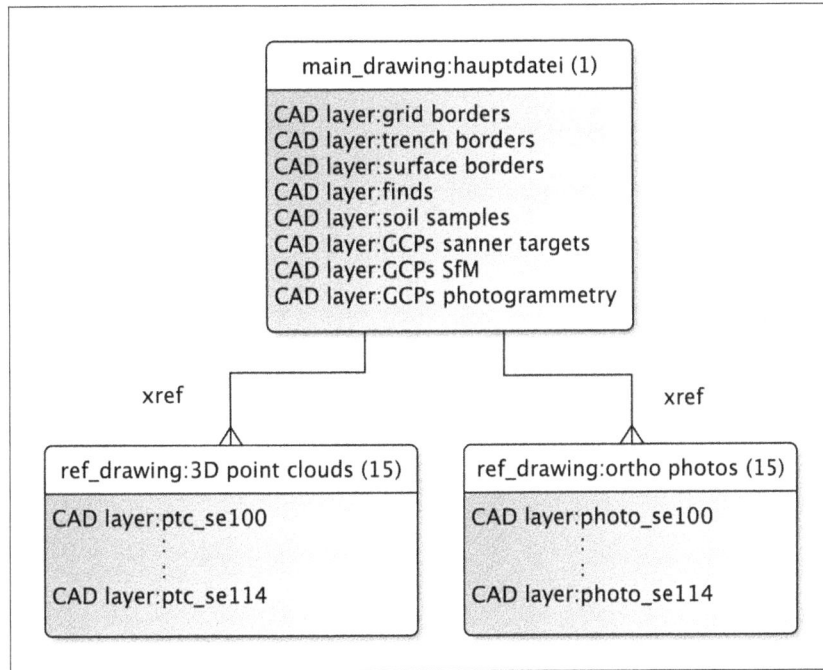

Figure 2.17. AutoCAD® main drawing with reference drawings.

Table 2.8. WS xviii

pedological sample preparation, off-site documentation:

Process No.	Detailed Description with Hardware & Software
xviii)* **chemical analysis**	# ICP-OES-analysis ('inductively coupled plasma optical emission spectrometry') 205 soil samples were analysed for major elements (Ca mg/g, Fe mg/g, K mg/g, Mg mg/g, Mn mg/g, Na mg/g, PO4 mg/g, Zi mg/g, S mg/g, Sr µg/g) using ICP-OES spectrometer (ICP-OES Perkin Elmer Optima 2100DV).
xviii)	# combination of analysis table with geometry detailed WSs:

*The process numbers are identical with the numbers (Roman numerals) in the workflow charts of process chain 1–4 (figs.2.8, 2.16, 2.18, 3.1). The graphical workflows in the tables show always only one typical example of each data type.

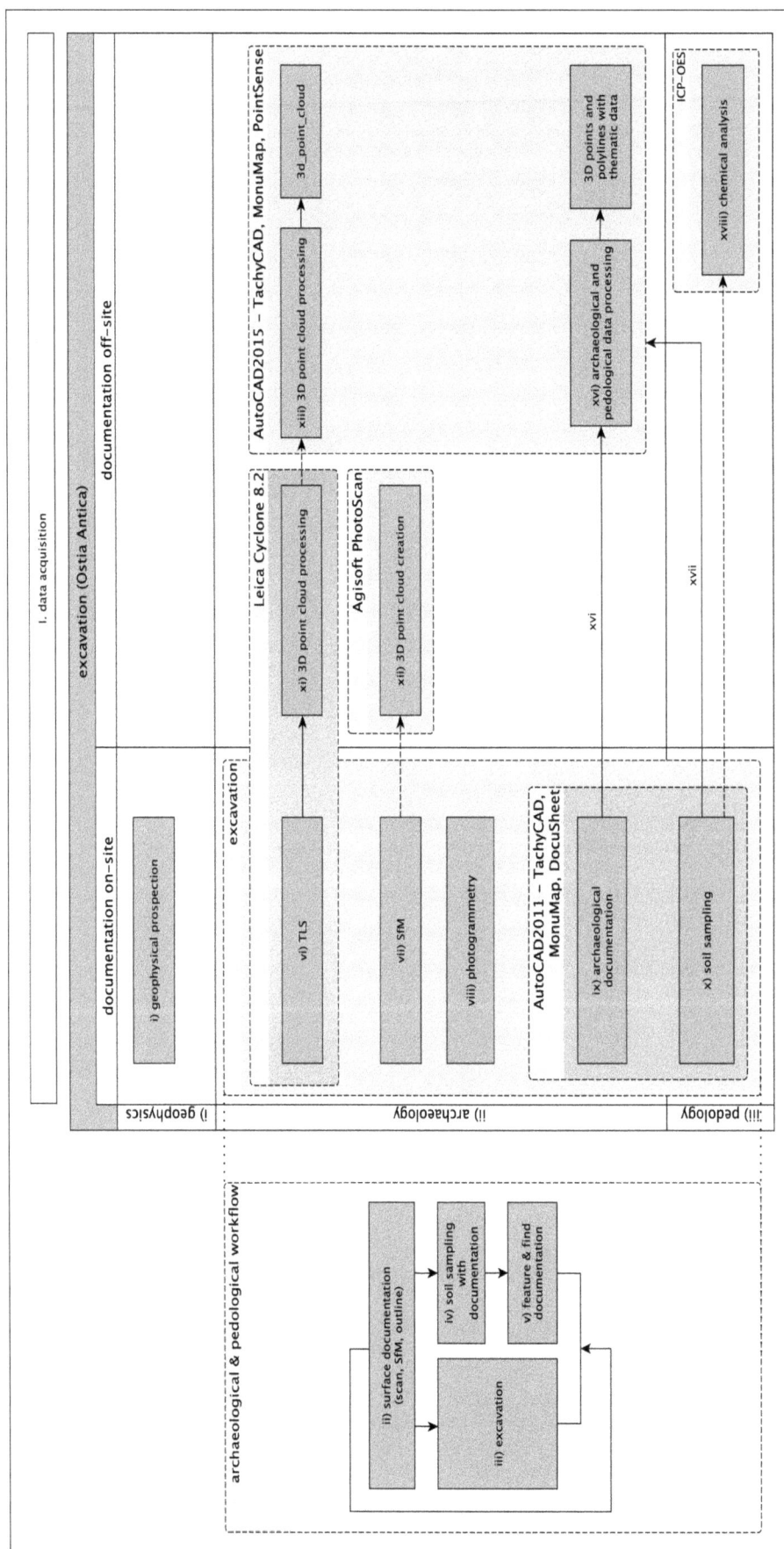

Figure 2.18. Process chain 3: general workflow of on-site data acquisition *Ostia Antica* and off-site data processing with pedological laboratory analysis. With reference to the tables 2.2, 2.3, 2.6, 2.7 and 2.8.

3

3D Data Modelling

The aim of this part of the study was to model excavation trench 1 as a first example of the campaign. All documented data from the three subjects archaeology, geophysics and pedology should be summarised in one 3D GIS model.

The modelling process in this chapter starts with importing all acquired data from chapter 2 into the 3D GIS environment 'GRASS GIS' (fig. 3.1). The processes of converting data into GIS-readable formats is described in detail. Some data had to be imported; some needed preparations beforehand.

To obtain raster surfaces of archaeological layers (top surfaces) out of the 3D point clouds (generated by TLS or SfM) several calculation steps had to be done. They were also required for the voxel of archaeological deposits (WS xx in table 3.2). In a last step, all data were exported as ParaView©-readable format (VTK (visual tool kit)-files), the viewer for the following analysis. This format is required by the scientific analysis environment ParaView©. This visualisation and analysis software is recommended by GRASS GIS itself when it comes to its limits to visualise voxel or complex 2.5D representations. The VTK-format is generally used by several scientific graphic analysis programs, for example 3D Slicer (Fedorov et al., 2012), CMake (CMake, 2018) and MeshLab (ISTI-CNR, 2018).

All processes are described in detail as working steps in tables 3.1, 3.2 and 3.3, respectively. The chart figure 3.1 gives an overview of the modelling workflow embedded within the study's workflow. The graphical workflows in the tables show a typical example of each data type.

The geophysical data made an exception in the modelling process. They were provided by the company Eastern Atlas® already as a VTK voxel model. Hence, no conversion had to be done except in scale (described in detail in chap. 3.1).

Since all data (archaeological and pedological) came as vectors, decisions had to be made as to how they should be treated in GIS, e.g. point data scans to be calculated into continuous raster surfaces as in 2D GIS (see also Scianna and Villa 2011, p. 340 tab.1). Hence, similar considerations as used in common 'GIS in archaeology' had to be made in terms of which representation format is best for modelling the real world – in this case the excavation trench.

3.1 Geophysical data modelling

The modelling of the geophysical data was already carried out by the company Eastern Atlas® (WS xix in table 3.1 and fig. 3.1). Eastern Atlas® provided, besides the common geophysical images (see chap. 2.2.1), a complete voxel model of the GPR reflection amplitude value of trench 1. The model was calculated by the interpolation of the reflection amplitude of 25 georadar timeslices showing values from 3 to 19686. The chosen voxel size is a resolution 2 cm horizontally by 5 cm vertically. This resolution has been chosen for two reasons:

– according to the data acquisition resolution and
– the calculation time of the software.

The model had been handed over already in a VTK-format which is readable by the viewing and analysis software ParaView© (fig. 4.9).

In order to combine the geophysical with the archaeological model, the geophysical had to be transformed into the final coordinate system 'short_ED50'. Transformation details are provided in table 3.1. The term 'short_ED50' is explained in detail in sec. 4.1.

3.2 Archaeological data modelling

To model the archaeological trench 1 from an archaeological point-of-view all archaeological vector data (WS xxiii, xxiv in tables 3.2 and 3.3) and 3D point clouds of archaeological surfaces (multipoint vector data) (WS xx, xxi in table 3.2) from the AutoCAD®-3D floor plan were imported into GRASS GIS. The vectors did not need any editing. In GIS they were converted into a VTK-files for importing into ParaView©.

Table 3.2 describes the import processes and data conversion of each archaeological data type into GRASS GIS, respectively ParaView©.

Additionally, the statistical software program RStudio© (RStudio Team, 2020), (RStudio, 2018) was used to assist GRASS GIS when no suitable algorithm was available (fig. 3.1). Fortunately, both programs share an interface which makes import-export procedures obsolete. RStudio© is an efficient calculation program with limited

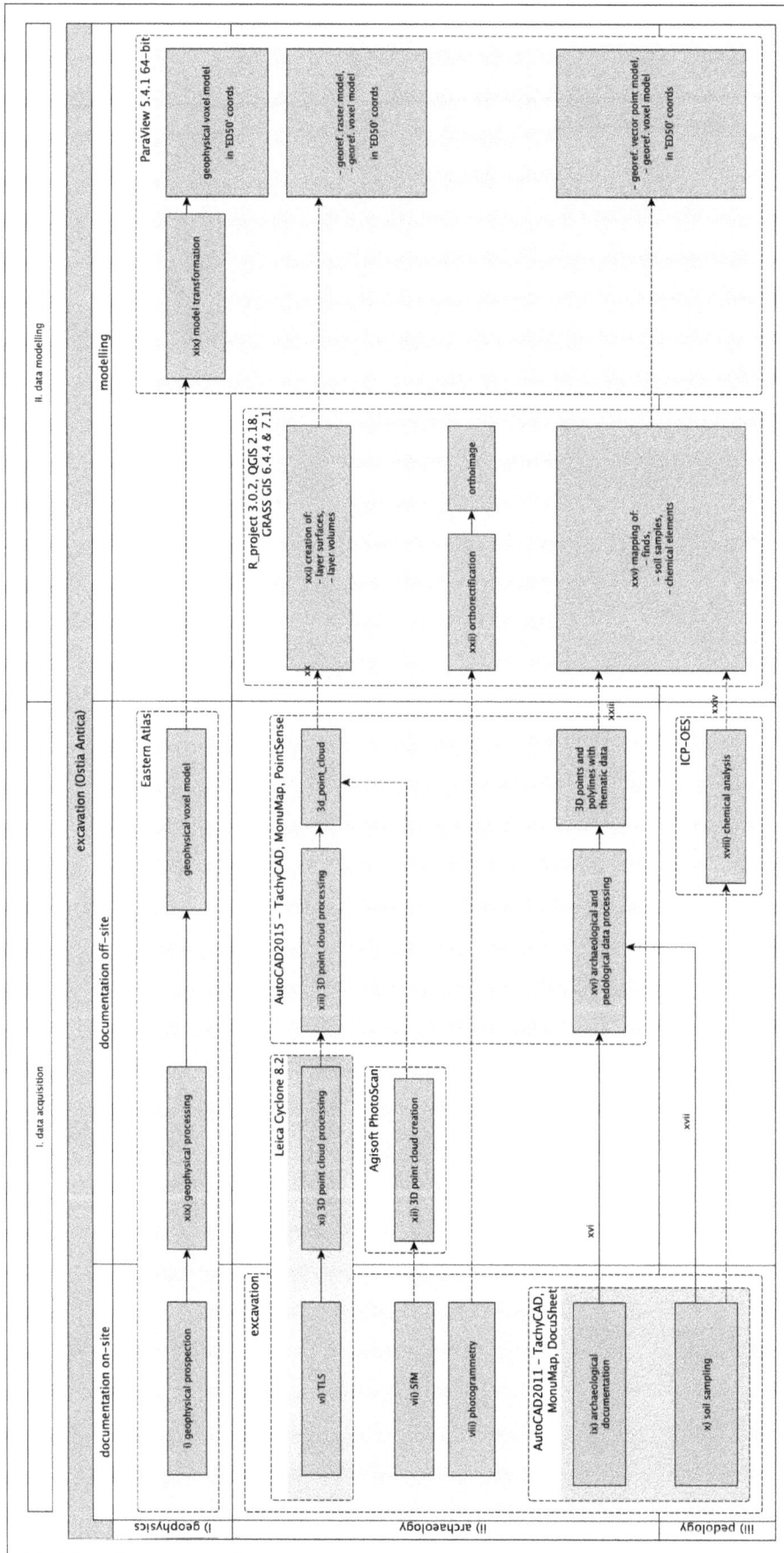

Figure 3.1. Process chain 4: general workflow of on-site data acquisition, off-site data processing and modelling of *Ostia Antica* excavation data. With reference to the tables 2.2, 2.3, 2.6, 2.7, 2.8, 3.1, 3.2 and 3.3.

Table 3.1. WS xix

geophysical model transformation:

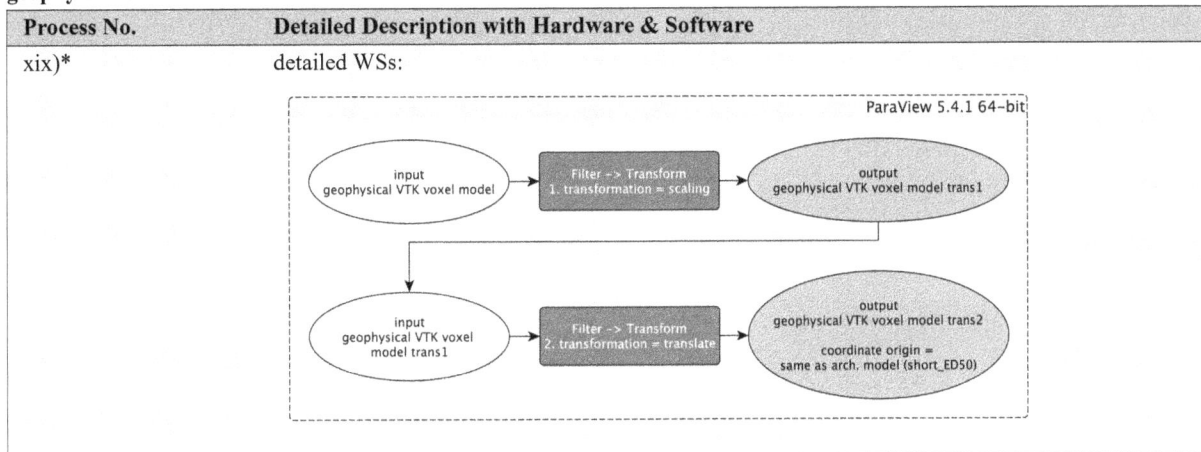

Process No.	Detailed Description with Hardware & Software
xix)*	detailed WSs:

*The process numbers are identical with the numbers (Roman numerals) in the workflow chart of process chain 4 (see fig. 3.1).

Table 3.2. WS xx–xxiii

archaeological data import & conversion – 3D vector points, 3D vector lines, 3D point clouds:

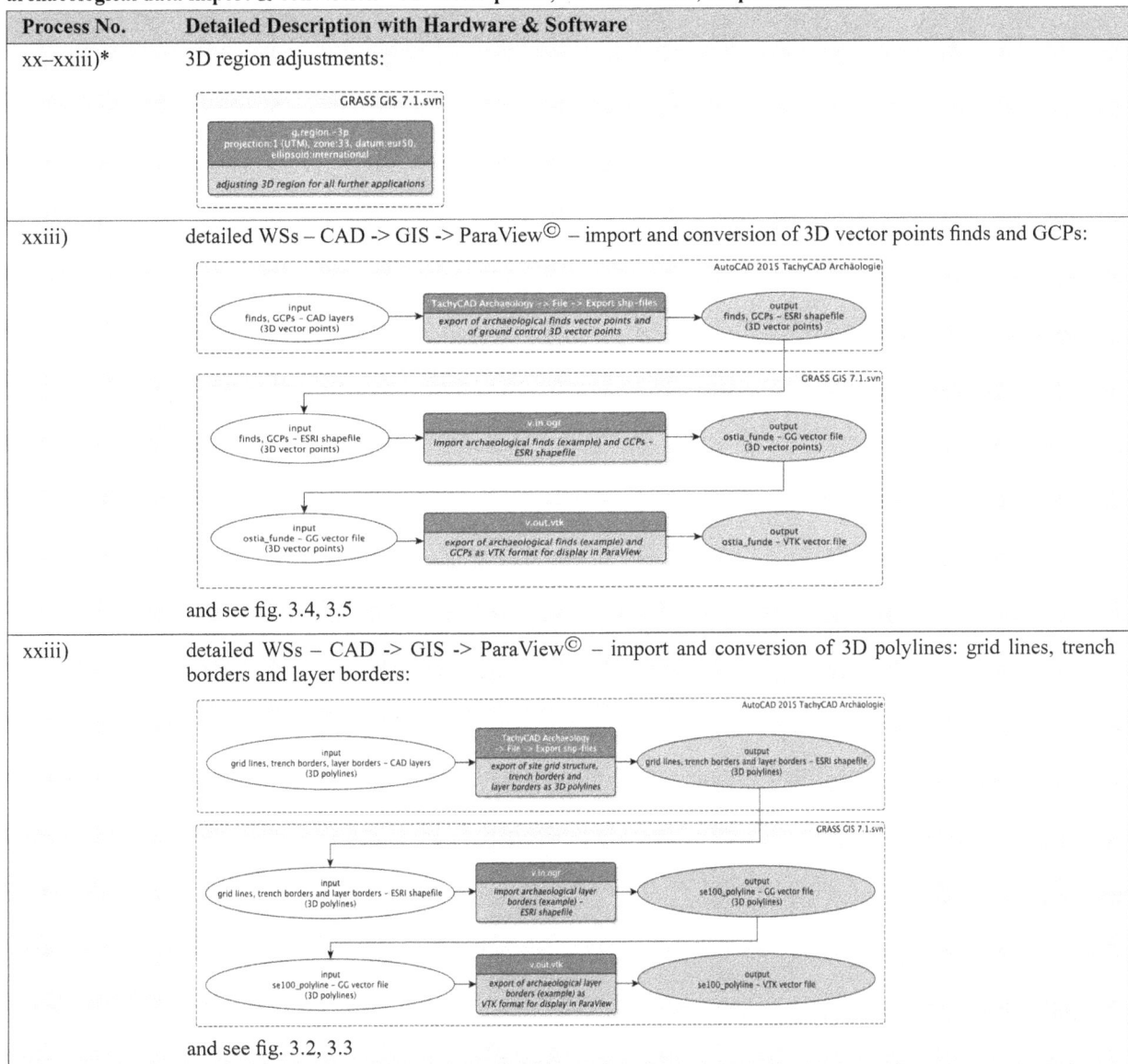

Process No.	Detailed Description with Hardware & Software
xx–xxiii)*	3D region adjustments:
xxiii)	detailed WSs – CAD -> GIS -> ParaView© – import and conversion of 3D vector points finds and GCPs: and see fig. 3.4, 3.5
xxiii)	detailed WSs – CAD -> GIS -> ParaView© – import and conversion of 3D polylines: grid lines, trench borders and layer borders: and see fig. 3.2, 3.3

(continued)

Table 3.2. WS xx–xxiii *(Continued)*

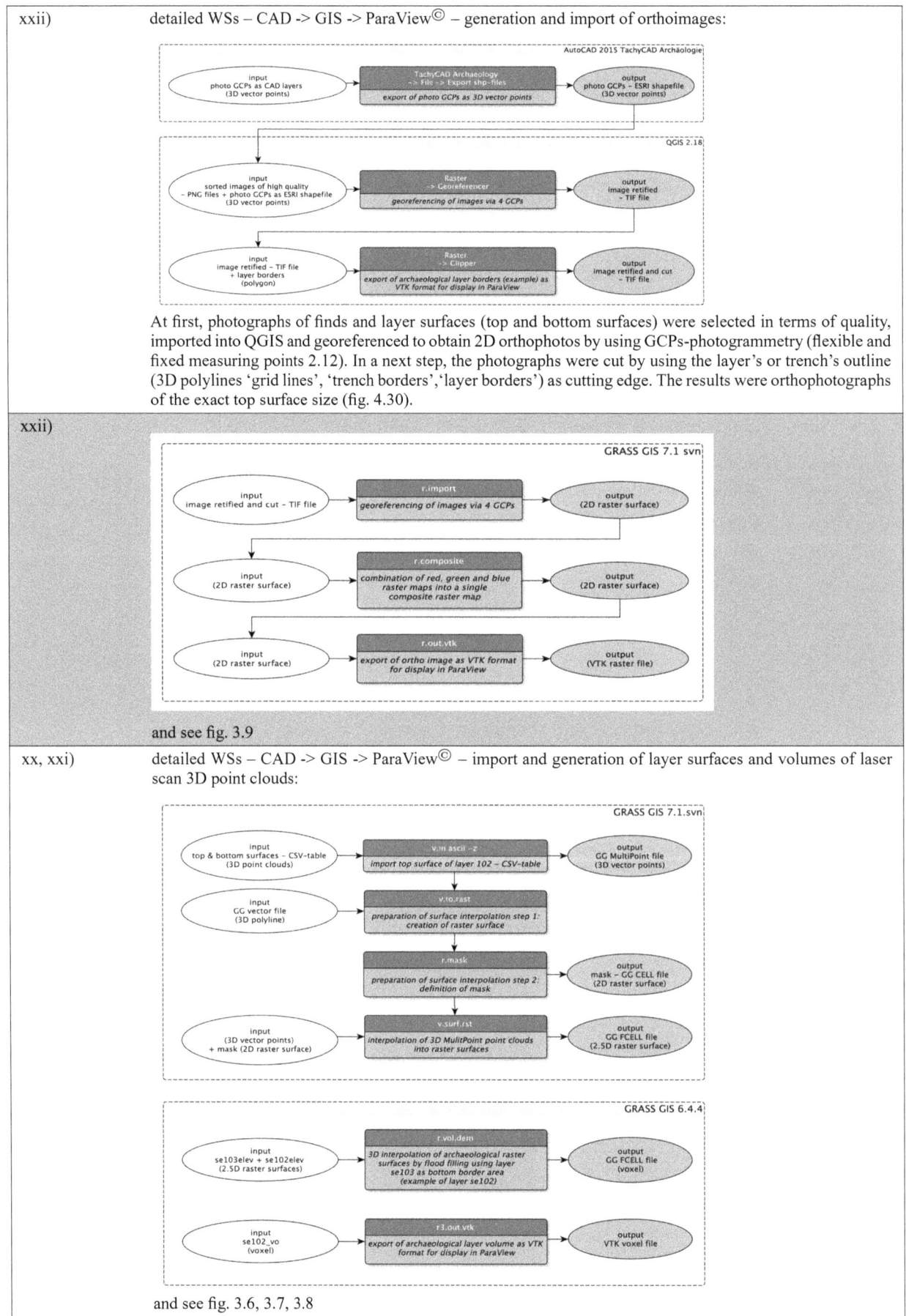

xxii)	detailed WSs – CAD -> GIS -> ParaView© – generation and import of orthoimages: At first, photographs of finds and layer surfaces (top and bottom surfaces) were selected in terms of quality, imported into QGIS and georeferenced to obtain 2D orthophotos by using GCPs-photogrammetry (flexible and fixed measuring points 2.12). In a next step, the photographs were cut by using the layer's or trench's outline (3D polylines 'grid lines', 'trench borders', 'layer borders') as cutting edge. The results were orthophotographs of the exact top surface size (fig. 4.30).
xxii)	 and see fig. 3.9
xx, xxi)	detailed WSs – CAD -> GIS -> ParaView© – import and generation of layer surfaces and volumes of laser scan 3D point clouds: and see fig. 3.6, 3.7, 3.8

*The process numbers are identical with the numbers (Roman numerals) in the workflow chart of process chain 4 (see fig. 3.1).

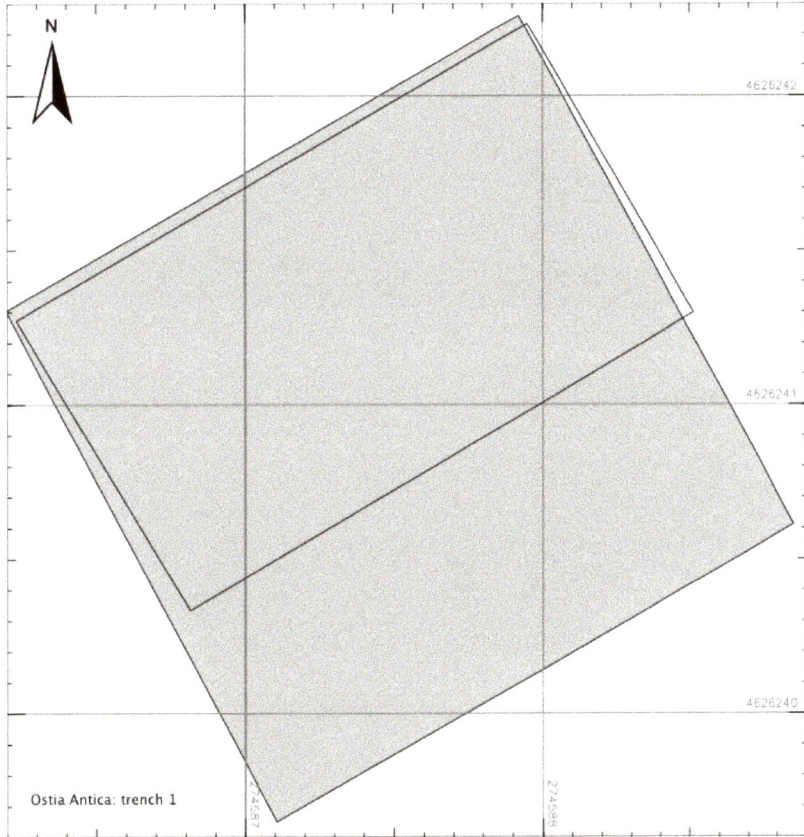

Figure 3.2. Trench 1: grid line as polygon, trench 1b: grid line as polyline in GRASS.

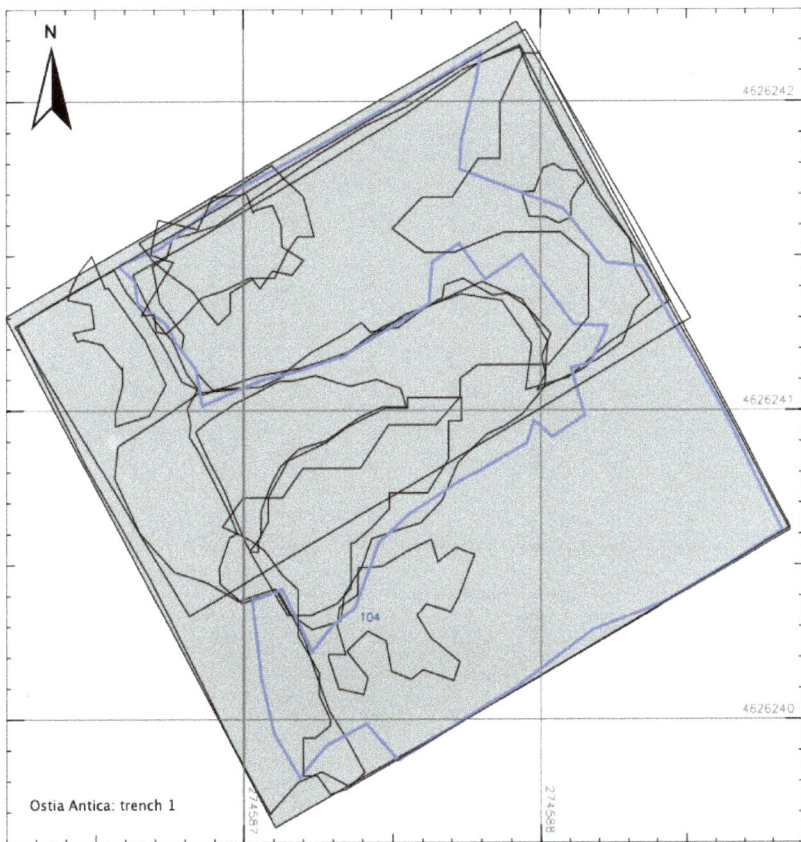

Figure 3.3. Trench 1: grid line as polygon, trench 1b: grid line as polyline, layer outlines as 3D polylines in GRASS.

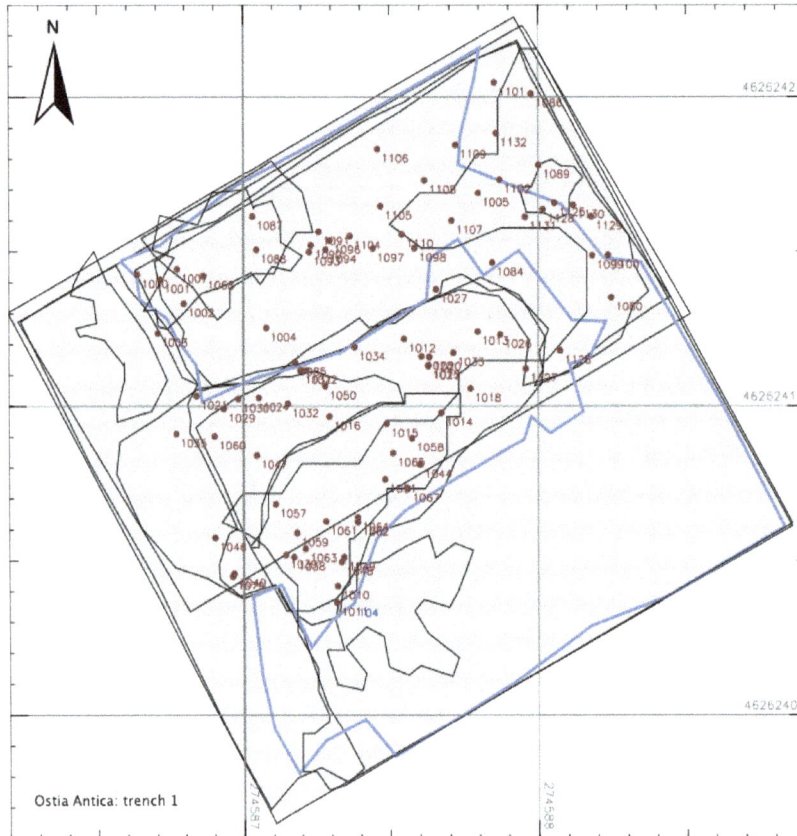

Figure 3.4. Trench 1: grid line as polygon, trench 1b: grid line as polyline, layer outlines as 3D polylines, archaeological finds with find number as 3D vector points in GRASS.

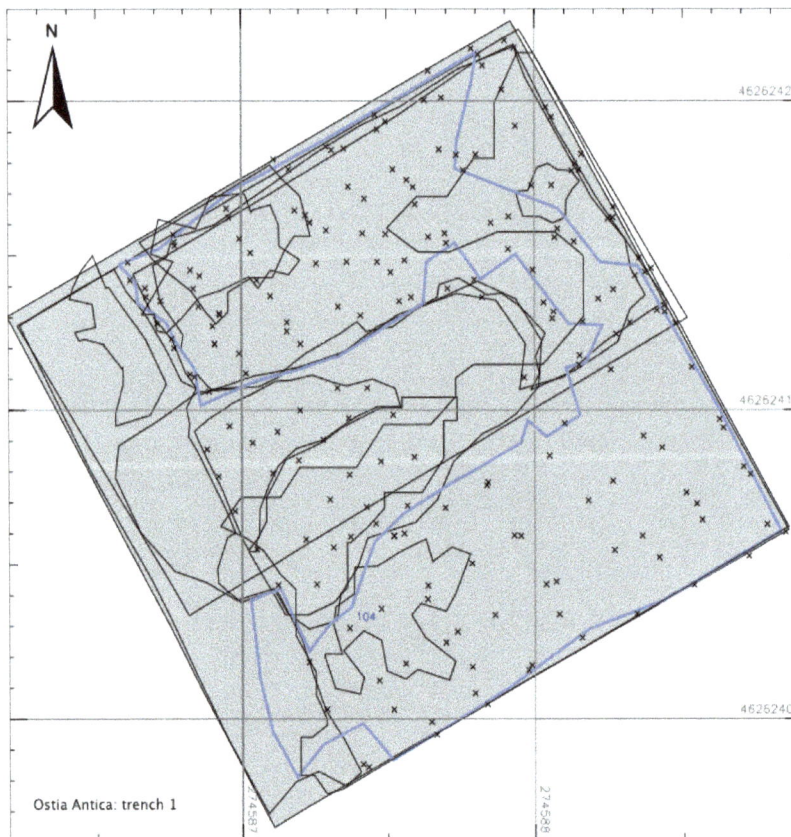

Figure 3.5. Trench 1: grid line as polygon, trench 1b: grid line as polyline, layer outlines as 3D polylines, soil sample locations as 3D vector points in GRASS.

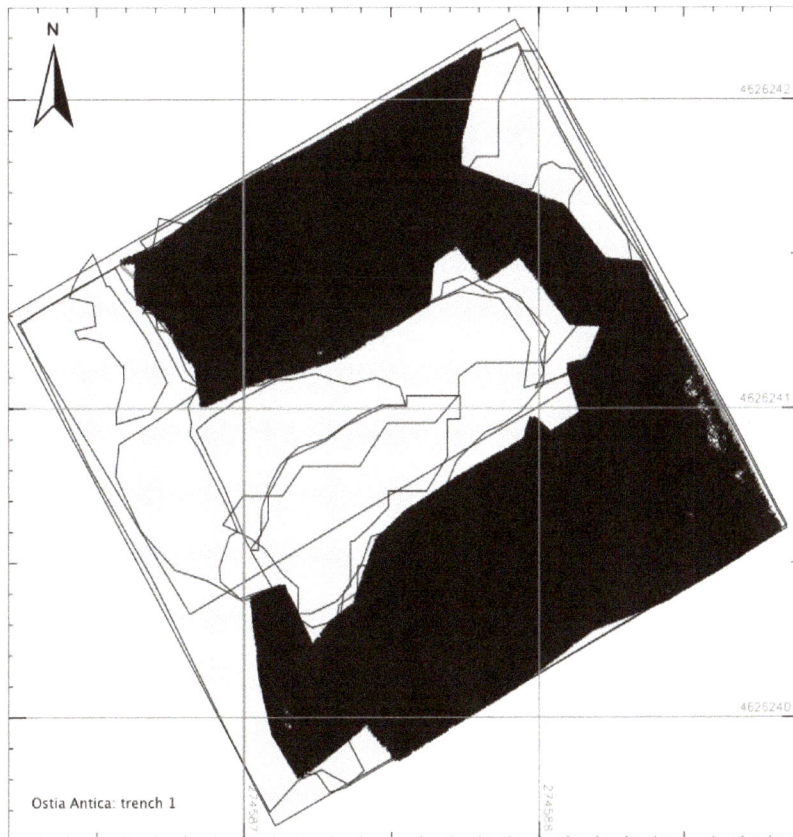

Figure 3.6. Trench 1: grid line as polygon, trench 1b: grid line as polyline, layer outlines as 3D polylines, layer 'se104' as 3D multipoint in GRASS.

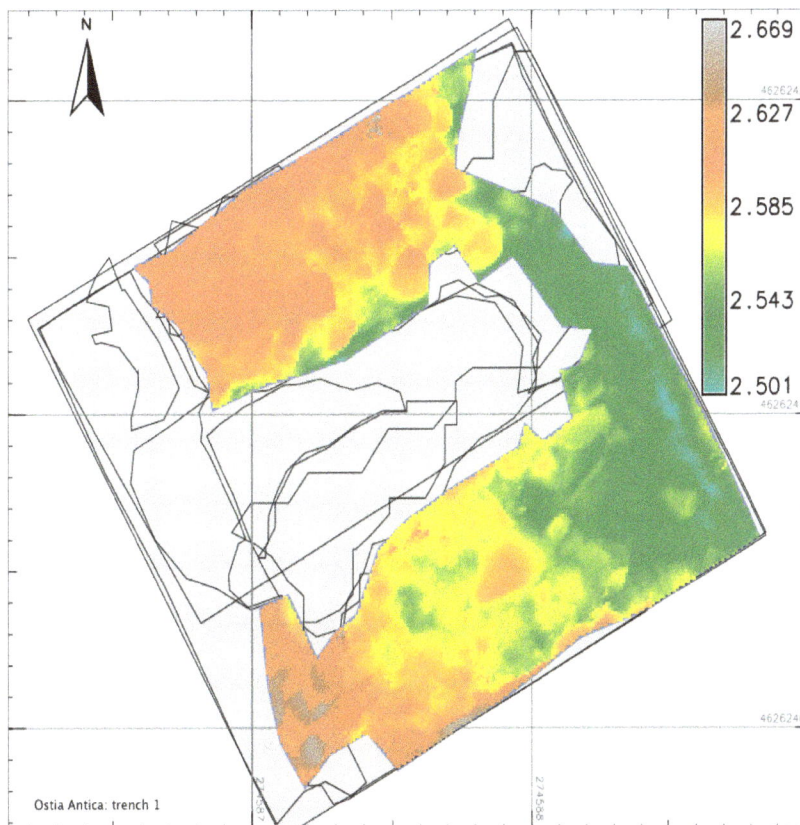

Figure 3.7. Trench 1: grid line as polygon, trench 1b: grid line as polyline, layer outlines as 3D polylines, layer 'se104' as raster surface in GRASS.

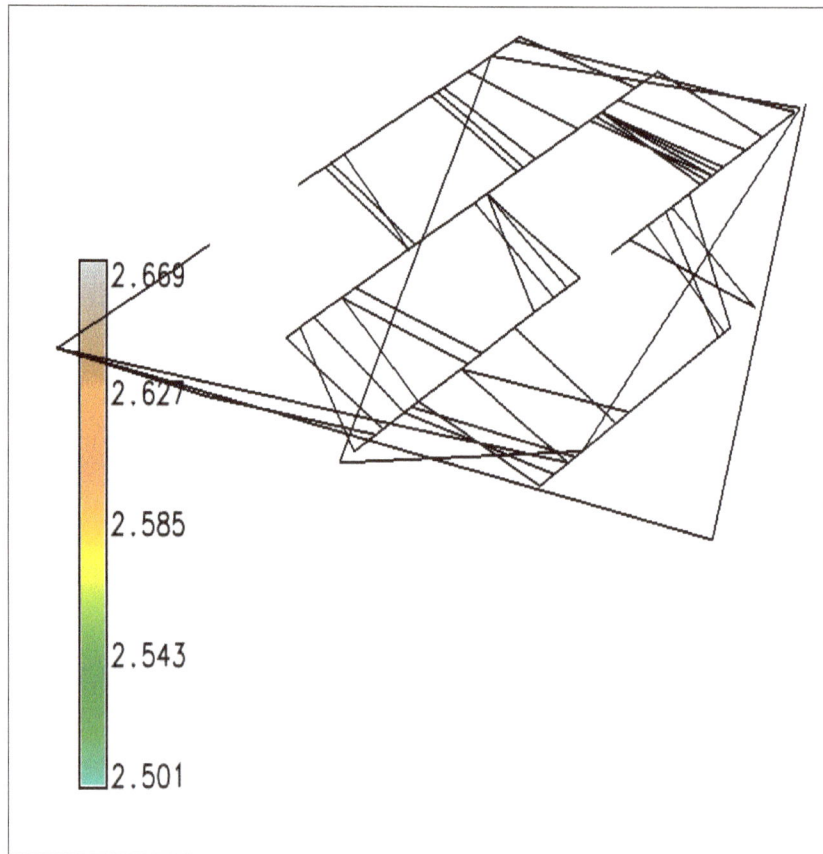

Figure 3.8. Trench 1: grid line as polygon, raster and volume in GRASS.

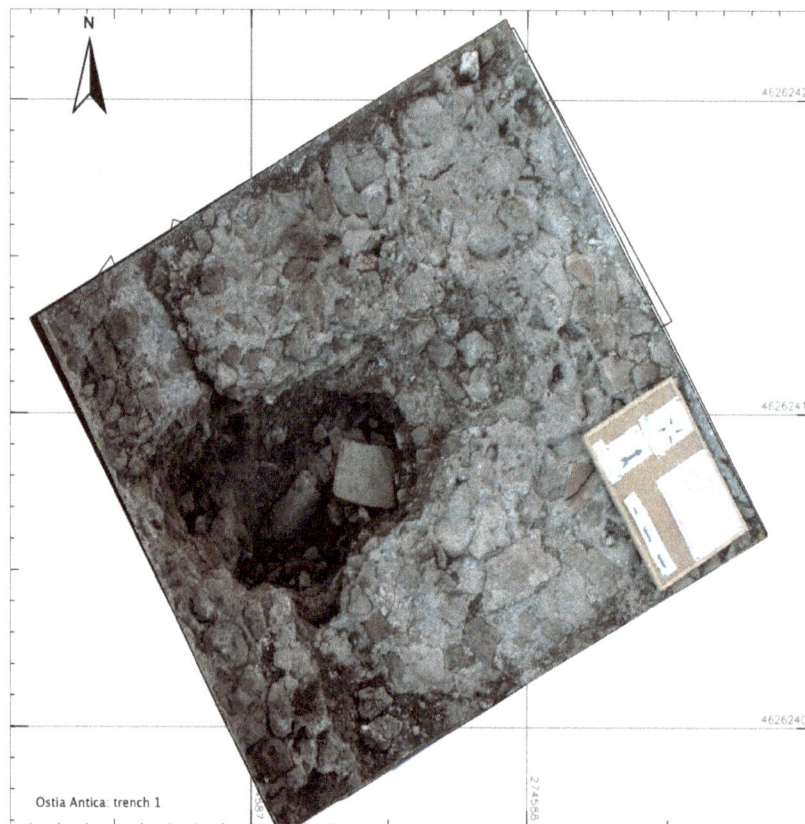

Figure 3.9. Trench 1: grid line as polygon, layer 'se104' as orthophoto in GRASS.

```
r3.info map=ostia_bp_s1_ca_vo_global@schnitt1
+----------------------------------------------------------------------+
| Layer:    ostia_bp_s1_ca_vo_global@schn  Date: Wed Feb 17 17:10:49 2016 |
| Mapset:   schnitt1                       Login of Creator: undine    |
| Location: Osita_ed50                                                 |
| DataBase: /Volumes/Elements/Finale_Daten_Diss/grassdata3            |
| Title:    ostia_bp_s1_ca_vo_global                                  |
| Units:    none                                                       |
| Vertical unit: units                                                 |
| Timestamp: none                                                      |
|----------------------------------------------------------------------|
|                                                                      |
|   Type of Map:  raster_3d          Number of Categories: 0           |
|   Data Type:    FCELL                                                |
|   Rows:         270                                                  |
|   Columns:      270                                                  |
|   Depths:       82                                                   |
|   Total Cells:  5977800                                              |
|   Total size:        7761037 Bytes                                   |
|   Number of tiles:   1000                                            |
|   Mean tile size:    7761 Bytes                                      |
|   Tile size in memory: 26244 Bytes                                   |
|   Number of tiles in x, y and  z:   10, 10, 10                       |
|   Dimension of a tile in x, y, z:   27, 27, 9                        |
|                                                                      |
|       Projection: UTM (zone 33)                                      |
|           N:  4626242.3   S:  4626239.6  Res:  0.01                  |
|           E:  274588.9    W:  274586.2   Res:  0.01                  |
|           T:       2.8    B:         2   Res: 0.0097561              |
|   Range of data:   min = 71.38214874 max = 215.57272339             |
|                                                                      |
|   Data Source:                                                       |
|                                                                      |
|                                                                      |
|                                                                      |
|   Data Description:                                                  |
|    generated by v.vol.rst                                            |
|                                                                      |
+----------------------------------------------------------------------+
```

Figure 3.10. Metadata: volume statistics for 3D raster map (voxel model) 'soil samples' of GRASS module *r3.stats*.

```
r3.univar map=ostia_bp_s1_ca_vo_global@schnitt1
total null and non-null cells: 7312760
total null cells: 4315160
Of the non-null cells:
----------------------
n: 2997600
minimum: 71.3821
maximum: 215.573
range: 144.191
mean: 104.078
mean of absolute values: 104.078
standard deviation: 10.2712
variance: 105.498
variation coefficient: 9.86874 %
sum: 311985469.494072
```

Figure 3.11. Metadata: univariate statistics from the non-null cells of 3D raster map (voxel model) 'soil samples' of GRASS module *r3.univar*.

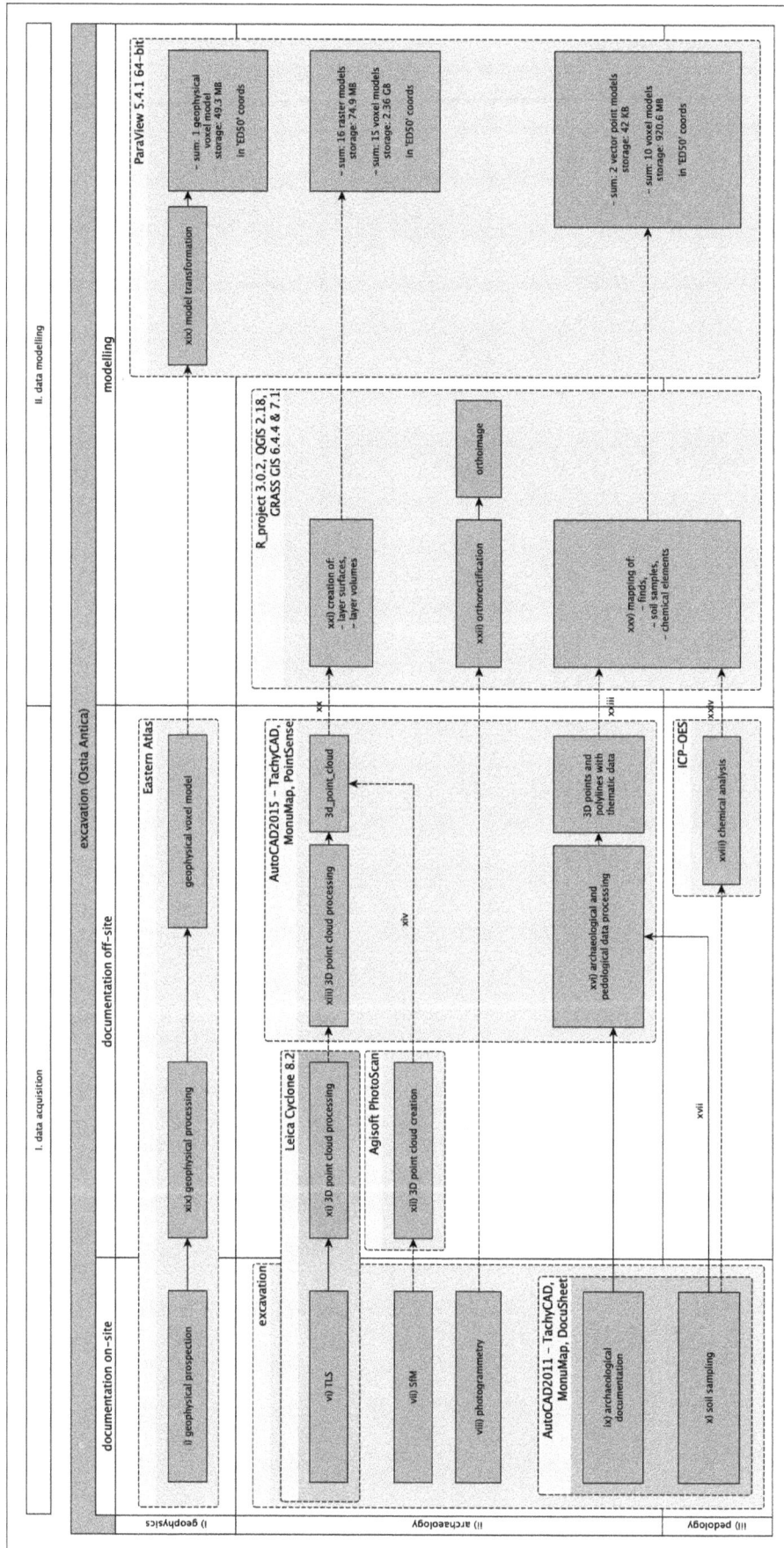

Figure 3.12. Process chain 4-results: general workflow of on-site data acquisition, off-site data processing and modelling of *Ostia Antica* excavation data. With reference to the tables 2.2, 2.3, 2.6, 2.7, 2.8, 3.1, 3.2 and 3.3.

Table 3.3. WS xxiv-xxv

pedological data conversion – laboratory analysis results and 3D vector points:

Process No.	Detailed Description with Hardware & Software
xxiv–xxv)*	detailed WSs – CAD -> GIS -> ParaView© – calculation of 3D distribution of chemical elements:

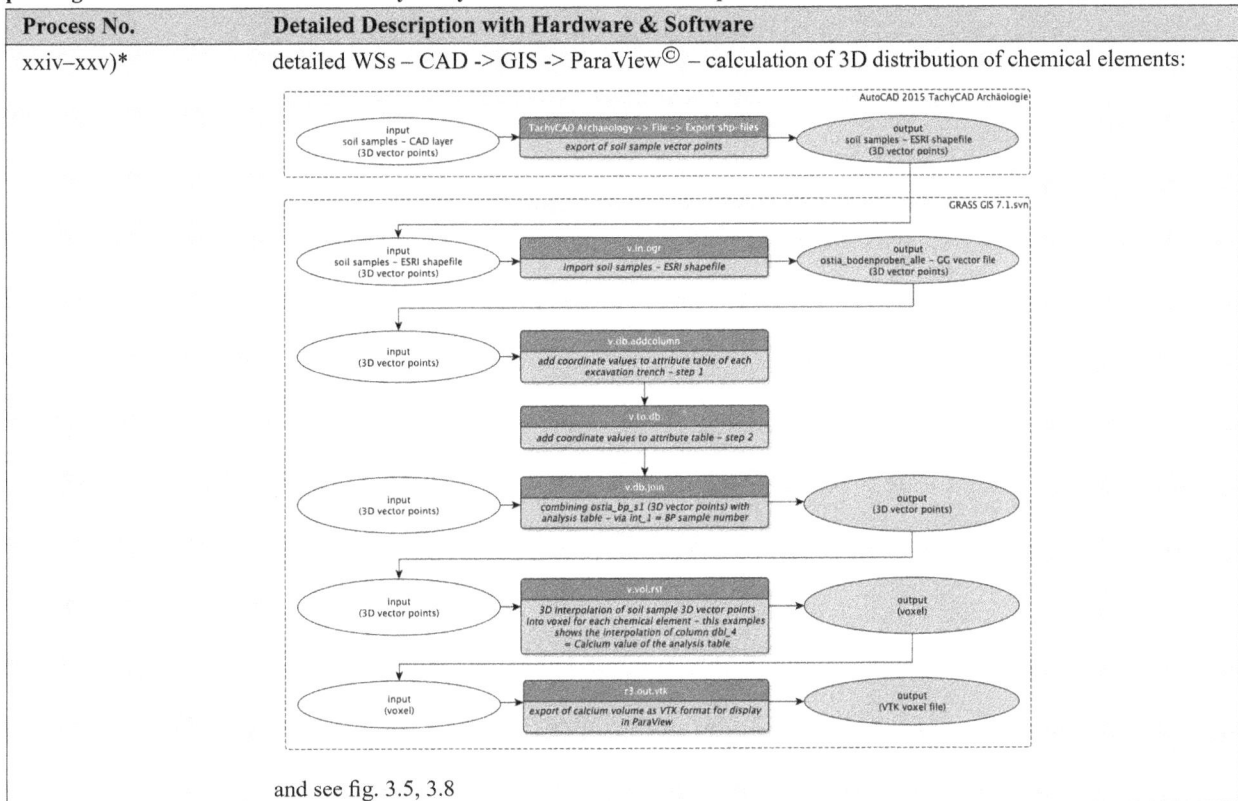

and see fig. 3.5, 3.8

*The process numbers are identical with the numbers (Roman numerals) in the workflow chart of process chain 4 (see fig. 3.1).

graphical output but great compute power. In this case study, it was used to solve two tasks:

1. shortening the coordinate digits and
2. combining the RGB-values of the laser scan point clouds.

The first application became necessary after a first test run. The model's world coordinates produced distorted results (figs. 4.1 and 4.2). The modelling worked fine after the coordinate digits were shortened (analysis sec. 4.1).

The second application was a planned experiment to differentiate archaeological layers by colour (see research question RQ x in sec. 1.2.2 and analysis section 4.3.1).

Orthophotos were generated by a detour with QGIS (WS xxii table 3.2 and see also discussion in sec. 5.1.12.

3.3 Pedological data modelling

The aim of this working step was to model the distribution of each selected chemical element inside the 3D space of the archaeological trench. The pedological information of the 205 soil samples of trench 1 was interpolated in the complete 3D space of trench 1 to show the 3D distribution of the chemical element information (figs. 4.7 and 4.18).

The following table 3.3 describes in detail the working steps of this volume calculation. Figures 3.10 and 3.11

show lists with metadata as descriptive statistics of the generated voxel models. They can be seen as representative examples for all other eight elements of the 205 soil samples in trench 1. Minimum and maximum values of the final voxel model present the range of the interpolation calcium values ('Range of data' in fig. 3.10). They differ slightly from the measured values due to the interpolation algorithm (see discussion in sec. 4.2.3 and the description of the interpolation algorithm v.vol.rst in sec. 1.2.2 and Conolly and Lake 2006, chap. 6).

The modelling section for geochemical data ends with the conversion of VTK-format which is used for the analysis in chapter 4.

All WSs of data modelling, their results and preparation for visualisation in ParaView© are summarised in the chart figure 3.12.

4

3D Data Analysis

The analysis chapter starts with the import of all trench 1's modelled data into ParaView©. Additionally to visualisation functionalities (Ayachit, 2018, chap. 4), this software provides several navigation and analysis options regarding filters (Ayachit, 2018, chap. 5) and selections (Ayachit, 2018, chap. 6) which were used for analysing.

The analysis of the archaeology, geophysics and pedology calculated in GRASS GIS is now visible as one common model. Its analysis is divided into a technical and an archaeological inspection. It starts with an overview of technical functionality visibility. They are applied in the second part where they are used to answer specific questions regarding the excavation site (section 4.2). The third part of this chapter describes planned (according to RQs) and unplanned (ideas which came up during the study) analysis experiments (section 4.3).

For structural reasons, the analysis approaches are sorted by numbers. The final 'code' is a combination of the letters AN (for 'analysis') and Roman numerals (e.g. 'AN i'). The range of the numerals has no hierarchy.

The results are visualised in thematic videos (fig. 4.6, 4.7, 4.8, 4.9, 4.10, 4.11, 4.18, 4.30) with detaild explanations.

4.1 Technical analysis

Besides 3D modelling, the study explores also analysis options of 3D voxel models concerning archaeological structures. In this section, I describe the options of ParaView©, the viewer software used here, from a technical point-of-view for all sample data types of trench 1.

Figures 4.1, 4.2 show the first attempts (AN i) which ended in negative results. The distorted models had no labels at the coordinate axes. The solution of this visualisation problem was to reduce the coordinate digits to a maximum of seven (fig. 4.3 ff.) because current versions of ParaView© support only floating point precision (Segal & Akeley, 2010). The same is true for all other scientific FOSS-viewers mentioned in chap. 3.

The problem is known by GRASS developers. Therefore, each GRASS VTK-export module has the option to 'Correct the coordinates'. But 'this works only with data from the SAME location' (e.g. https://grass.osgeo.org/grass74/manuals/r3.out.vtk.html -c flag option).

Therefore, a further WS xxvi had to be included to shorten the coordinates for each VTK-file (fig. 4.5). The coordination manipulation was only done for the export VTK-format in order to avoid manipulation of the original GIS-data (fig. 3.10). The new artificial coordinate system in this monograph is called 'short_ED50'. figures 4.3 and 4.4 show finally the same data as figures 4.1 and 4.2 without distortion after successful coordinate manipulation.

Due to the unexpected visualisation problems in ParaView© a further working step (process chain 5 in fig. 4.5) had to be added in order to shrink the latitude and longitude coordinates. The final results are reduced to a maximum of five digits in order to visualise VTK-files (coordinates e.g. in fig. 4.3 and ff.).

4.2 Archaeological analysis

This section explores the analysis options of ParaView© from an archaeological point-of-view by using all archaeological excavation data in combination with the geophysical and geochemical results of trench 1.

4.2.1 Analysis: geophysics & archaeology

This subsection is focused on combining and comparing geophysical and archaeological results in the digital analysis environment ParaView©.

The videos 4 and 5 (fig. 4.9 and 4.10) show representative examples investigating the stratigraphy of trench 1 by displaying geophysical GPR-wavelengths from a macroscopic point-of-view and by applying value threshold intervals. The geophysical results are compared with the representation of archaeological stratigraphy (surfaces in 2.5D and layers as 3D volumes).

Video 4 (fig. 4.9) shows the interpolated geophysical results of trench 1 as a cuboid. The frequency distribution of these GPR-wavelength values inside the trench indicate a clear tendency towards lower values. High wavelength reflection values are rare in trench 1. They are separated for better visibility by adjusting threshold values and intervals (fig. 4.10-01:38 ff.). Thresholds create 3D volume models of defined value ranges. The selected range clearly shows the shape of the archaeological pit (layer 108) in 3D. This geophysical shape is congruently to the archaeological result (fig. 4.10).

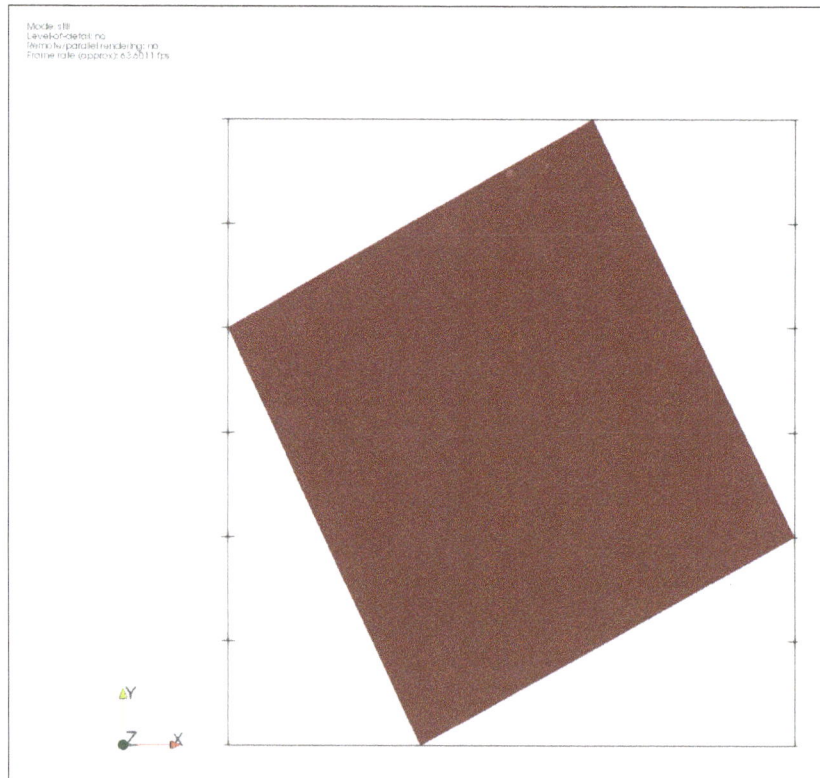

Figure 4.1. Trench area of trench 1 as polygon VTK-file (coordinate system ED50) in ParaView© – camera topview.

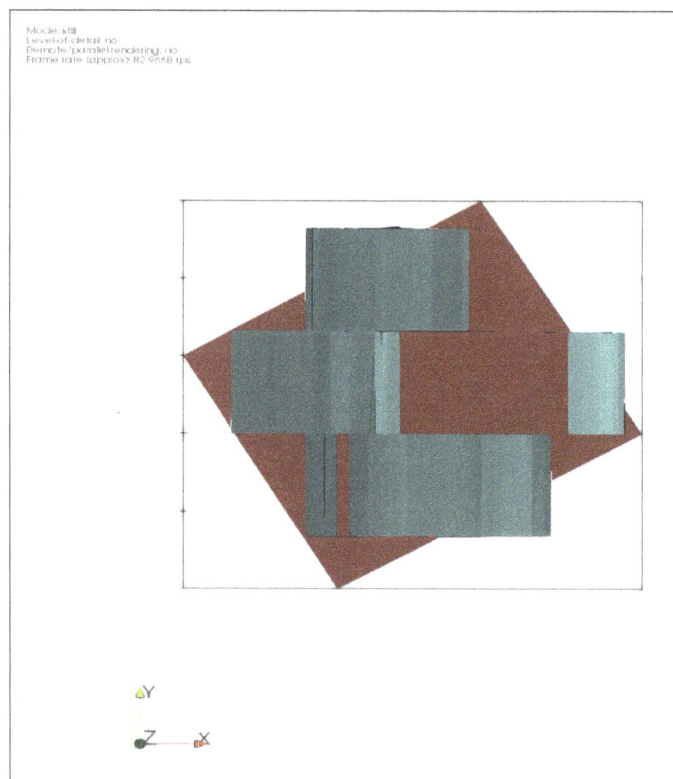

Figure 4.2. Trench area of trench 1 as polygon VTK-file in combination with top surface 'se104' of trench 1 as raster VTK-file (coordinate system ED50) in ParaView© – camera topview.

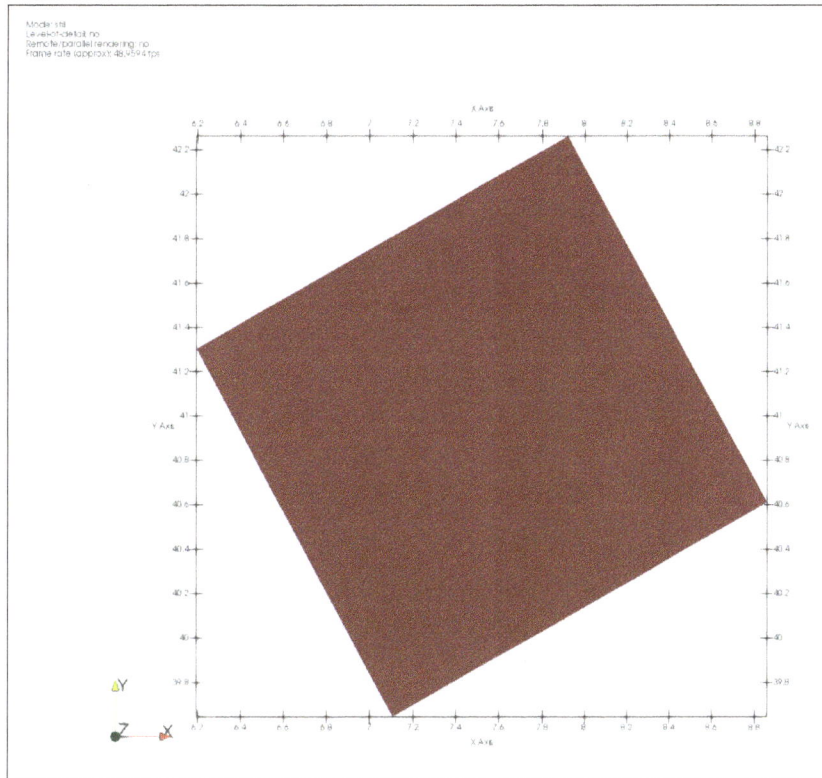

Figure 4.3. Trench area of trench 1 as polygon VTK-file (coordinate system 'short_ED50') in ParaView© – camera topview.

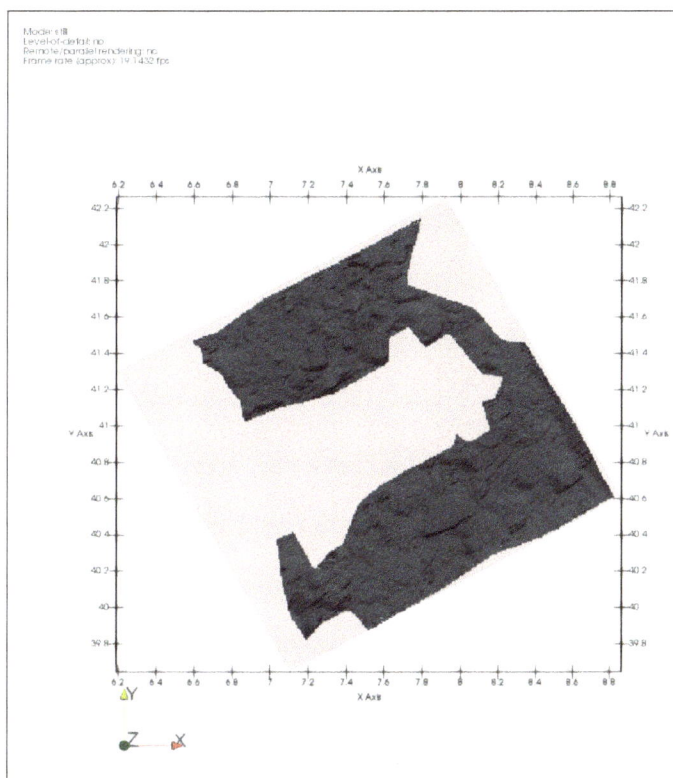

Figure 4.4. Trench area of trench 1 as polygon VTK-file in combination with top surface 'se104' of trench 1 as raster VTK-file (coordinate system 'short_ED50') in ParaView© – camera topview.

I. data acquisition | II. data modelling

documentation on-site | documentation off-site | modelling

excavation (Ostia Antica)

i) geophysics

i) geophysical prospection

xix) geophysical processing

geophysical voxel model

Eastern Atlas

geophysical voxel model

ParaView 5.4.1 64-bit

xix) model transformation

geophysical voxel model in 'ED50' coords

xxvi) reducing coordinate digits to 'short_ED50'

ii) archaeology

excavation

vi) TLS

vii) SfM

viii) photogrammetry

Leica Cyclone 8.2)

xi) 3D point cloud processing

Agisoft PhotoScan

xii) 3D point cloud creation

AutoCAD2015 – TachyCAD, MonuMap, PointSense

xiii) 3D point cloud processing

3d_point_cloud

xiv

AutoCAD2011 – TachyCAD, MonuMap, DocuSheet

ix) archaeological documentation

xi) soil sampling

xvi

xvii

xvii) archaeological and pedological data processing

3D points and polylines with thematic data

xxiii

R_project 3.0.2, QGIS 2.18, GRASS GIS 6.4.4 & 7.1

xxi) creation of: - layer surfaces, - layer volumes

xxii) orthorectification

orthoimage

xxv) mapping of: - finds, - soil samples, - chemical elements

- georef. raster model, - georef. voxel model in 'ED50' coords

- georef. vector point model, - georef. voxel model in 'ED50' coords

iii) pedology

xviii) chemical analysis

ICP-OES

xxiv

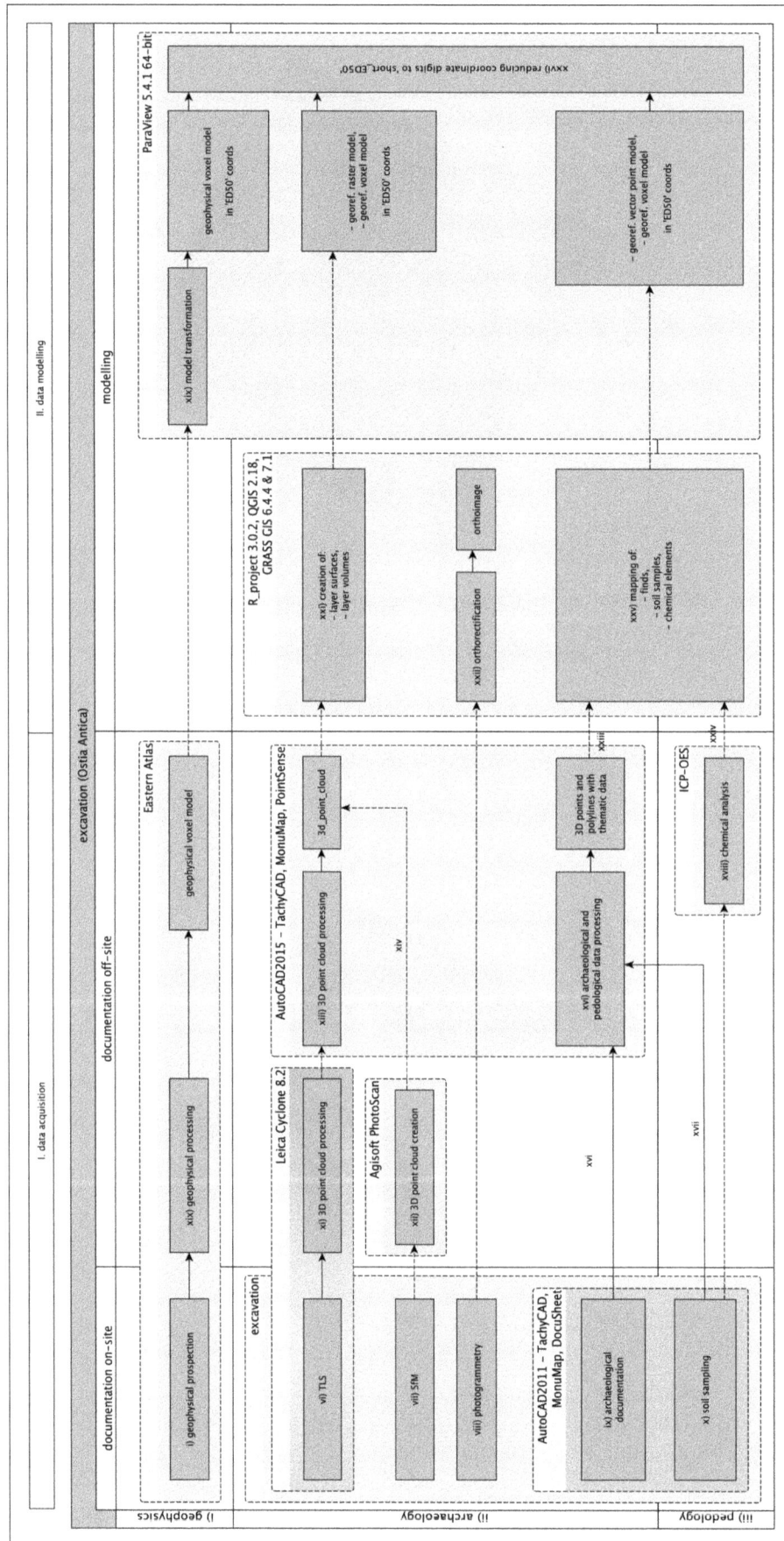

Figure 4.5. Process chain 5: general workflow of data acquisition on-site, data processing off-site, modelling and coordinate reduction of *Ostia Antica* excavation data. With reference to the tables 2.2, 2.3, 2.6, 2.7, 2.8, 3.1, 3.2 and 3.3.

Table 4.1. Analysis approaches: AN ii

visualisation ii

Analysis no. Figures & Videos	Description of Operations	Results
AN ii) # video fig. 4.6	# Open -> Apply -> Representation: wireframe # Open -> Apply -> Representation: surface	**3D vector polylines** # trench 1: grid line, reduced trench 1 = trench 1b, layer borders
AN ii) # video fig. 4.7	# Open -> Apply -> Representation: points	**3D vector points** # trench 1: finds, soil samples
AN ii) # video fig. 4.8	# Open -> Apply -> Representation: multipoint # Open -> Apply -> Representation: surface	**2.5D raster surfaces** # trench 1: layer top surfaces
AN ii) # video fig. 4.7	# Open -> Apply -> Representation: volume	**voxel volumes versus extrusion** # trench 1: layer volumes
AN ii) # video fig. 4.8, 4.9	# Open -> Apply -> Representation: volume	**voxel volumes versus interpolation** # trench 1: geophysics, pedology
AN ii) # video fig. 4.6	# selections: selection by table in 'Spreadsheet view' or geometry via 'Selection Inspector' # labelling: selection -> Display Inspector -> 'Point Labels', select the variable of table for labelling	**DB link** # selections # labelling

The viewer offers the possibility of slicing (*'clip'*) the model at any place (horizontally, vertically, diagonally – see video 4, fig. 4.9, and 5, fig. 4.10, and AN iv, v in table 4.3). This option not only gives insight into the geophysical and archaeological structures at any place of the trench but also creates digital sections and plans of outlines and surfaces. Video 5 (fig. 4.10) shows the clip of the geophysical data in combination with the top surface of archaeological layer 'se108'. This 3D map shows again very clearly the conformity of high GPR-values and the pit's shape formed by layer 'se108'.

Separations are also possible by the creation of isosurfaces (video 5, fig. 4.10-02:24 ff.). Isosurfaces are polyhedrons, so-called 3D boundaries, which follow a certain value inside 3D space. Compared to voxel models they are hollow objects.

In summary, the geophysical voxel model shows a horizontal layer of high GPR-values at the same course as the archaeological layer 'se101' which consists mainly of mortar (fig. 4.9-01:59 and written information in docu-sheet 'se101'). The same is true for the lowest point of the pit shaped by surface 'se108' (fig. 4.9-01:55 ff.). It contained a great amount of rubble and stones of marble or limestone which are represented with the high GPR-value (fig. 4.12 und docu-sheet).

4.2.2 Analysis: archaeology

The transparent geophysical volume in the videos 4 to 8 (figs. 4.9, 4.10, 4.11, 4.18 and 4.30) serves as 3D background orientation for the visualisation of archaeological layers and surfaces. The combination of the layer volume 'se109' with the surfaces of layers 'se108'

and 'se103' is an example of the visualisation options of ParaView© to represent the spatial relationships of archaeological stratigraphy. Videos 6 and 8 show the younger layer deposit 'se108' (figs. 4.11 and 4.30). Layer 'se109' was built later and hence lies above layer 108. However, both layers reach the same depth. This result can be compared by either highlighting the bottom layer as voxel or raster, e.g. in video 6 (see attribute tables with layer numbers and z-values in 4.11-01:18 ff.).

In contrast to the 3D interpolation used for the geophysical and geochemical voxel models, the archaeological voxel layers are calculated by extrusion (GRASS module *r.vol.dem* see WS xx, xxi in tab. 3.2). Hence, each voxel in the layer has the same value – the layer number e.g. '109' (figs. 4.11 and 4.30).

The video shows also that layer volume 'se101' is above 'se109' and 'se108'. The model shows also all the finds from different perspectives. Their colour corresponds to the archaeological layer. Their numbers are the find numbers of the database. Both values (layer number and find number) are obtained from the connected attribute table.

Adding the layer surface 'se112' the relationship to layer 'se108' becomes visible. Layers 'se102' and 'se103' are small deposits of similar shape above each other closely beneath the stone pavement. They contained several finds but could not yet be interpreted archaeologically or linked to other structures.

The archaeological investigation of the relationship of archaeological layers in the viewer ParaView© resulted in a revised Harris Matrix diagram (fig. 4.14). This 'second

Figure 4.6. Video 1 – **https://doi.org/10.30861/9781407357867.video1: 3D model of trench 1 – 3D vectors & geospatial DB-link.**

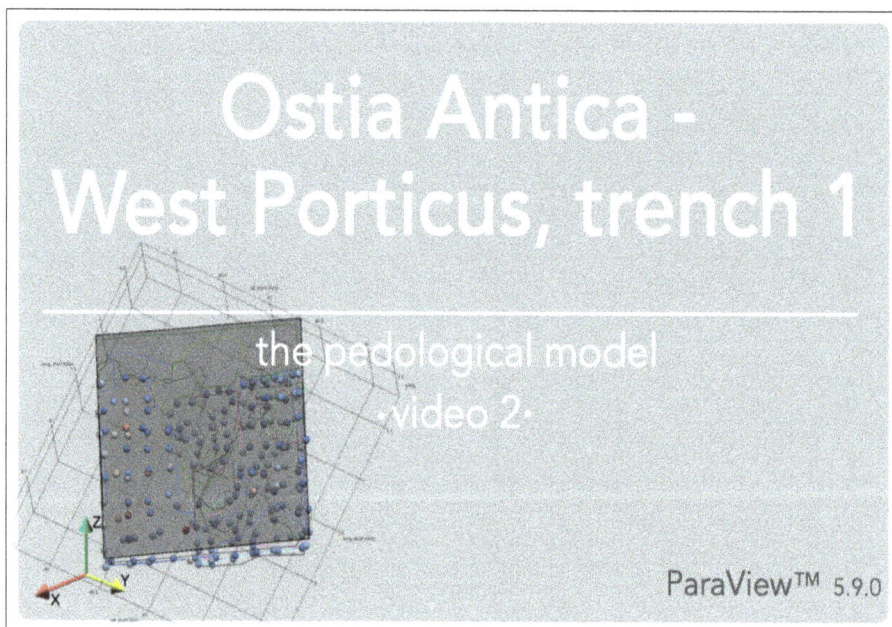

Figure 4.7. Video 2 – **https://doi.org/10.30861/9781407357867.video2: 3D model of trench 1 – the model of geochemical data.**

edition' shows more connections than the *'most immediate relationships'* (compare fig. 2.14 in chapter 2 created during excavation, Harris 1989). The precise 3D visualisation of all deposits now makes it possible to draw a complete Harris Matrix diagram displaying every spatial contact.

Furthermore, if the macroscopic estimation via viewer does not suffice, a verification can be made by the mapcalculator in GRASS (*r.mapcalc*) by calculating the difference between two raster layers. If a subtraction results in a difference (positive or negative) there is an overlay which can be interpreted as a connection (fig. 4.15).

Plane raster surfaces like orthophotos can also be visualised in ParaView© (fig. 4.12). Their incorporation might be a good start for getting an overview from topview. However, 3D measurements and assignments are difficult due to the 2D plane structure.

Alternatively, textured 2.5D surfaces (generated with the SfM method in this study, sec. 3.2) might be an option in the near future when the false colour visualisation (fig. 4.13) can be replaced by true-colour from photographs in ParaView©). The same colour problem affects also orthophotos (4.12).

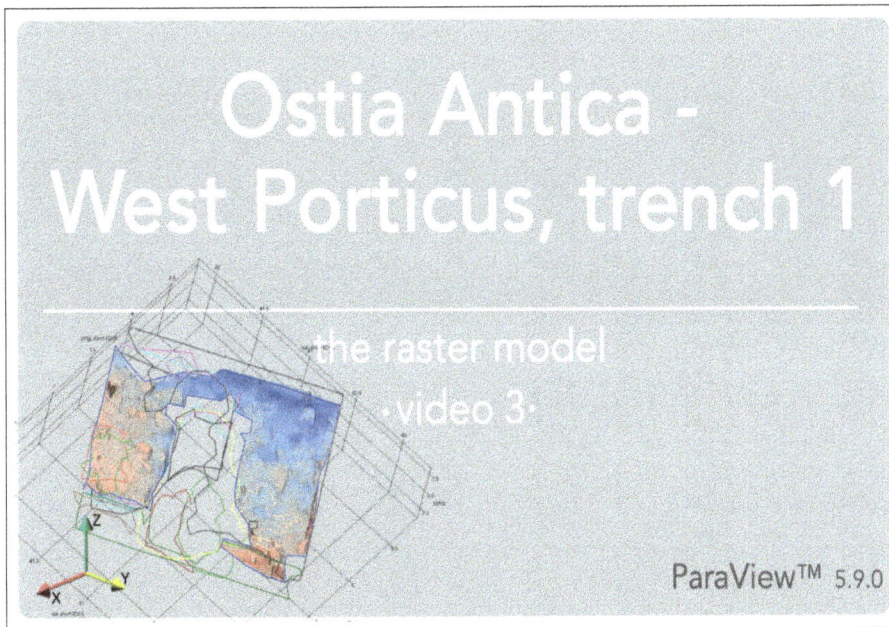

Figure 4.8. Video 3 – https://doi.org/10.30861/9781407357867.video3: 3D model of trench 1 – raster surfaces.

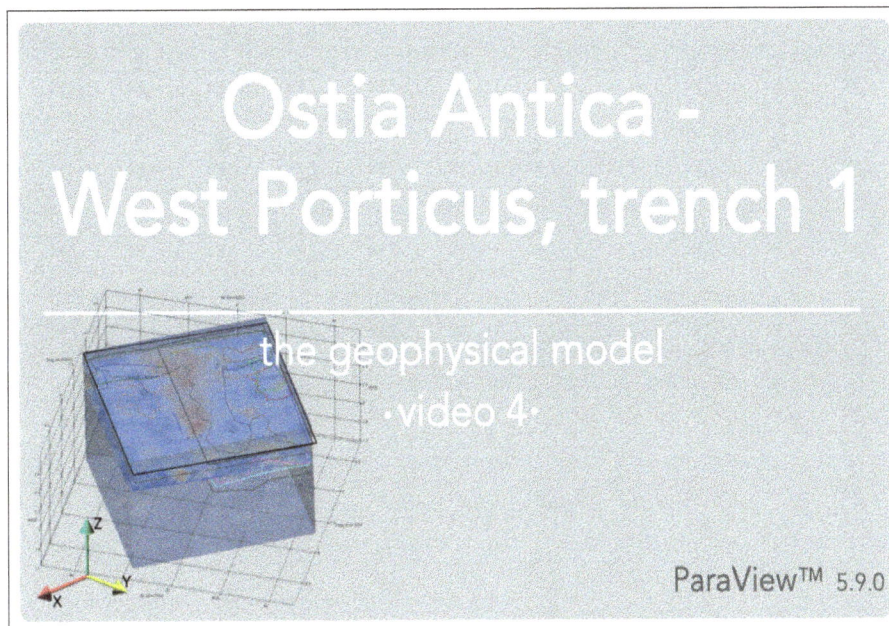

Figure 4.9. Video 4 – https://doi.org/10.30861/9781407357867.video4: 3D model of trench 1 – the geophysical model.

4.2.3 Analysis: pedology & archaeology

The visualisation of geochemical soil elements in this study is exemplified by the element 'calcium'. The calcium value taken from the 205 soil samples was interpolated inside the space of the whole of trench 1 (figs. 4.7 and 4.18). According to this calculation process of the GRASS module *v.vol.rst* (table 3.3), the result is a cuboid, e.g. the geophysical voxel model (compare with 4.9). The histogram can be generated in order to get an overview of the calcium's frequency distribution. Figures 4.19 and

4.20 show the calcium voxel amount inside trench 1 sorted in value categories as a Normal Distribution curve.

However, histogram results depend on the scale and scope of the investigated area (Conolly & Lake, 2006, chap. 8). The same is true for statistical analysis in 3D space (Ripley, 1981, 1988). Hence, the 3D bounding box of the calculation region adjusted in GRASS (table 3.2 *g.region* adjustments for top and bottom, table 3.3) and the 'maskmap' in the 3D interpolation module *v.vol.rst* (adjusts position coordinates) define the 3D scope of the calculation area

Table 4.2. Analysis approaches: AN iii

visualisation iii: – geophysics & archaeology

Analysis No. Figures & Videos	Description of Operations	Results
AN iii)		**voxel volume vers. interpolation, 3D polyline, raster surface**
# video fig. 4.10	# Open -> Apply -> Representation: volume (geophysical volume)	# trench 1: combination of geophysical volume with archaeological layer volume, layer surfaces and layer outlines
# video fig. 4.11	# Open -> Apply -> Representation: volume (geophysical volume) with transparency	# trench 1: combination of geophysical volume with archaeological layer volume, layer surfaces and layer outlines
# video fig. 4.10	# Open -> Apply -> Representation: surface (archaeological top surface)	# trench 1: combination of geophysical volume with archaeological layer volume, layer surfaces and layer outlines

Table 4.3. Analysis approaches: AN iv-vii

3D data analysis: geophysics & archaeology

Analysis No. Figures & Videos	Description of Operations	Results
AN iv)		**voxel volume versus interpolation, 3D polyline, raster surface**
# video fig. 4.10	# Filter -> Clip (geophysical volume), Type: Plane	# trench 1: vertical clipping west-east of geophysical model further examples in combination with archaeological layers as outline and raster surface
		# trench 1: combination of geophysical volume with vertical clipping (west-east, twice) with visualisation of archaeological layer surface and outlines
AN v) # video fig. 4.10	# Filter -> Clip (geophysical volume), Type: Plane + Ruler	**see above** # trench 1: vertical clipping south-north + one slice in 1.22m parallel distance
AN vi) # video fig. 4.10	# Open -> Apply -> Representation: volume (geophysical volume), Threshold: 5000–13000	**see above** # trench 1: combination of geophysical volume with GPR-wavelength threshold and archaeological layer surfaces and layer outlines
	# Open -> Apply -> Representation: volume (geophysical volume), Threshold: 5000–19686	
AN vii) # video fig. 4.10	# Filter -> Isosurfaces (geophysical volume), value: 7500	**see above** # trench 1: combination of geophysical volume with GPR-wavelength threshold as isosurfaces, archaeological layer surfaces and layer outlines
	# Filter -> Isosurfaces (geophysical volume), value: 9844.5	

and influence the statistical result. For comparison with model1, a tailored 3D bounding box region with the same distances to the outer borders in all three directions as the distance between the soil samples (20cm – table 2.6) served as the calculation boundary for a second 'model2' of the calcium distribution in trench 1. Its histogram shows a similar Normal Distribution curve as that of 'model1' and no bias in contrast to the value selection by threshold intervals (figs. 4.21 to 4.26).

Further confirmation of model1 can be found by overlaying both models with the same threshold range 110.5–180. The voxel geometry confirms expectations after studying the 'Range of data' in the metadata of both models. Model2 shows a wider value range than model1. Furthermore, their range even goes beyond the original values between 67.1 and 243.2 (figs. 4.23 and 4.24). The reason is the wider scope for interpolation and extrapolation at the edges and

unchanged interpolation algorithm adjustments (compare the buffer area for model2 calculation in fig. 4.22 in 2D and in 3D in fig. 4.25 with the calculation area of model1 in fig. 4.21 for 2D and for 3D in figs. 4.19, 4.25).

To summarise, when both models are compared, the central argument of high concentration areas within the archaeological layer 'se104' is maintained by both calculations. Anomalies would be places where both models have no overlay. This is not the case with calcium in trench 1. The only difference is the wider range of calcium values in model2.

Similar comparisons can be done with the geophysical model. Further studies applying the same procedure are possible with all other elements of the geochemical investigation (table 2.8).

Table 4.4. Analysis approaches: AN viii–x

3D data analysis: archaeology

Analysis No. Figures & Videos	Description of Operations	Results
AN viii) # video fig. 4.11, 4.18	# Open -> Apply -> Representation: volume (archaeological layer)	**voxel volume vers. interpolation, 3D polyline, raster surface** # trench 1: combination of geophysical volume with archaeological layer volume, layer surfaces and layer outlines
AN ix) # video fig. 4.11	# selection: selection by geometry -> 'Selection Inspector'	**DB link** # trench 1: selection of volume voxels by geometry displaying voxel category value '109'
AN x) # video fig. 4.11	# labelling: selection -> Display Inspector -> 'Point Labels', selection of variable 'find no.' of attribute table for labelling + legend display of variable 'layer no.' of attribute table 3D vector points	**see above** # trench 1: labelling (find no.) and colouring (layer no.) of archaeological finds

Figure 4.10. Video 5 – https://doi.org/10.30861/9781407357867.video5: 3D model of trench 1 – archaeology & geophysics.

Figure 4.11. Video 6 – https://doi.org/10.30861/9781407357867.video6: 3D model of trench 1 – volumes & geospatial DB-link.

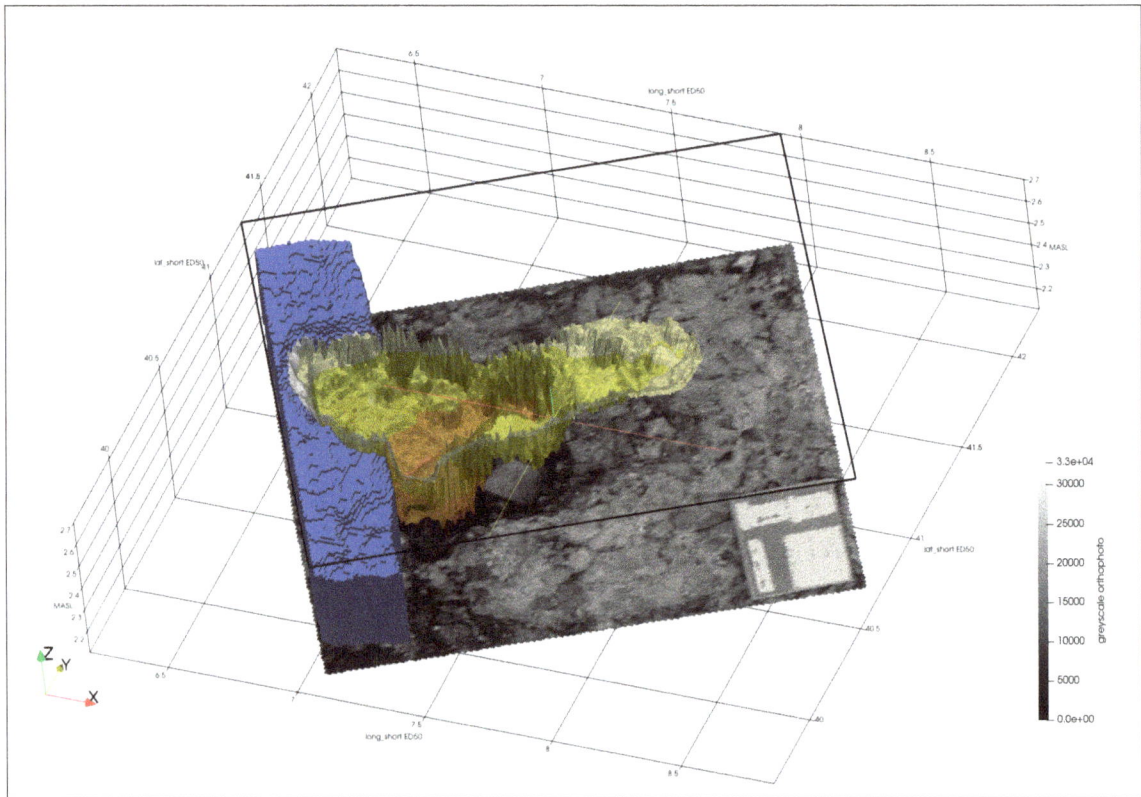

Figure 4.12. Orthophoto: 2D orthophoto of top surface 'se108' in false colour (grey) with clipped volume of layer 'se109' (darkblue-transparent) and raster surface of 'se108' (yellow) in ParaView© – camera view from east angle 45°. The legend shows the greyscale.

The location of the calcium concentration can be displayed with threshold values or threshold intervals of the voxel models (table 4.5). A further option is to clip these models to get an insight into the distribution of the concentration value. Combining these thematic 3D maps of geochemical concentrations with archaeological structures, the 3D map can generate additional information and lead to new conclusions compared to the pure excavation model (fig. 4.18).

In this study, the highest calcium concentration values correspond exactly with the archaeological layer 'se104' (fig. 4.18-01:58 ff.). If one needs to know the exact values at certain places in 3D space, interesting voxels can be selected by geometry and their database content displayed either as labels or as attribute table (fig. 4.11).

In the model, layer 'se101' lies directly above layer 'se104' and contains a similar amount of calcium concentration. The clipping option enables a precise insight into where the highest concentration belongs. In this example, the archaeological model and the geochemical model confirm the geophysical results described in subsection 4.2.1.

Additionally, threshold values can be presented as single values forming so-called isosurfaces. They can be technically compared with 'isolines' which follow a

defined value through space. In contrast, isosurfaces follow the value in 3D space by creating a continuous mesh hull. Such hollow objects can also be created by ParaView©. The example here shows the minimum and maximum values of calcium inside trench 1 (fig. 4.18-01:40 to 02:02).

In contrast, 'isovolumes' are solid objects representing not just one value as isosurfaces but a value range where the outer surface is built by the lowest value. It can be clipped like voxel objects, providing an insight into the structure. The variation of the continuous values within an isovolume can be displayed by a 'plot over line' diagram (figs. 4.16 and 4.17). This representation format is suitable for continuous values (e.g. measured values like geophysical and geochemical), in contrast to e.g. archaeological deposits which are built with only one value (fig. 4.11).

The final results of VTK-files with short coordinates are summarised in the 'process chain 5-results' (fig. 4.32). The chart shows the processing of these data until their representation in ParaView©. A sample set of uploaded VTK-files is shown in figure 4.31 (yellow rows) with their metadata. White rows in the table show model derivatives of the adjacent VTK-file created by analyses in ParaView©.

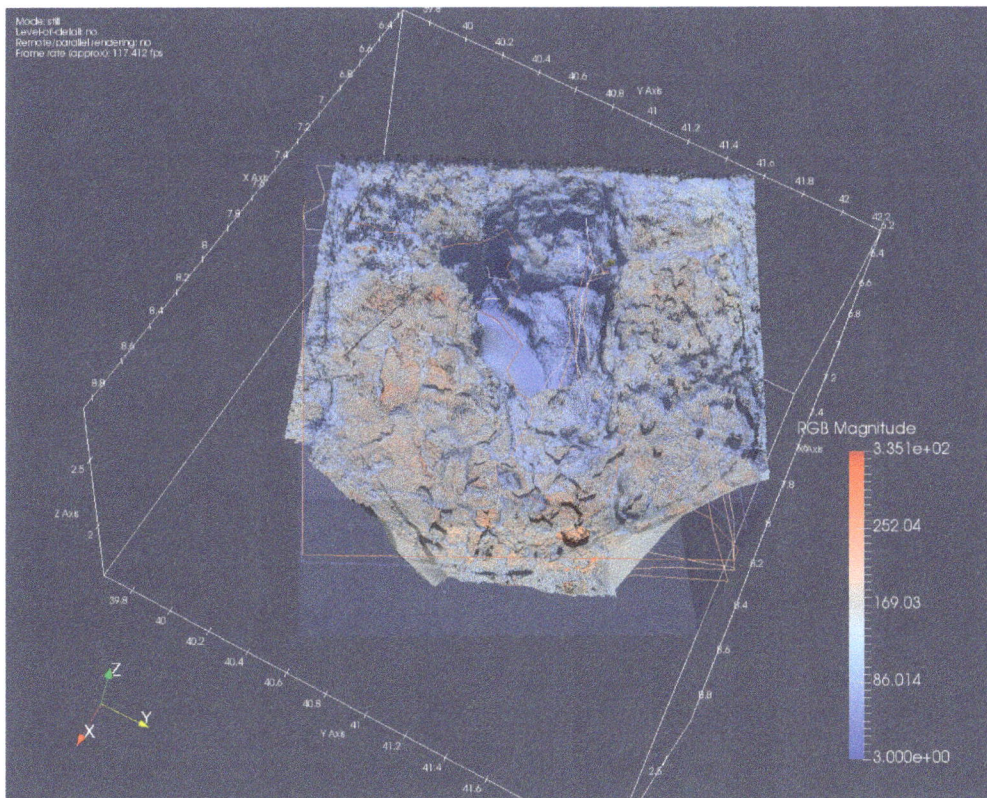

Figure 4.13. Textured model: model with SfM texture of top surface 'se104' and 'se108' in false color in ParaView© – camera view from east angle 45°. The legend shows the range of RGB values.

Table 4.5. Analysis approaches: AN xi–xiv

3D data analysis: pedology & archaeology

Analysis No.	Detailed Description of Operations	Results & Figure No.
AN xi) **geochemistry: calcium**	# Open -> Apply -> Representation: volume, Threshold range: 120–215	# trench 1: calcium distribution in combination with archaeological layers and surfaces, video fig. 4.18
	# Open -> Apply -> Representation: volume + Filter -> Clip volume (horizontal on z-height 2.45m)	# see above with volume insight video fig. 4.18, 4.30
AN xii) **see above**	# Open -> Apply -> Representation: Isosurfaces, Threshold: 112, 120, 125	# trench 1: calcium distribution in combination with archaeological layers and surfaces, video fig. 4.18
AN xiii) **see above**	# Filter -> Isovolumes, Threshold range: 110.5–180, Representation: volume	# trench 1: calcium distribution in combination with archaeological layers, video fig. 4.18
	# Filter -> Data Analysis -> Plot over Line	# with volume insight, video fig. 4.18 # with cross section showing variation of calcium values along a line, position and direction; see arrow in fig. 4.16 and curve in fig. 4.17 displaying the height of the arrow on the x-axis in meters and the variation of the calcium value on the y-axis
AN xiv) **see above**	# Open -> Apply -> Representation: volume # Filter -> Data Analysis -> Histogram	# trench 1: calcium distribution of model1 in video fig. 4.18 and of model2 in video fig. 4.30

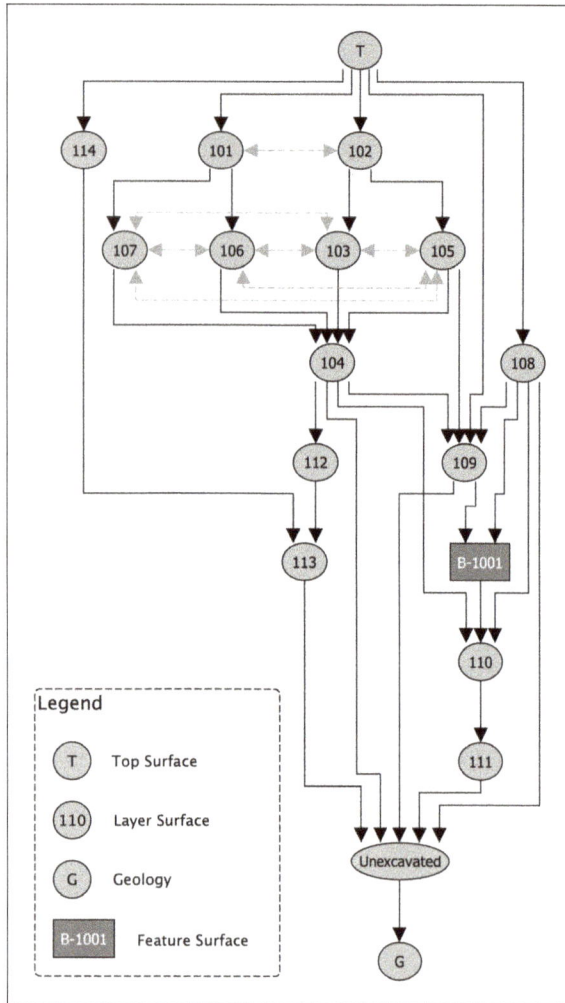

Figure 4.14. **Revised Harris Matrix of trench 1 of fig. 2.14.**

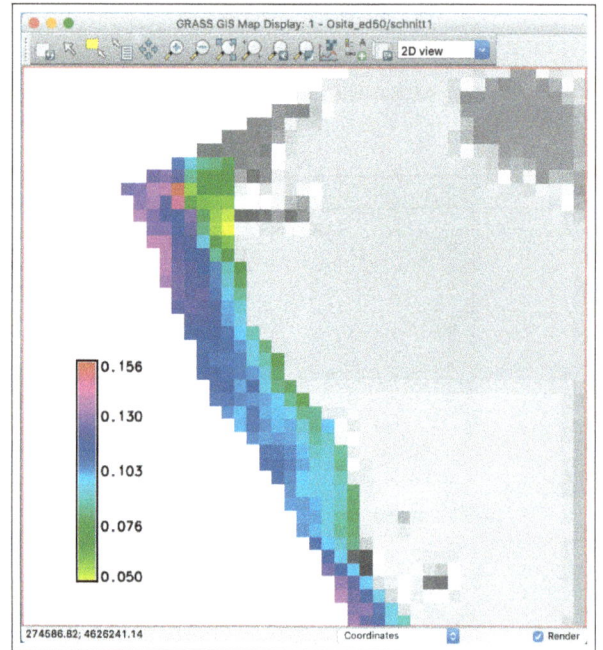

Figure 4.15. Difference calculation by GRASS module *r.mapcalc.*

'Data Type's in the second column can be 'translated' into GIS-data types as follows:

– Image (Uniform Rectilinar Grid) = voxel volume,
– Unstructured Grid = voxel volume,
– Polygonal Mesh = 2.5D raster surface,
– Table = histogram according to attribute table.

The 'No. of Cells' refers to the amount of voxel or pixel. It changes with the chosen representation type (compare amount in column 'No. of Points'). The 'Spatial Bounds' always show the minimum bounding box around a 3D object.

Analysis results like threshold values, filters, selections, isosurfaces and isovolumes can be exported as:

– VTK-files or other common 3D object exchange formats like X3D, SVG etc. (Ayachit, 2018, chap. 8.2.2),
– screenshots like in this study (Ayachit, 2018, chap. 8.2.1),
– animations in AVI-video format (Ayachit, 2018, chap. 8.3) and
– complete status files combining all uploaded VTK-files with visualisation adjustments, styles and scale (= state of visualisation pipeline (Ayachit, 2018, chap. 8.4)) in a ParaView©-internal format (not exchangeable).

In general, the export format depends on research questions and further use. Since the aim of this study was to only explore different analysis options, the analysis ends at this working step.

4.3 Experiments

4.3.1 Colour test

According to research question RQ x of this study (section 1.2.2), the colour of each archaeological surface was measured in order to quantify archaeological stratigraphy by RGB-values.

Due to the calculation requirements for voxel volumes of the GRASS module *v.vol.rst*, a so-called *w-value* for interpolation is necessary (see also the interpolation process of geochemical elements in sec. 3.3). The dilemma between these requirements and archaeological stratigraphy is to express archaeology in a quantified way.

One of my suggestions, discussed already in (Lieberwirth, 2008a), to overcome this problem is to measure colour information as RGB-value. Since the beginning of archaeology, colour and colour combinations had always been used to differentiate archaeological stratigraphy. Hence, the problem in this study was not to 'see' the colour but to measure it. Fortunately, every TLS takes digital photographs of the area of interest before scanning. During an internal TLS-post-process, these images are combined with the measured coordinate information where the image's colour information (RGB-value) is assigned to each 3D point after scanning. Hence, by exporting TLS-points as tables, each point (row) contains not only coordinates but also three more columns with a R, G and B value (fig. 4.33).

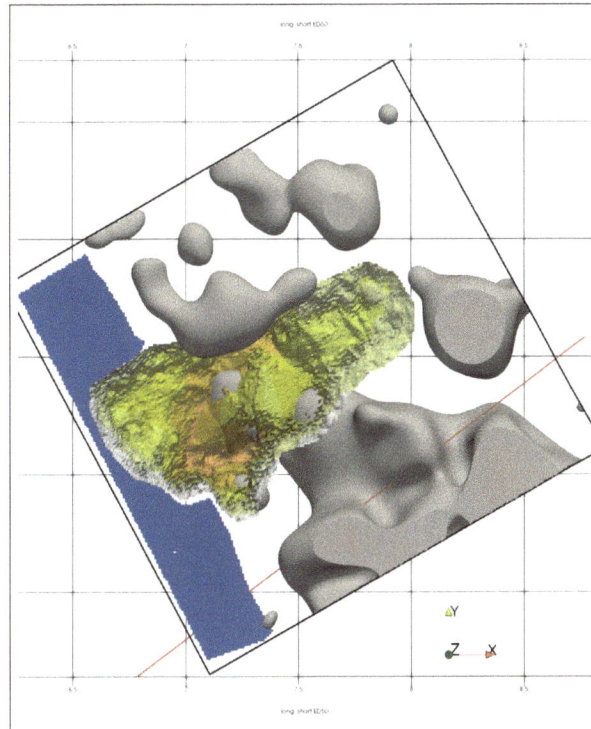

Figure 4.16. Isovolumes: calcium distribution of value range 110.5–180 as isovolumes in white with line as yellow arrow for plotting (see plot in fig. 4.17) in combination with archaeological layers: 'se109' in claret as volume and 'se108' as raster in yellow in ParaView© – camera topview.

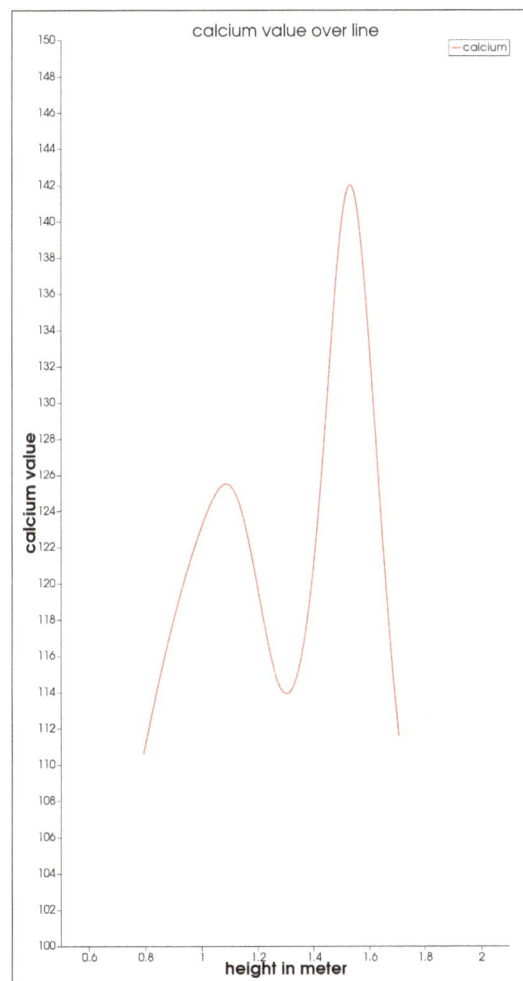

Figure 4.17. Isovolumes: diagram of calcium values along the line in fig. 4.16.

Figure 4.18. Video 7 – https://doi.org/10.30861/9781407357867.video7: 3D model of trench 1 – the geochemical model.

In a next external post-processing step, these three columns were combined into one for generating a single w-value for each row (see formula and procedure in table 4.6). These modified tables of each layer surface were then imported into GRASS and combined to one single 3D point cloud-table of all surfaces of trench 1. The w-value of this table could thus be used for the generation of the voxel volume (table 4.6).

Finally, the resulting VTK-file was edited in order to shorten the coordinates (section 4.1) and visualised in ParaView©. Figures 4.34 and 4.35 show the resulting volume of RGB-distribution inside trench 1 with different threshold intervals (see legend). To summarize, only the interval of high values in fig. 4.35 allows for some interpretation: there are clusters of high-value concentrations at the places of layer 'se103' (compare fig. 4.30). However, this interpretation should be taken with caution. The downside of this procedure was the unstandardised colour documentation. Due to changing light conditions during documentation, colour results change even within one surface dramatically. Furthermore, no colour matching was done to balance these values because of time constraints.

Nevertheless, the test shows that the procedure works in general from a technical perspective. RGB-values can be documented, combined and interpolated to obtain a high-resolution colour distribution of archaeological stratigraphy in 3D space.

The same test was done with RGB-values obtained by the SfM method. The result was similar, for the same reason mentioned above.

4.3.2 SfM post-processing – Agisoft PhotoScan® versus VSFM versus BundlerTools

To overcome the limitations of the TLS (the Leica ScanStation 2 we used only provides a vertical angle of

270° – see also product specifications Leica 2009), which turned out to be an obstacle while scanning small and deep pits, the new documentation method *Structure from Motion* was applied for three archaeological layer surfaces of trench 1 (section 2.2.2).

At the time of excavation and post-processing, several FOSS and proprietary software programs were available but not many studies published so far. Therefore, we decided to start our own study during the *Ostia Antica* excavation campaign in order to test the precision and accuracy of the resulting 3D point clouds. As reference, we used the high-precision measurements of the TLS and GCPs taken by total station in trench 1 (Lieberwirth et al., 2015).

The TLS-point clouds and SfM-point clouds were generated with different software programs:

as proprietary
– Cyclone® (Leica, 2011) for TLS,
– Agisoft PhotoScan® (Agisoft, 2014) for SfM,

as FOSS,

– BundlerTools (Schwarz, 2014) and
– VSFM (Wu, 2014) for SfM.

To summarise the comparison of their results, the VSFM-model was more precise but Agisoft PhotoScan® produced the highest resolution. Since the precision deviation was only millimetre units I decided to use the proprietary software Agisoft PhotoScan® in this thesis because additionally it made the most out of the legacy data. Furthermore, the software provides a georeferencing option and several common export formats – see more details in Lieberwirth (2015).

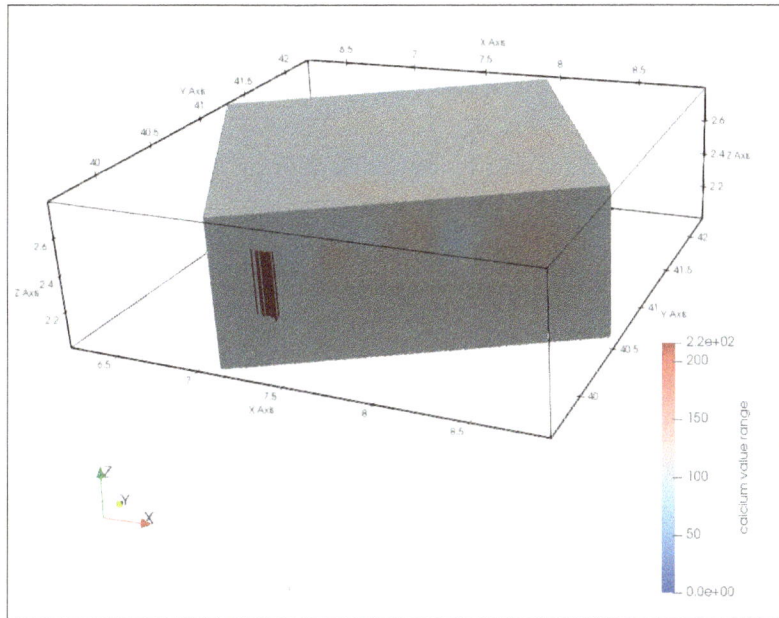

Figure 4.19. **Voxel: calcium distribution 'model1' of trench 1 as volume in ParaView© – camera view from south angle 20°. The legend shows the range of calcium values. Dark red structures show parts of layer deposit 'se109' as voxel model.**

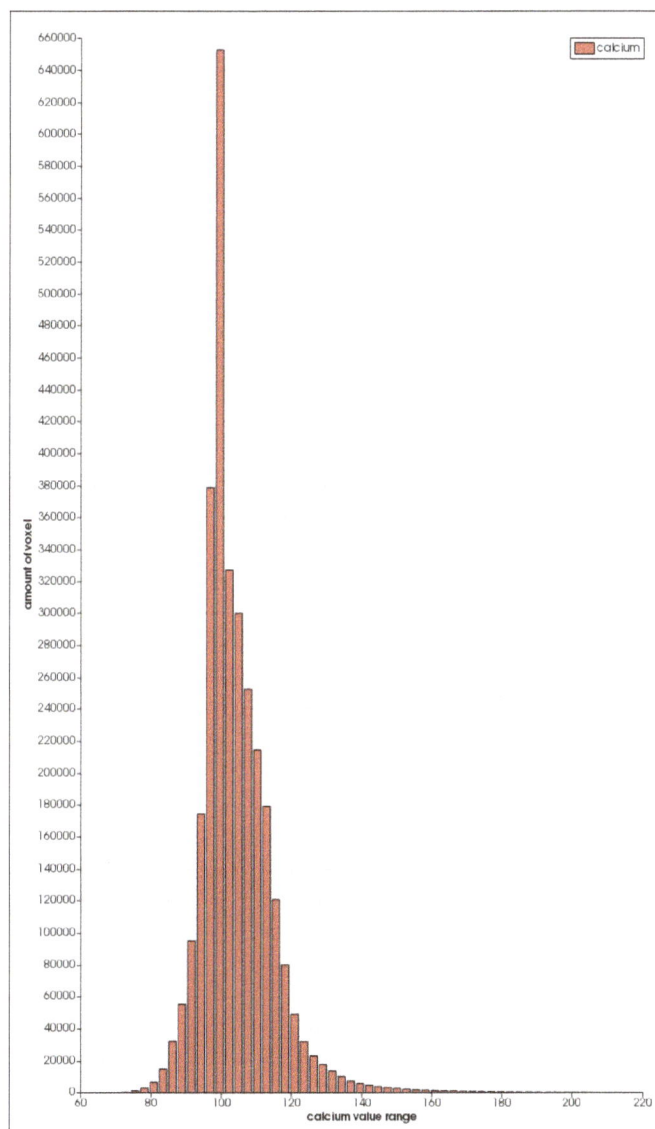

Figure 4.20. Voxel: histogram of calcium distribution 'model1' of trench 1 in ParaView©.

59

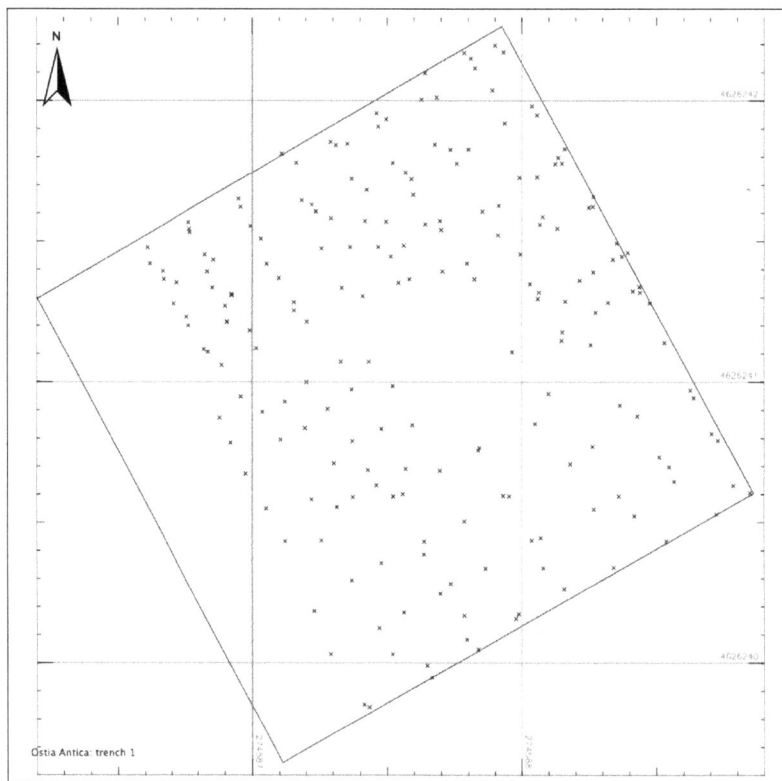

Figure 4.21. 3D points – model1: 2D distribution of soil samples and calculation scope in GRASS.

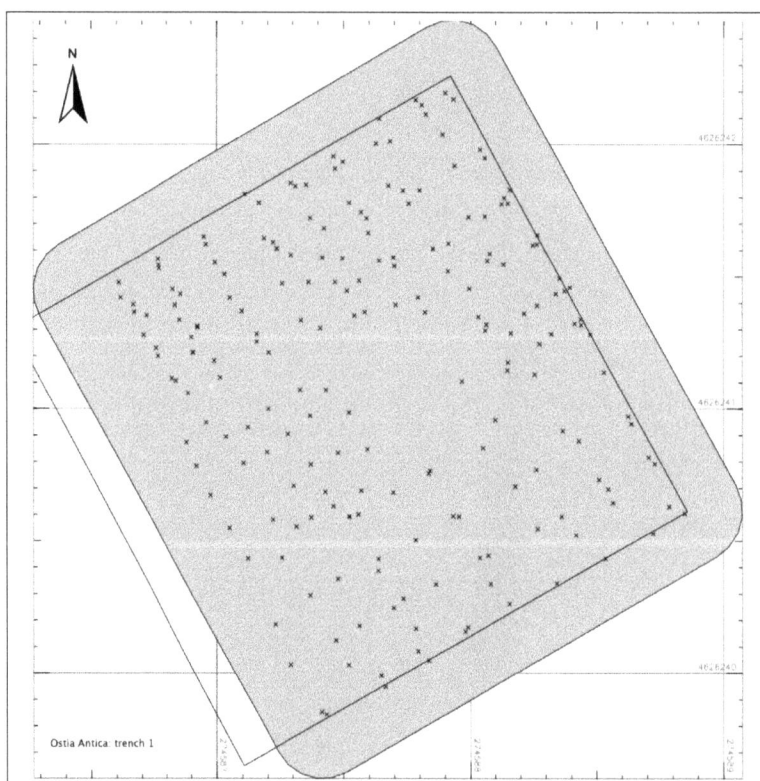

Figure 4.22. 3D points – model2: 2D distribution of soil samples and calculation scope with buffer in GRASS.

```
r3.info map=ostia_bp_s1_ca_vo_global@schnitt1
+----------------------------------------------------------------------+
| Layer:    ostia_bp_s1_ca_vo_global@schn  Date: Wed Feb 17 17:10:49 2016 |
| Mapset:   schnitt1                       Login of Creator: undine    |
| Location: Osita_ed50                                                 |
| DataBase: /Volumes/Elements/Finale_Daten_Diss/grassdata3            |
| Title:    ostia_bp_s1_ca_vo_global                                   |
| Units:    none                                                       |
| Vertical unit: units                                                 |
| Timestamp: none                                                      |
|----------------------------------------------------------------------|
|                                                                      |
|  Type of Map:  raster_3d          Number of Categories: 0            |
|  Data Type:    FCELL                                                 |
|  Rows:         270                                                   |
|  Columns:      270                                                   |
|  Depths:       82                                                    |
|  Total Cells:  5977800                                               |
|  Total size:        7761037 Bytes                                    |
|  Number of tiles:   1000                                             |
|  Mean tile size:    7761 Bytes                                       |
|  Tile size in memory: 26244 Bytes                                    |
|  Number of tiles in x, y and  z:   10, 10, 10                        |
|  Dimension of a tile in x, y, z:   27, 27, 9                         |
|                                                                      |
|       Projection: UTM (zone 33)                                      |
|           N: 4626242.3    S: 4626239.6   Res:  0.01                  |
|           E:  274588.9    W:  274586.2   Res:  0.01                  |
|           T:      2.8     B:       2     Res: 0.0097561              |
|  Range of data:   min = 71.38214874 max = 215.57272339              |
|                                                                      |
|  Data Source:                                                        |
|                                                                      |
|                                                                      |
|                                                                      |
|  Data Description:                                                   |
|   generated by v.vol.rst                                             |
+----------------------------------------------------------------------+
```

Figure 4.23. **Metadata model1: descriptive statistics of model1 displaying metadata of study examples in GRASS module** *r3.stats.*

```
r3.info map=ostia_bp_s1_ca_vo_small@schnitt1
+----------------------------------------------------------------------+
| Layer:    ostia_bp_s1_ca_vo_small@schni  Date: Tue Oct  9 16:19:43 2018 |
| Mapset:   schnitt1                       Login of Creator: undine    |
| Location: Osita_ed50                                                 |
| DataBase: /Volumes/Elements/Finale_Daten_Diss/grassdata3            |
| Title:    ostia_bp_s1_ca_vo_small                                    |
| Units:    none                                                       |
| Vertical unit: units                                                 |
| Timestamp: none                                                      |
|----------------------------------------------------------------------|
|                                                                      |
|  Type of Map:  raster_3d          Number of Categories: 0            |
|  Data Type:    FCELL                                                 |
|  Rows:         287                                                   |
|  Columns:      280                                                   |
|  Depths:       91                                                    |
|  Total Cells:  7312760                                               |
|  Total size:        10541793 Bytes                                   |
|  Number of tiles:   1000                                             |
|  Mean tile size:    10541 Bytes                                      |
|  Tile size in memory: 32480 Bytes                                    |
|  Number of tiles in x, y and  z:   10, 10, 10                        |
|  Dimension of a tile in x, y, z:   28, 29, 10                        |
|                                                                      |
|       Projection: UTM (zone 33)                                      |
|           N: 4626242.47   S: 4626239.6   Res:  0.01                  |
|           E:  274589.07   W:  274586.27  Res:  0.01                  |
|           T:      2.82    B:     1.91    Res:  0.01                  |
|  Range of data:   min = 37.80387115 max = 238.6784668               |
|                                                                      |
|  Data Source:                                                        |
|                                                                      |
|                                                                      |
|                                                                      |
|  Data Description:                                                   |
|   generated by v.vol.rst                                             |
+----------------------------------------------------------------------+
```

Figure 4.24. **Metadata model2: descriptive statistics of model2 displaying metadata of study examples in GRASS module** *r3.stats.*

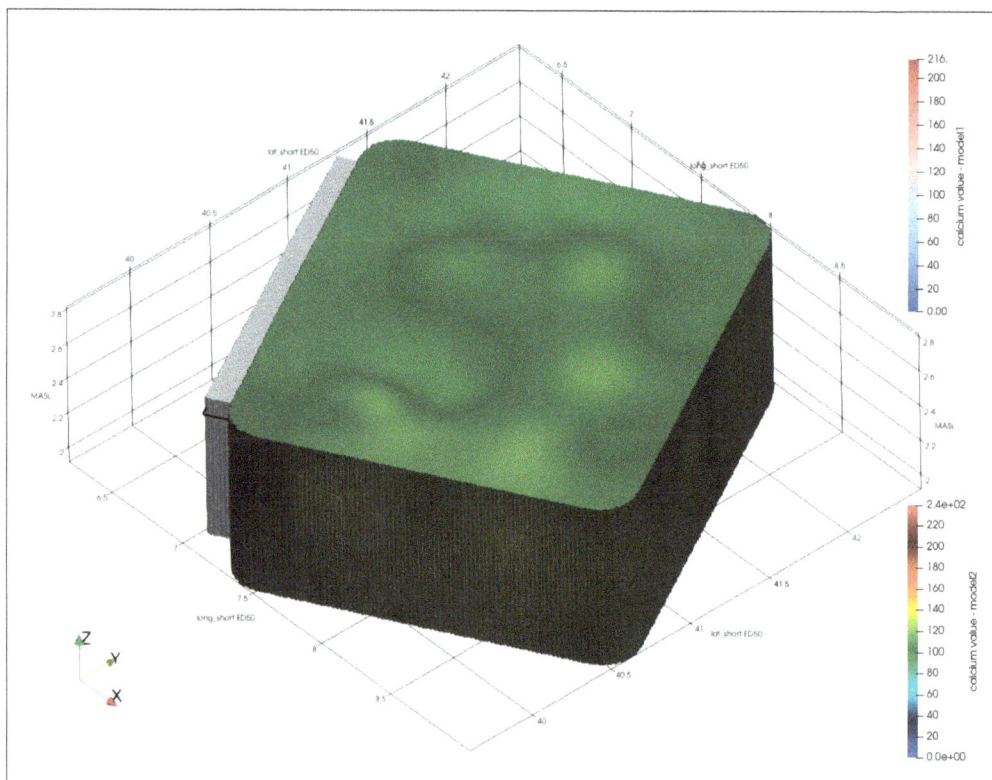

Figure 4.25. Model1 & Model2: calcium distribution as volume for model1 (grey) and model2 (green) in ParaView© – camera view from south-east angle 60°. The upper legend shows the range of calcium volume values for model1. The lower legend shows the same value for model2.

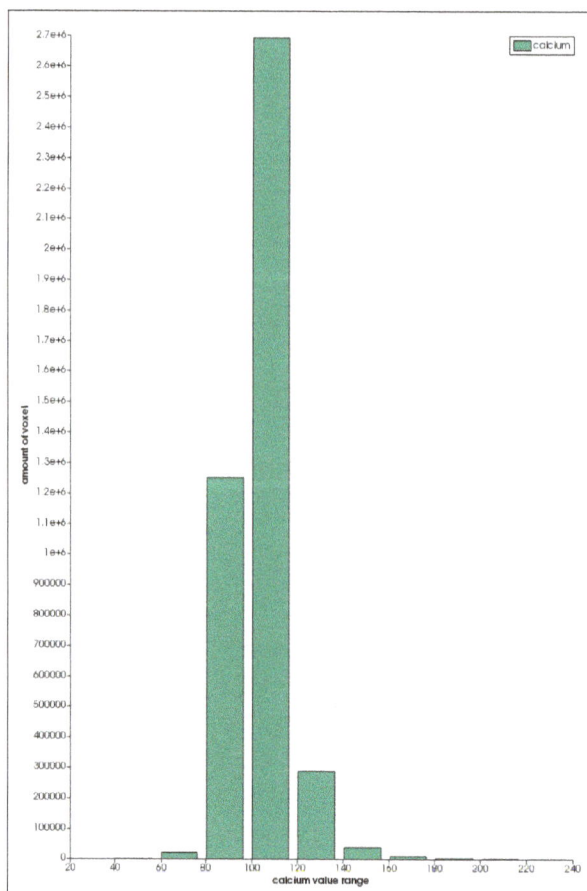

Figure 4.26. Voxel model2: histogram of calcium distribution of model2 according to the voxel volume displayed in fig. 4.25 in ParaView©.

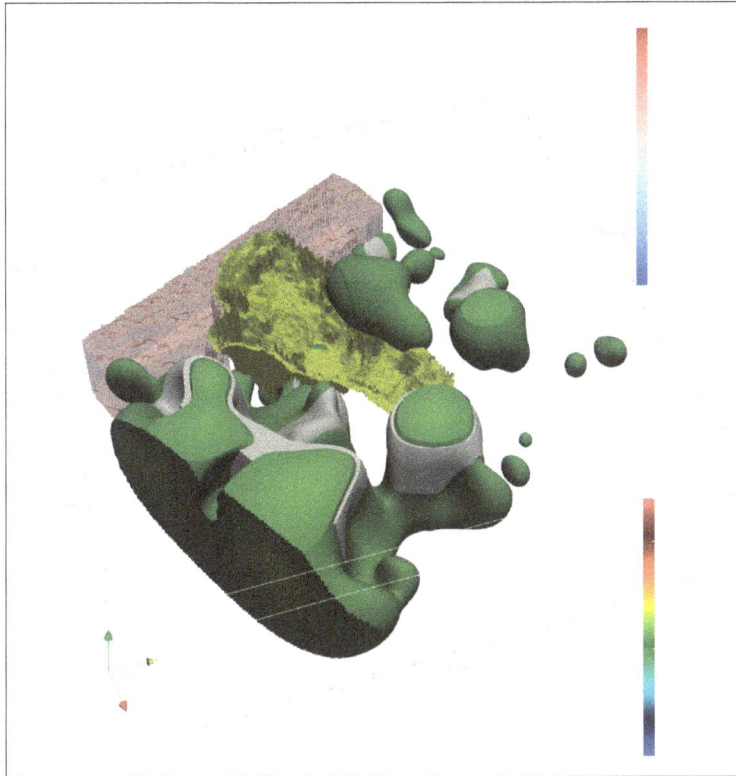

Figure 4.27. Model1 & Model2: calcium distribution as volume for model1 (grey) and model2 (green) in combination with archaeological layers: 'se109' in claret-transparent as volume, 'se108' as raster in yellow in ParaView© – camera view from south-east angle 45°. The upper legend shows the range of calcium volume values for model1. The lower legend shows the same value for model2.

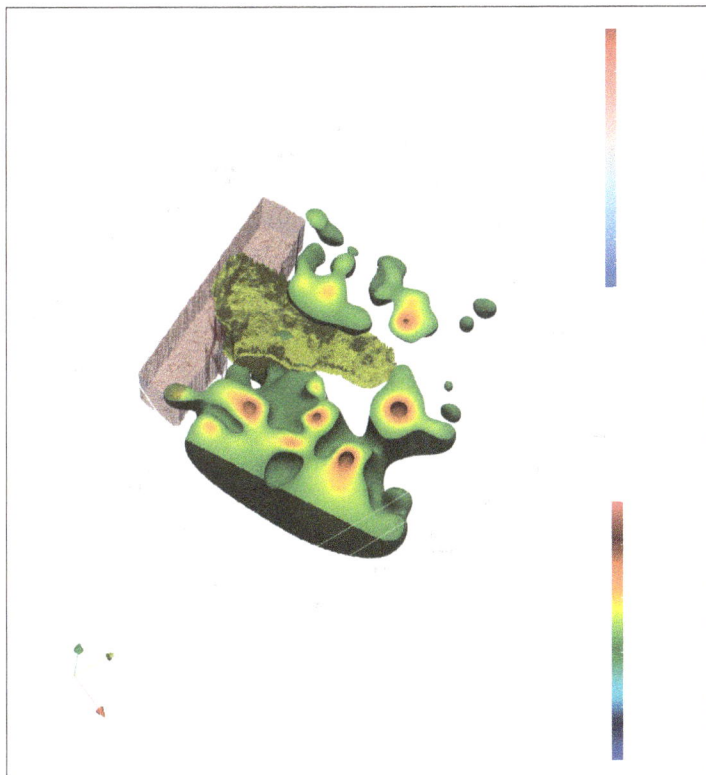

Figure 4.28. Clipped model2: clipped calcium distribution as volume (green to red) at height 2.6m in combination with archaeological layers: 'se109' in claret-transparent as volume, 'se108' as raster in yellow in ParaView© – camera view from south-east angle 60°. The upper legend shows the range of calcium volume values for model1. The lower legend shows the same value for model2.

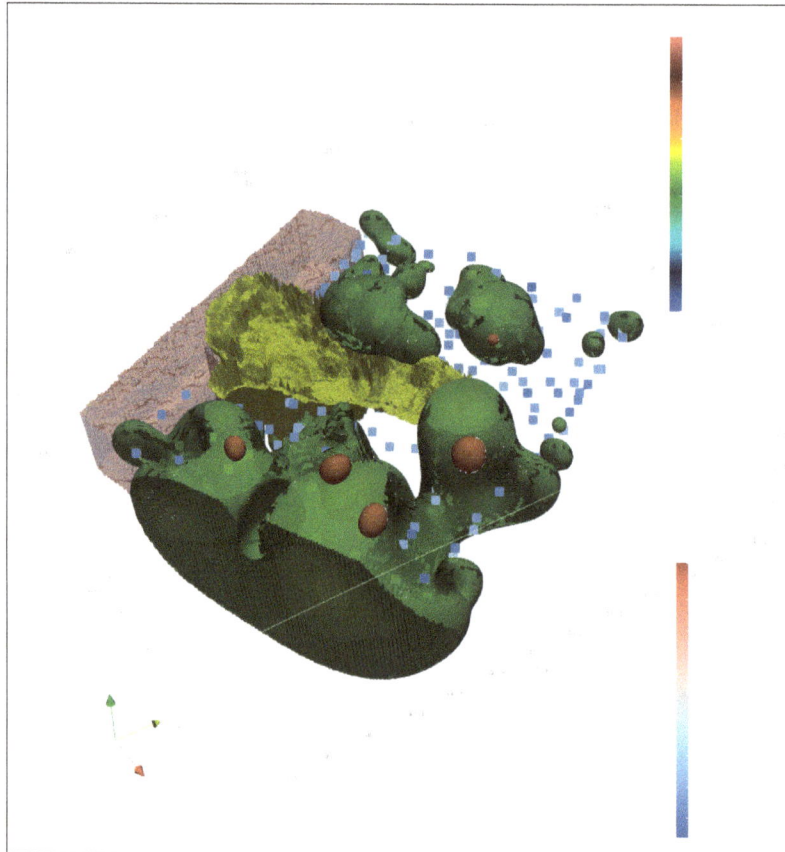

Figure 4.29. Model2: calcium distribution as volume (green) in combination with archaeological layers: 'se109' in claret-transparent as volume, 'se108' as raster in yellow and soil samples as 3D points in ParaView© – camera view from south-east angle 45°. The upper legend shows the range of calcium volume values. The lower legend shows the same value for the points.

Figure 4.30. Video 8 – https://doi.org/10.30861/9781407357867.video8: 3D model of trench 1 – combination of the digital archaeological model with excavation photographs.

	Name	Data Type	No. of Cells	No. of Points	Memory (MB)	Geometry Size (MB)	Spatial Bounds
					Statistics Inspector		
	schnittgrenze1_polyg_kk1.vtk	Polygonal Mesh	3	11	0.008	0.01	[6.2, 8.86] , [39.6, 42.3] , [2.7, 2.7]
	ostia_funde_s1_kk.vtk	Polygonal Mesh	0	0	0	Unavailable	[1e+299, -1e+299] , [1e+299, -1e+299] , [1e+299, -1e+299]
	schnittgrenze1_polyg_kk1.vtk	Polygonal Mesh	0	0	0	Unavailable	[1e+299, -1e+299] , [1e+299, -1e+299] , [1e+299, -1e+299]
	SEs_Schnitt1_1_kk.vtk	Polygonal Mesh	0	0	0	Unavailable	[1e+299, -1e+299] , [1e+299, -1e+299] , [1e+299, -1e+299]
	se108_1a_kk.vtk	Polygonal Mesh	72361	72900	6.26	Unavailable	[6.2, 8.9] , [39.6, 42.3] , [0, 2.67]
	Threshold1	Unstructured Grid	0	0	0.018	Unavailable	[1e+299, -1e+299] , [1e+299, -1e+299] , [1e+299, -1e+299]
	Threshold2	Unstructured Grid	8305	8564	0.469	Unavailable	[6.57, 8.02] , [40.3, 41.4] , [2.13, 2.67]
	se103_3_kk.vtk	Polygonal Mesh	0	0	0	Unavailable	[1e+299, -1e+299] , [1e+299, -1e+299] , [1e+299, -1e+299]
	Threshold3	Unstructured Grid	0	0	0.018	Unavailable	[1e+299, -1e+299] , [1e+299, -1e+299] , [1e+299, -1e+299]
	Threshold4	Unstructured Grid	0	0	0.018	Unavailable	[1e+299, -1e+299] , [1e+299, -1e+299] , [1e+299, -1e+299]
	Flaeche_A_S1_trans.vtk	Unstructured Grid	807840	850700	91.134	Unavailable	[6.2, 8.7] , [39.6, 42.2] , [1.58, 2.78]
	se109vo_kk.vtk	Image (Uniform Rectilinear Grid)	11226600	11383355	43.854	Unavailable	[6.2, 8.9] , [39.6, 42.3] , [1.5, 3]
	Threshold5	Unstructured Grid	151784	170055	14.073	Unavailable	[6.26, 7.39] , [39.7, 41.4] , [2.1, 2.64]
	ExtractSelection1	Unstructured Grid	0	0	0.018	Unavailable	[1e+299, -1e+299] , [1e+299, -1e+299] , [1e+299, -1e+299]
	se101_vo_kk.vtk	Image (Uniform Rectilinear Grid)	11226600	11383355	43.854	Unavailable	[6.2, 8.9] , [39.6, 42.3] , [1.5, 3]
	Threshold6	Unstructured Grid	266535	301070	24.751	Unavailable	[6.95, 8.81] , [39.9, 42.1] , [2.19, 2.81]
	ostia_bp_s1_ca_vo_global_kk.vtk	Image (Uniform Rectilinear Grid)	5861241	5977800	23.351	Unavailable	[6.21, 8.9] , [39.6, 42.3] , [2, 2.8]
	Threshold7	Unstructured Grid	0	0	0.018	11.166	[1e+299, -1e+299] , [1e+299, -1e+299] , [1e+299, -1e+299]
	Threshold8	Unstructured Grid	627185	680127	55.341	Unavailable	[6.55, 8.85] , [39.8, 42.2] , [2, 2.8]
	Clip1	Unstructured Grid	109774	128577	9.804	Unavailable	[6.72, 8.69] , [39.9, 41.9] , [2.13, 2.61]
	se104_3_kk.vtk	Polygonal Mesh	0	0	0	Unavailable	[1e+299, -1e+299] , [1e+299, -1e+299] , [1e+299, -1e+299]
	Threshold9	Unstructured Grid	0	0	0.018	Unavailable	[1e+299, -1e+299] , [1e+299, -1e+299] , [1e+299, -1e+299]
	IsoVolume1	Unstructured Grid	0	0	0.018	Unavailable	[1e+299, -1e+299] , [1e+299, -1e+299] , [1e+299, -1e+299]
	IsoVolume2	Unstructured Grid	0	0	0.018	Unavailable	[1e+299, -1e+299] , [1e+299, -1e+299] , [1e+299, -1e+299]

Figure 4.31. Metadata: statistics inspector of ParaView© displaying metadata of study examples.

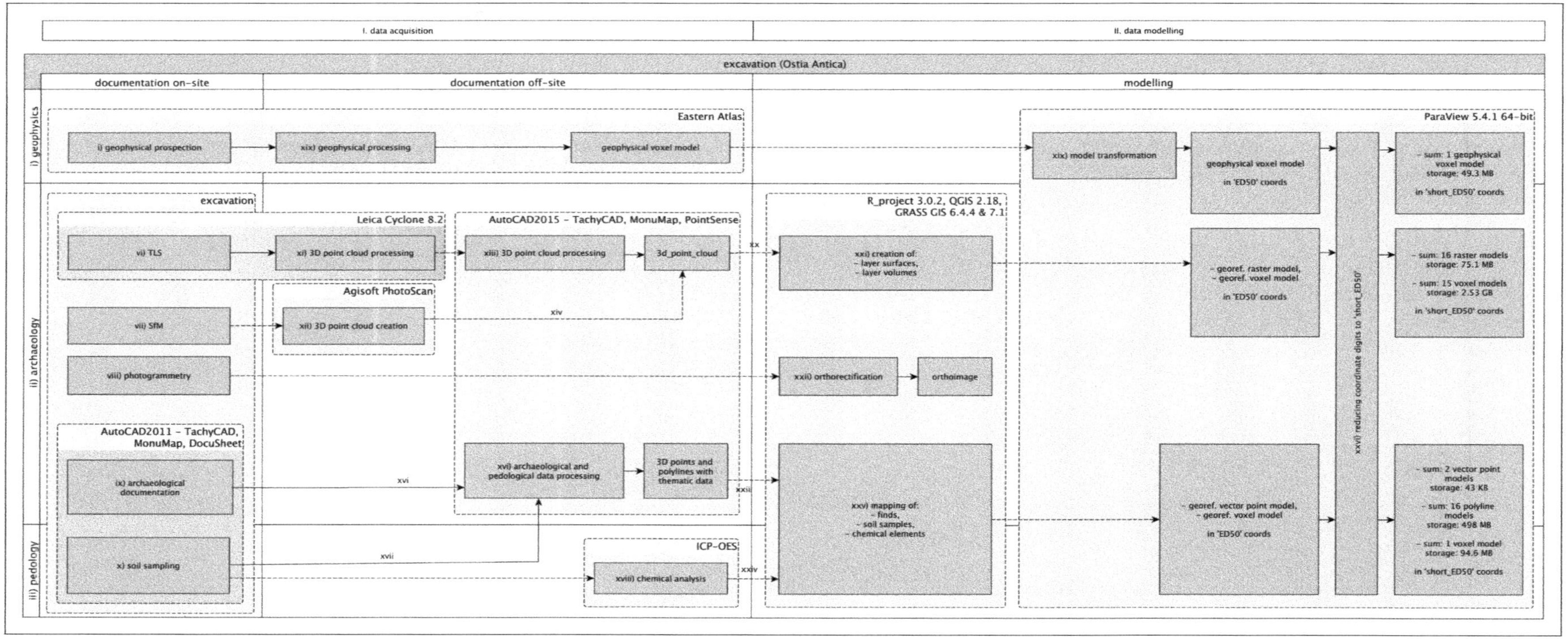

Figure 4.32. Process chain 5-results: general workflow of on-site data acquisition, off-site data processing, modelling and coordinate reduction with results (VTK-files with short coordinates) of *Ostia Antica* excavation data. With reference to the tables 2.2, 2.3, 2.6, 2.7, 2.8, 3.1, 3.2 and 3.3.

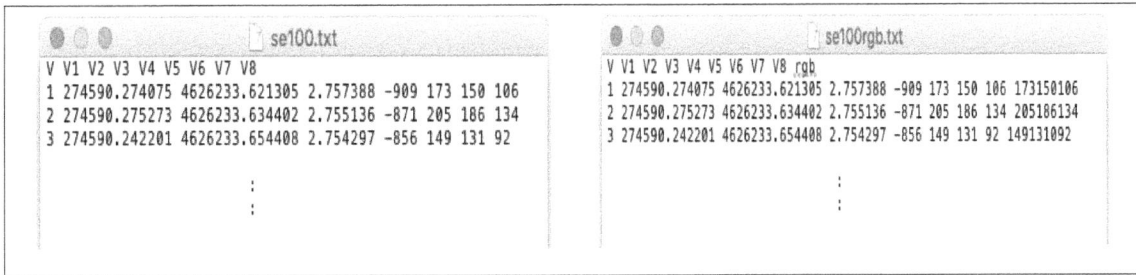

Figure 4.33. Colour test: original TLS-export file with RGB-values (left) and with combined RGB-values (right).

Table 4.6. Working steps of colour test

experiments: colour test

Process	Detailed Description with Hardware & Software
working steps: color test	# combination of three RGB columns into one and calculation of RGB-value distribution: 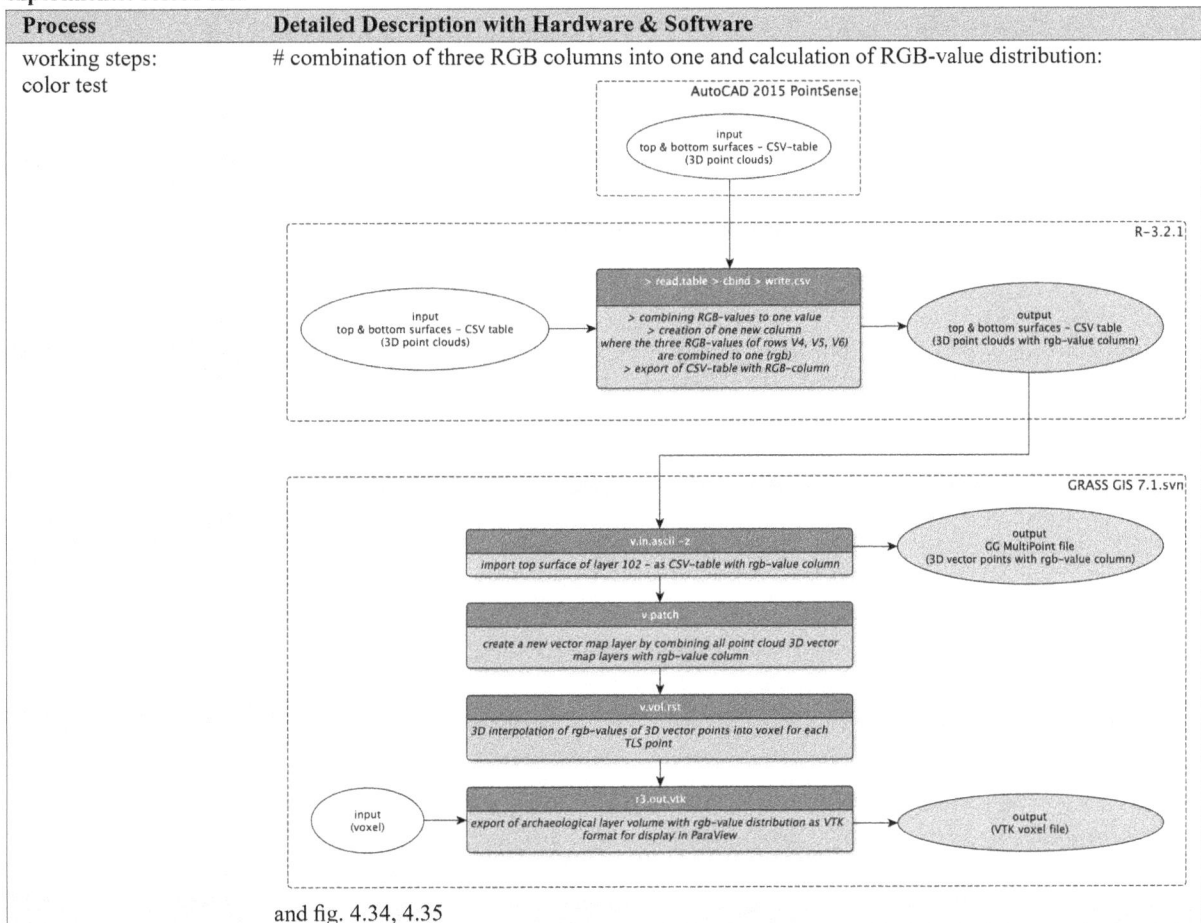 and fig. 4.34, 4.35

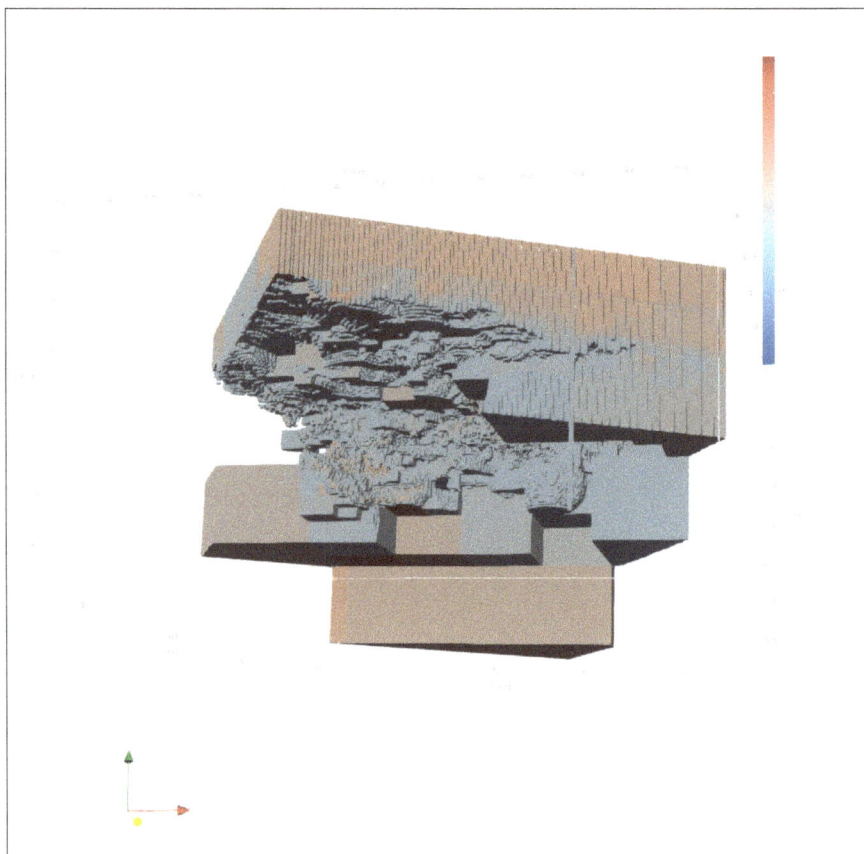

Figure 4.34. Colour test: RGB-colour distribution of TSL-colour values with threshold I in ParaView© – camera view from north angle −45°. The legend shows the range of RGB-column values.

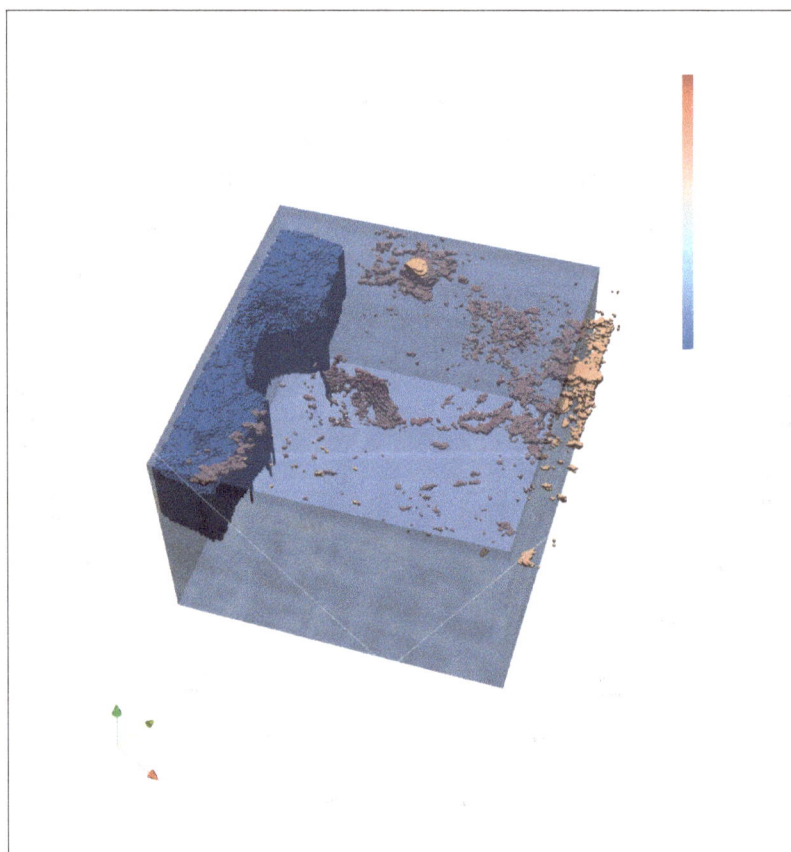

Figure 4.35. Colour test: RGB-colour distribution of TLS-colour values with threshold II and volume layer 'se109' (darkblue) in ParaView© – camera view from south angle 70°. The legend shows the range of RGB-column values.

5

Discussion & Conclusion

The last chapter of this study discusses all applied working steps, analysis and theoretical considerations in detail as a critical investigation of pros and cons. It provides summarised conclusions and suggestions for further developments and experiments as an outlook.

Discussions are divided into advantages and disadvantages for each working step of the data acquisition and the data modelling. They contain a critical description of the experiences with new technologies and approaches in comparison with common procedures.

It is followed by a conclusion which contains a final evaluation of the results.

Each paragraph ends with an outlook with either methodological or archaeological suggestions.

This compact study summary follows the same pattern as in the previous chapters by using the WS numbers from chaps. 2 and 3. The process chain graphs using the processing time in order to provide a temporal overview for each part of the study.

The analysis summary in section 5.3 is sorted into the different approaches using the same table structure and series numbers (AN) as in chapter 4.

The last subsection of each section answers the research questions (RQs) from each chapter by discussing theories and perceptions.

5.1 Discourse: 3D data acquisition

5.1.1 Geophysical prospection – WS i)

advantages

The two geophysical measurement resolutions for georadar wavelengths have proven very useful. The first/rough with a point distance of 0.05m and section distance of 0.25m gave a useful overview of the whole site. Thus the fine resolution could be applied to places of archaeological interest.

disadvantages

Geophysical investigations with this precision and with the result of a voxel model were only made available (at this time) by the Eastern Atlas® company.

conclusion

Carrying out geophysical investigations before an archaeological excavation is standard procedure and has proven once again to be very meaningful. The acquisition and analysis by an external cooperation partner should be considered in the planning campaign costs.

outlook

There is no doubt that geophysics will continue to play an important role in archaeology.

5.1.2 Surface documentation – WS ii, vi, vii)

advantages

The best way to document the curve of a top or bottom surface is to cover it with a net of 3D points. Such a 'cloud' can be generated by a TLS (see WS vi) or the SfM method (see WS vii). Both methods are well suited for this task. Combined with a 3D polyline as an outline for defining the top and bottom borders, they make a perfect digital documentation option.

disadvantages

Both methods need additional measuring points (GCPs) and separate targets (specially designed TLS-targets readable only by the adjusted TLS-type, and specially designed markers for measuring the photographs for SfM (Lieberwirth & Bussilliat, 2017, chap.3) for referencing. Their measurements need extra time for documentation.

conclusion

Alternative 3D measurement options for the curve of a surface relief would be point-to-point measurement by e.g. total station or with a metric tape and yardstick. However, the latter lacks precision; the first takes a great amount of time – depending on the roughness of the surface. Hence, the application of a TLS was a meaningful decision until it reached its limits (see discourse on WS vi). The final conclusion of this application is that a total station (measuring the layer's outline) and a device for creating a precise point cloud of the surface are necessary to digitally document on excavations.

outlook

Nowadays, technological developments tend to more flexible devices like handhelds for small scales and objects (e.g. Trimble DPI-8, FARO Freestyle3D or even smartphone apps like EyeCue Qlone, Trnio Inc., SmartMobileVision Scann3D) which might also be suitable for excavations but need to be tested. There main advantage is the creation of an on-the-fly point cloud which makes it possible to immediate verify the documentation. The acquisition of GCPs is still necessary for precise georeferencing.

5.1.3 Excavation – WS iii)

advantages

The excavation was executed in the single-context-recording method in order to generate top and bottom surfaces of the layers. On one hand, this was compulsory according to the requirements of the Soprintendenza Archeologica Italia; on the other hand, it well suited our experimental setup which needed an exposed surface for measurement (see WS ii, vi, vii – surface documentation). In combination with the HM the high amount of archaeological stratigraphical layers could be easily managed.

disadvantages

The methods reach their limits on surfaces with less-visible structures. In this case, a digital reconstruction of the curved surface is only possible by post-excavation analysis of the plana and sections drawings but would lack precision and accuracy (Lieberwirth, 2008b).

conclusion

The single-context-record excavation has proven ideal for this study and for the purpose of digital reconstruction. Planum excavation is possible in general (see Lieberwirth 2008a) and would save digging time. However, digital reconstruction takes much more post-processing time and lacks precision because the digital model has to be built up through the documentation of section drawings. Since section drawings take in greater distances than point clouds, one will lose the information in between (Lieberwirth, 2008b).

outlook

Current trends are moving towards the 3D point cloud documentation of archaeological surfaces by TLS or SfM (see discussion on WS ii, vi, vii). Hence, one can assume an increased use of single-context-recordings since 3D point measurement methods cannot be applied.

5.1.4 Soil sampling & documentation – WS iv, x)

advantages

There is no advantage at the excavation itself.

disadvantages

Taking samples (including measurement) took about 20min per layer (see fig. 5.2). A special challenge at *Ostia Antica*

was the urban soil composition (more rubble and mortar than soil). Hence, samples sometimes had to be taken slightly out of line.

conclusion

For the first time, this study tested whether it is possible to predict the course of archaeological layers by reconstructing the curve and shape of natural layers as 3D volumes. Hence, taking soil samples had the same intention as the geophysical investigation, particularly to generate independent quantified information compare with the archaeological record. The storage of the sample material in white paper bags was ideal for soil drying and labelling. Considering the extra time needed for sampling, it took away excavation time but proved a worthwhile investment afterwards.

outlook

Since the method had proven very successful, it could be used in surveys as a precise 3D preparation of an archaeological excavation. Alternatively, it can be used as a non-destructive excavation method for generating geochemical volumes out of core drills. In some ideal cases, it might replace an archaeological excavation itself, e.g. when there is a great diversity of soil composition such as at *Ostia Antica*.

5.1.5 Feature & find documentation – WS v)

advantages

At the *Ostia Antica* excavation only the archaeological categories 'layers' and 'finds' were documented because 'features' were rare and large enough to be treated like a 'layer'.

Every find got a separate ID number in the DB. Hence, they could be easily identified amongst other geometry in the CAD-floor plan. The connection to the DB also allowed for a detailed text description of the shape and position of the finds and their reference to the layer. With this procedure, the geometry and database were always up-to-date and did not need any extra editing at post-processing.

The application of CAD with the plug-in TachyCAD Archäologie® has proven very useful. The drawing and the attribute-DB were completed when the excavation ended. Due to the real 3D coordinate system, the documentation can be verified from any perspective. The MonuMap®-DB offers the opportunity to store attribute data for each vector separately. Hence, all acquired single point data and polylines could be linked to the geometry and grouped into entities. Additionally, I used the AutoCAD®-layer structure to sort all DB-entities on thematic CAD-layers. The combination of AutoCAD® and TachyCAD® is a very flexible tool which can be adjusted on-the-fly to different excavation situations in the field.

disadvantages

The recording of finds with attributes in the attached DB took extra excavation time on-site.

The applied software combination is the best tool for documentation at the moment. However, several working steps could be spared if GIS were capable of 3D documentation with a real 3D coordinate system.

conclusion

Digitally documenting finds by a total station with a connected CAD-DB turned out to be a successful tool combination. Due to the clear DB-structure and the real 3D view, it was easy to verify documented data on-the-fly. Errors were discovered in time. Students became quickly familiar with the equipment. Considering their few experiences, they made very few mistakes. Only the vector types 3D point and 3D polylines were used. Polygones were not suitable since they are *per definition* flat 2D structures which did not occur at site.

TachyCAD® in combination with MonuMap® is a strong tool for documenting, storing and managing data in 3D space. The systems fit best for the requirements of this study with including the interface with GIS.

outlook

General main doubts about storing the data only digitally are security concerns. In this case study, I solved this problem by backing up external drives daily. With the increase in internet transmission speed there might be an opportunity to save data in a cloud on a remote server. From a technical perspective, there exists already an established workflow of transforming all archaeological information into a digital environment. Hence, the trend towards complete digitalisation is probably unstoppable (Lock 2003, chap. 6, ARCHES 2013, IANUS 2017). Except TachyCAD®, there are several documentation software programs available which provide an archaeological excavation-friendly structure (e.g. ArchaeoCAD®).

Improvements could be made by making GIS ready for 3D documentation.

5.1.6 TLS – WS vi)

advantages

A great advantage is the live-tracking option of the scan process. The software calculates the scan time in advance according to the chosen area and scan resolution. This makes it possible to plan the workflow for the excavation.

The scan workflow is straightforward with all-in-one software. Once the TLS is programmed, it works independently. The results can be georeferenced with high precision (in our study with a deviation of 2cm

(Lieberwirth et al., 2015)). The TLS Leica Geosystems® AG ScanStation2 offers the opportunity to adjust the point distance up from 1×1mm. Due to the surface topography's great variety within short distances and for economy of time (which would double by the highest possible resolution), I chose 1×1cm.

The control software Cyclone® is equipped with an internal DB which can be structured individually. The TLS-file names were documented in the docu-sheets for double-checking and non-digital backup. For merging point clouds and precise georeferencing, specially designed scanner targets (only recognisable for the specific TLS-type) had to be measured, too.

disadvantages

The TLS method requires a bunch of hardware devices (3D TLS with tripod, additional laptop, batteries or independent power supply) and proprietary software (control software and post-processing software) which were very expensive at the time of application. The devices require a high amount of energy. Hence, two batteries were included as accessories by the supplier. However, both cover just 8 working hours. In practical terms, this is not enough for a whole excavation day. According to our first experience with the TLS two years ago at the Hornsburg excavation (see Acknowledgements), we took a mobile generator with us with an additional weight of 20 kg. All devices were not easy to transport onto the site, which was only accessible on foot.

In summary, there are several arguments against the use of a 3D TLS on an excavation site:

– approx. 60 kg weight (TLS + additional devices),
– need for a permanent power supply,
– extra targets for georeferencing,
– on a diverse surface, at least three scans per surface were necessary = time consuming,
– the limitation of 270° vertical angle at ScanStation2 = the greatest disadvantage at this site.

Hence, documenting small and deep pits/layer surfaces was not possible even with the use of a tripod extension. (An additional tripod of a max. height of 1.80 m was the recommended solution by Leica Geosystems® AG but it did not work well due to susceptibility to wind.) Finally, the scanning process of one 'ScanWorld' (scanning one part of a surface from one perspective) at the adjusted resolution took approximately 20 min. According to the very differentiated surfaces, we generally needed at least two 'ScanWorlds' from different positions for one surface (sometimes even three when we reached greater depths). Including the time for TLS setup and dismantling, we had to plan for about 1 h scanning time per surface. This scanning time was extended even more by documenting the scanner targets at high resolution. Leica Geosystems® AG recommends a minimum of two targets. Based on our experiences at Hornsburg, we used at least five targets after each new stationary to avoid registration problems and to maintain precision (fig. 2.5).

conclusion

Creating a 3D point cloud of an archaeological surface is the ideal approach for describing it in a quantitative way. It offers a wide range of post-excavation analysis possibilities for archiving, restoration, reconstruction, protection, heritage management, etc. The number of its applications in a cultural heritage context has increased considerably over the past couple of years (Boardman & Bryan, 2018), but it is still rarely used to document archaeological surfaces (Fera et al., 2013). However, based on the many disadvantages described here it is worth looking at alternative methods (see outlook). The documentation time of approximately 1h had a great influence on the whole excavation workflow. This needs to be considered in advance for planning. My solution for the team was to split and move excavation teams to trench 2 or 3 during the scanning.

outlook

Prices for TLS-hardware and software are getting lower (e.g. FARO Laserscanner FOCUS 3D X30®). Thus TLSs might still be an option for archaeological excavations. Furthermore, total station combinations with laser scan options are available nowadays (e.g. Leica NOVA MS60®). However, there is a general unsolvable physical problem that high-resolution scanners provide low distance ranges and vice versa. The 'Landesamt für Archäologie Sachsen' overcame this limitation by sourcing two different TLS-devices (http://www.archaeologie.sachsen.de/951.htm).

Since SfM can conquer these limitations and taking into consideration the cumbersome handling of TLS, the trend is towards SfM in archaeology (Reinhard, 2016) and heritage management (Hixon et al., 2018).

5.1.7 SfM – WS vii)

advantages

The equipment, just a digital camera, is already included into the archaeological documentation features. Hence, there are no additional costs for hardware. Even FOSS for data processing is available e.g. VisualSFM. However, the proprietary software Agisoft PhotoScan® I used in this study creates better results and provides an interface between GIS and can hence be recommended (Lieberwirth et al., 2015).

disadvantages

Unfortunately, the method does not provide immediate results for verification. Therefore, one cannot be sure if documentation and resolution will prove satisfactory. Resolution cannot be adjusted in advance such as with

a TLS. It depends on the amount and quality of the photographs (Lieberwirth & Bussilliat, 2017, chap.2.2).

Due to this uncertainty, users tend to create more pictures than necessary. This leads to a very high number of them, which claims greater memory space than usual. We needed an extra external hard drive of 500 MB at *Ostia Antica*.

For georeferencing, numbered and specially designed GCPs have to be placed on and around the documented surfaces (at least four targets) separately measured by the total station (Lieberwirth et al., 2015).

conclusion

Due to the high-quality results generated from low-cost equipment and software, the method is very attractive for archaeological documenting. The described disadvantages were compensated for a tailored workflow at *Ostia Antica* (see outlook). To summarise, experiments executed during the excavation revealed that SfM-results are very reliable, in part even better than TLS-results (Lieberwirth et al., 2015). They have therefore been used for layers 108, 112 and 113 in this study. These layers could not been documented by the TLS because of it's vertical angle limitations (see sec. 2.2.2).

outlook

Using only SfM at an excavation, the following workflow is suggested:

> At first, a rough SfM-model with low resolution should be created from approximately 10 overlapping pictures. This amount can be managed in a reasonable short time in order to generate a first model for verification. Secondly, a dense point cloud from about 20–25 overlapping photographs can be created. According to our experiences at *Ostia Antica* and other places, I recommend an overlap of 60% (Lieberwirth & Bussilliat, 2017, chap. 2.2 slide 19).

5.1.8 Photogrammetry – WS viii)

advantages

The photogrammetry at the site of *Ostia Antica* required no new component compared to common archaeological excavation procedure. Digital photographs were created from topview.

disadvantages

The disadvantage of a flat documentation of a surface relief is the loss of distance information in 3D space concerning surface topography.

conclusion

Even in a 3D model, the overview of an excavation trench from a topview should not be neglected. At some points, the

2D flat overview of a site might be more informative than a detailed 2.5D relief because of its information reduction.

outlook

Since SfM is capable of the production of orthophotographs out of 3D point clouds with texture (Agisoft PhotoScan®) it might replace photogrammetry in general. This can save documentation time and memory space, and removes one complete working step.

Future applications might replace orthophotogrammetry in general with more advanced 3D approaches overcoming the 2D projection (Traoré et al., 2018).

5.1.9 Archaeological documentation – WS ix)

advantages

For digital documentation, only the vectors 3D points and 3D polylines were needed, which older total station versions can provide. They are sufficient as long as they can export CAD-readable formats.

Filling out docu-sheets every working day had the advantage that all excavation members were always at the same information level. Furthermore, there was no other medium to create a sketch of the layer's horizontal position.

disadvantages

Filling the DB and docu-sheets directly on-site takes away much needed excavation time. Hence, one should think about an adequate and efficient workflow that does not occupy the total station and laptop with the AutoCAD® software too long (at least if there is only one device on-site).

conclusion

The generation of a real 3D floor plan makes it possible to view the site from different perspectives. This offered a permanent verification of measurements and led to very few documentation/measurement errors. The applied combination of digital geometry and DB plus a paper-based 'backup' proved meaningful because in some parts (at least in the sketch and HM-diagram) we had no equivalent at hand.

The documentation via total station with TachyCAD-archaeology® and the related MonuMap®-DB created an on-the-fly 3D floor plan with a complete DB. This combination proved very useful on-site and can be managed by students. The software stores and manages all information in one system.

Documentation sheets on one hand were used to create a backup on a different medium, while, on the other hand, they provided a place for information normally documented in a so-called 'excavation-diary'. In this study, they proved useful in terms of verification and summary of layer information. The sheets contain a summary of all data connected to each layer, such as 3D point cloud files and photographs. Secondly, the 'diary-information', like the sketch of the layer's location and the HM-diagram, could be documented in a structured way.

outlook

One might consider using a digital environment also for the docu-sheets using a digital form with a suitable digital device (e.g. tablets with a digital pencil). A further option could be to import surface photographs to draw sketches onto it directly (Taylor et al., 2018).

5.1.10 3D point cloud processing – WS xi, xiii)

advantages

Data processing laser scan point clouds in the attached control software Cyclone® 8.2 is very straightforward. The interface between Cyclone® and the CAD plug-in PointSense® worked without any problem, without loss of information or quality. For efficient handling of the 3D point clouds, CAD provides the category multipoint (besides single vector points).

disadvantages

The data processing (registration, georeferencing) of the laser scan point cloud can only be executed in the attached control software.

Both software applications are proprietary and expensive.

conclusion

The combination of the Leica control software Cyclone® and the CAD plug-in PointSense® was the only available solution for data post-processing at the time.

outlook

An alternative FOSS workflow from Cyclone® to GIS omitting PointSense® is possible and described in detail in the RGB-experiment 'colour test' (see sec. 4.3.1).

According to the described limitations and my research results, I generally recommend SfM for future applications instead of laser scanning. Efficient processing options are described in WS vii in this section.

5.1.11 3D point cloud creation – WS xii, xiv)

advantages

Creating a 3D point cloud out of overlapping photographs with georeferencing and export worked extremely well in Agisoft PhotoScan®. The result was a very precise model with a mean deviation (RMSE) of 0.01 m with sufficient resolution (compare with Lieberwirth et al. 2015, tab.1).

disadvantages

Processing SfM photographs in FOSS was not straightforward and the result not as good as in Agisoft PhotoScan®.

conclusion

The Agisoft PhotoScan® results were a georeferenced 3D point cloud describing the course of archaeological layer surfaces with a point resolution of approx. 1×1 cm. They were very satisfactory and could be used for further processing. The results of the FOSS software cannot yet compete with the Agisoft PhotoScan® results and need improvement in terms of a user-friendly workflow and the quality of results.

outlook

To overcome the limitations of the proprietary software available in this field, it is worth looking forward to improvements of VisualSFM or similar FOSS.

A third option (which has not been discussed here), the calculation of point clouds via web-interface (for examples see Lieberwirth and Bussilliat 2017, chap.2.3 slide 23), cannot be recommended for scientific data as long as the hosting server conditions do not agree the EU-GDPR (https://gdpr-info.eu/).

5.1.12 Orthorectification – WS xv)

advantages

Ortho-rectifying of photographs in AutoCAD® with e.g. the software PhoToPlan® is a common procedure in digital archaeology and works very well. However, the image rectification in this study was carried out by GIS. This had two advantages. The results are already in the final software and the resulting file formats are readable by the final processing software GRASS (which is not always the case). QGIS was chosen because it has a more user-friendly georeferencing GUI than GRASS.

disadvantages

There are two disadvantages concerning PhoToPlan®. The software is proprietary and the output format is not readable by GRASS.

conclusion

The aim of this study (to use only FOSS software) conflicted with the decision to use CAD during documentation because of its real 3D coordinate system. This implied a prior use of proprietary software. (AutoCAD® is proprietary and its FOSS-alternatives are not suitable.) So this aim could be pursued.

outlook

Ortho-rectification might not be necessary in the future – see outlook of WS viii in this section.

5.1.13 Archaeological & pedological data processing – WS xvi, xvii)

advantages

The AutoCAD® extension TachyCAD® has proven very useful during documentation and beyond. It even offers an interface to GIS with the export of the SHP-file format for vector data with their attached attributes from the MonuMap®-DB.

Furthermore, TachyCAD® provides an advanced ('erweiterte') HELMERT-Transformation tool for 3D transformation (scaling, moving and rotation of x,y, and z-coordinates) from a local coordinate system into the national coordinate system ED 50 PROIEZIONE UTM. This 3D transformation is not yet possible in GIS. From the three possible coordinate systems provided by the Soprintendenza Speciale, WGS84-ETRF2000, Gauss-Boaga Fuso Est and ED50 I chose ED50 because national grids have less distortion and they are available in all common GIS.

disadvantages

There was no disadvantage except that all the applications could not be done in GIS due to its lack of a 3D coordinate system.

conclusion

No further editing of the vector data was necessary either in TachyCAD® nor in MonuMap®. Exporting the data after the coordinate system transformation into GIS required only one WS.

outlook

The transformation WS might have been avoidable because every transformation leads to distortions.

A general alternative to CAD would be a real 3D GIS. For example QGIS provides an interface with several measurement devices (e.g. common total stations or DGPS) with the option of on-the-fly measurements like in TachyCAD® (unfortunately only in 2D). This would reduce the amount of WSs and applied software.

5.1.14 Chemical analysis – WS xviii)

advantages

The geochemical analysis of the soil samples was done by the Institute of Physical Geography at the Free University Berlin (see Preface). The result was a table which could be attached to the vector points with the soil sample ID number as a primary key.

disadvantages

The procedure of sample acquisition took up excavation time. The geochemical analysis cannot be carried out

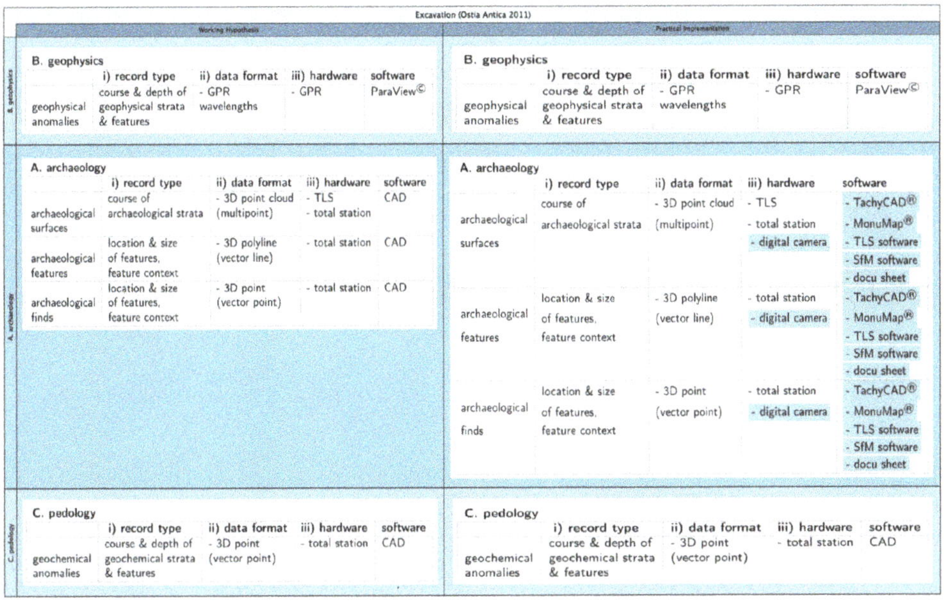

Figure 5.1. Comparison of working hypothesis (see table 1.1, 1.2, 1.3) with practical implementation.

by archaeologists and has to be paid for along with the geophysical investigation.

conclusion

The effort of taking soil samples can be neglected according to the outstanding results (see 4.2.3). The laboratory analysis should be considered by planning campaign costs.

outlook

See discussion analysis of soil samples in sec. 5.3

5.1.15 Summary of discourse: 3D data acquisition

The excavation site at *Ostia Antica* turned out to be a perfect test bed for the methodological challenges of this study. The data acquisition followed the **idea** of a complete digital excavation. This approach was not completely new (Lock, 2003, chap.3) but was in some parts still an experiment.

CAD again proved why it's qualified for this task due to its linked, interactive DB between the geometry and the real 3D coordinate system. The latter was and will probably still be a good choice as to why CAD will be chosen for documentation.

Furthermore, the **aim** was to document as precisely and as accurately as possible in the most advanced way, although no solution for processing and analysing data sets exists yet, but there will be one in the future.

For these tasks, a **working hypothesis** was formulated (see sec. 1.2.3). Compared to the practical implementation, it can be confirmed in most parts (55.7%); in 16.6% it could be specified and in 27.7% corrected (see fig. 5.1). The specification concerns only the CAD plug-in. TachyCAD® and MonuMap® were preferred over others because of their

open interface to further processing software. The 27.7% correction concerns

– the geophysical model transformation in ParaView©,
– the TLS software which had to be used for first processing steps of the laser scan results,
– the whole SfM method hardware and software because this method was created during excavation and was not part of the working hypothesis and
– the use of docu-sheets. At the time of the data acquisition the idea to use tablets for digital docu-sheets had been developed already but the hardware was not yet available at reasonable price (see the paper-less project in Pompeii where the tablets were sponsored by Apple Inc.© (Wallrodt, 2016)).

From a technical perspective, the theoretical workflow has proven feasible in general. However, by planning and managing an excavation, one must also consider **time** management. Hence, the workflow steps should be arranged not only in right succession but also according to the time needed (fig. 5.2). The time diagram gives an overview of the working hours for each process on-site in this study (fig. 5.3). This structure helps to discover time gaps at excavation which I closed by moving teams between three trenches. The diagram is also an indicator on method efficiency, e.g. data acquisition time between TLS and SfM. The latter proved favourable on-site and even during off-site procession (fig. 5.4).

The target to materialise archaeological excavation via digital approach was achieved. Concerning only archaeological data, the idea of gaining more objectivity had to be dismissed because decisions over which kind of information should be documented still had to be made by me. This confirms the conclusion of Merlo (2016, p.69).

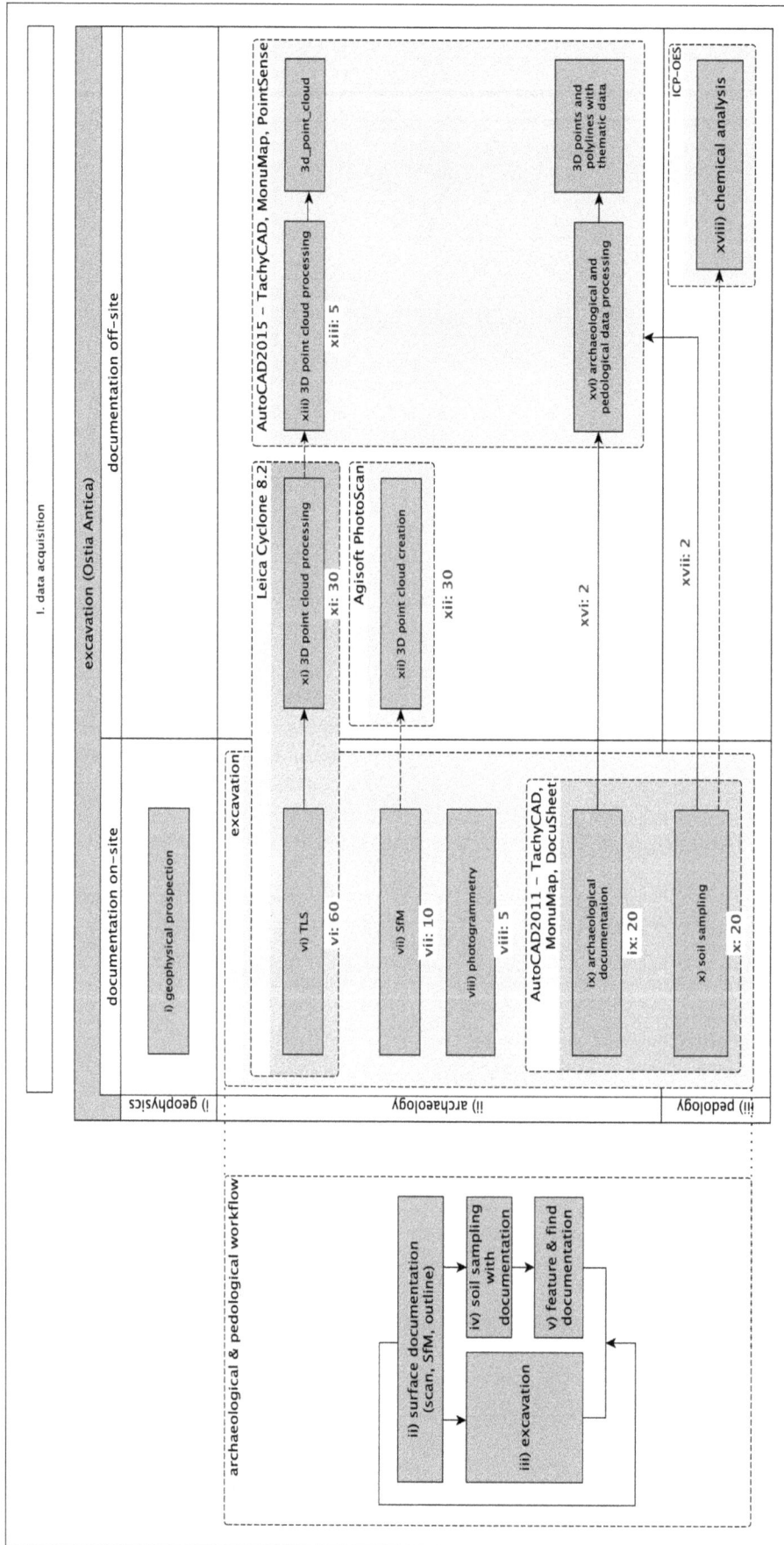

Figure 5.2. Process chain 3-time, copy of fig. 2.18: general workflow of on-site data acquisition, off-site data processing and modelling of Ostia Antica excavation data with average processing time for one layer in minutes. With reference to the tables 2.2, 2.3, 2.6, 2.7 and 2.8.

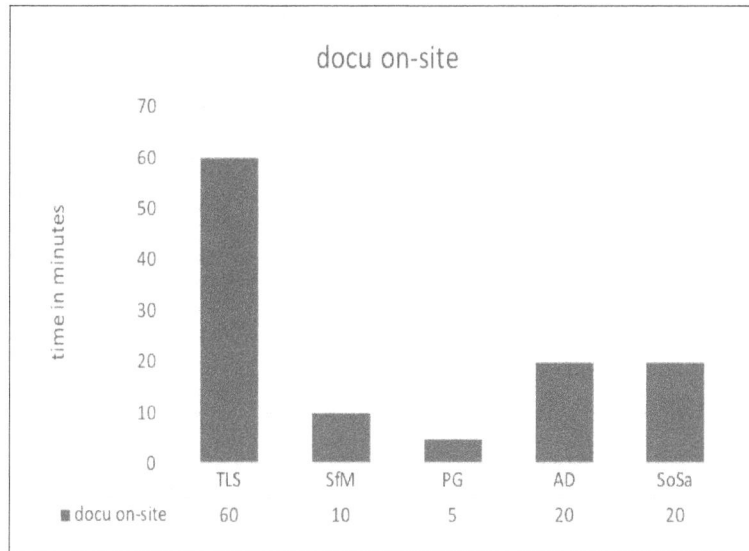

Figure 5.3. Time diagram of WS 'documentation on-site'. Times are average values for one layer (see also process chain 3-time, fig. 5.2). Legend: TLS = terrestrial laser scanner, SfM = *Structure from Motion*, PG = photogrammetry, AD = archaeological documentation, SoSa = soil sampling.

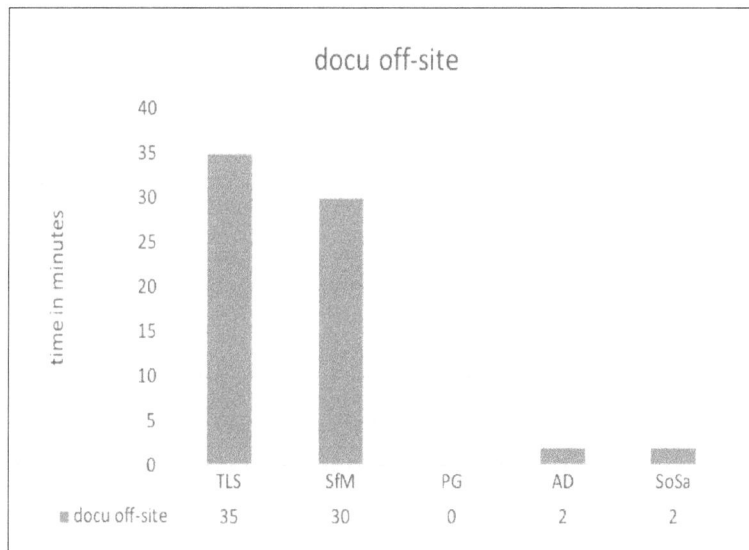

Figure 5.4. Time diagram of WS 'documentation off-site'. Times are average values for one layer (see also process chain 3-time, fig. 5.2). Legend: TLS = terrestrial laser scanner, SfM = *Structure from Motion*, PG = photogrammetry, AD = archaeological documentation, SoSa = soil sampling.

In contrast, the pedological and geophysical data were taken without any bias. Their results are summarised in section 5.3.7.

5.2 Discourse: 3D data modelling

5.2.1 Geophysical model transformation – WS xix)

advantages

The viewer software ParaView© provides not only 3D visualisation but also analysis. Both options were successfully applied in the visualisation and 3D transformation (advanced Helmert transformation) of the geophysical voxel model provided by the company Eastern Atlas®.

disadvantages

No disadvantages in this working step

conclusion

The first visualisation of the geophysical model worked because it was implemented in a local coordinate system (set up by the company Eastern Atlas®). After the model's transformation into 'ED50' I got the same errors as described in sec. 4.1. Only after the second transformation into 'short_ED50' did the model fit together with all other data.

outlook

The first transformation could have been avoided by providing the coordinate system to cooperation partners beforehand. The second can be avoided as soon as the OpenGL library problem in ParaView© is solved.

5.2.2 Model building of layers – WS xx, xxi)

advantages

The viewer software ParaView© provides not only 3D visualisation but also analysis. Both options were successfully applied in the visualisation and 3D transformation (advanced Helmert transformation) of the geophysical voxel model provided by the company Eastern Atlas®.

disadvantages

Due to the requirements of the module, the calculation of the layer volumes needed time-consuming preparations beforehand: an additional virtual top or bottom raster surface had to be created to stop the voxel calculation (the filling process between two layer surfaces) in the up or down direction.

conclusion

The flood-fill algorithm in GRASS is still the only suitable solution for filling the volume of an object with non-measurable information.

outlook

The *v.vol.rst* algorithm might also be an option for archaeological layers if it could use polyhedra as calculation borders (3D mask).

5.2.3 Generation of orthophotos – WS xxii)

advantages

QGIS© offers a very user-friendly GUI for georeferencing. Its interface with GRASS qualifies it for this study.

disadvantages

At the moment there is no interface between AutoCAD® with plug-in PhoToPlan® and GRASS GIS. Hence, the geographic reference of orthophotos generated in PhoToPlan® vanish after importing into GRASS.

Importing and exporting to and from QGIS© is an additional WS which can be avoided if GRASS offers a similar tool.

conclusion

Generating orthophotographs could have been done in AutoCAD® with the plug-in PhoToPlan® but was dismissed because of the requirements of GRASS. It worked with QGIS© as a FOSS but took additional processing time.

outlook

TLS as well as SfM could become a substitute for photogrammetry in the future. Both processing software programs offer export options of 2D topview screenshots of their textured 3D point cloud models. If the model is georeferenced beforehand, the result is an orthophotograph, a derivative of the model (Agisoft, 2018, chap.3). Nevertheless, the whole WS of generating an orthophoto will become obsolete the moment importing a coloured point cloud of textured mesh in ParaView© becomes possible because ParaView© offers the option of orthogonal topviews (see chap. 4).

5.2.4 Conversion of 3D vector points & 3D polylines – WS xxiii)

advantages

The chosen GIS system GRASS provides the two vector data types (3D point – including multipoint, 3D polyline) I used in CAD for documentation. Due to the interface and standardised exchange format SHAPEFILE (see 'The Open Geospatial Consortium' http://www.opengeospatial.org/); the import into the chosen system was no problem. No further editing was necessary.

disadvantages

There is no disadvantage except that the whole working step could be omitted – see outlook.

conclusion

This WS could be done in nearly no time and produced no errors. All attributes of the CAD-DB were maintained.

outlook

See outlook for WS xvi, xvii.

5.2.5 Calculation of 3D distribution of chemical elements in soil samples – WS xxiv-xxv)

advantages

GRASS is the only FOSS GIS which offers voxel generation. The 3D interpolation algorithms *v.vol.rst* is very useful for calculating volumes of continuous values in 3D space.

disadvantages

The algorithm calculates voxel only in the adjusted 3D region which can be only adjusted as a cube or cuboid.

conclusion

Besides the flood-fill algorithm, GRASS offers a second algorithm with different requirements. It needs an attribute value for interpolation. Hence, it is suitable for measuring values inside 3D space.

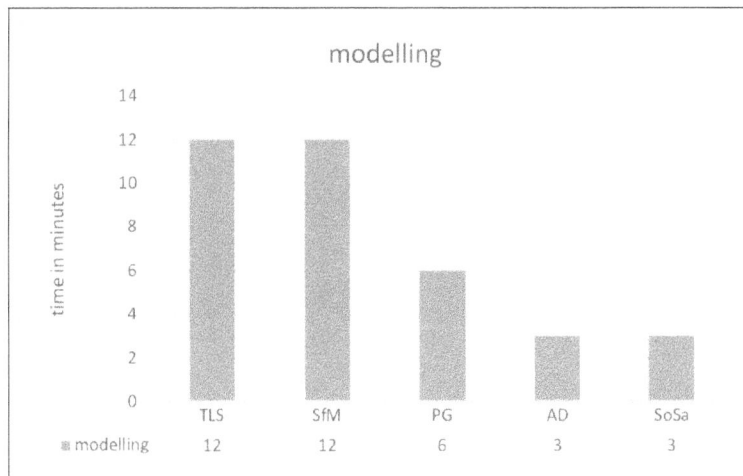

Figure 5.5. Time diagram of WS 'modelling'. Times are average values for one layer (see also process chain 4-time, fig. 5.8). Legend: TLS = terrestrial laser scanner, SfM = *Structure from Motion*, PG = photogrammetry, AD = archaeological documentation, SoSa = soil sampling.

outlook

Incorporating of polyhedra as 3D a calculation border (3D mask as buffer) will save calculation time and storage space because calculations be done for more specific 3D areas.

5.2.6 Summary of discourse: 3D data modelling

The **aims** of modelling all data in GRASS GIS, formulated in section 1.2.2, were achieved successfully. Compared with my work from 2007 (Lieberwirth, 2008a), new workflows had to be developed because I incorporated new data types from TLS and SfM. All other workflows were very similar to those of the former study because the relevant GRASS modules for 3D raster cells did not change profoundly.

The **time** diagram (fig. 5.5) of the modelled working steps (fig. 5.6) shows a clear outlier towards 3D point cloud processing where the modelling of SfM data was faster in terms of calculation and managing large data sets.

5.3 Discourse: 3D data analysis & visualisation

5.3.1 Visualisation i, ii – AN i, ii + WS xxvi)

advantages

After the incorporation of WS xxvi the import of all VTK-files (vector, raster, voxel) worked well with the individual working-coordinates system 'short_ED50'.

VTK-files have a human readable format in a table-like structure. Hence, manipulation is possible in programs which can handle tables and execute calculations (like RStudio© in this study). The latter was applied for all VTK-vector files. Raster and voxel files could just be edited by changing coordinate information in the header line.

The manipulation of the export format VTK-files has the advantage of maintaining the original data and coordinates

in a GIS-readable format until a solution for the viewer software is found.

disadvantages

The additional working step, to overcome the visualisation limitations of ParaView©, takes extra time. In particular, manipulating vector files due to the import and calculation operation in an external program is time consuming (see also fig. 5.8).

conclusion

To conclude, the calculation of voxel in GRASS using real coordinate systems is successful. However, their representation in ParaView© is not yet possible without manipulation.

By the time this study ended no FOSS GIS alternative either to calculate voxel or to represent them adequately existed. The compromise solution presented in this study for solving the presentation problem works fine. Its results are precise in proportion to all other data manipulated in the same way.

outlook

The alternative -c flag ('correcting the coordinates to match the VTK-OpenGL precision' – see e.g. https://grass .osgeo.org/grass74/manuals/r.out.vtk.html), suggested in all GRASS VTK-export modules (*v.out.vtk, r.out.vtk, r3.out.vtk*), does not work properly since it makes a random cut for each file (profoundly discussed by me with the developer).

A second solution presented by Merlo (2016, p.92 fig.5.15) using powers of ten ($\times 10^3$) does not resolve the general problem of digits limitations.

It might be a question of time until a suitable OpenGL library is incorporated into ParaView© and/or other scientific viewers. Meanwhile, the solution presented by

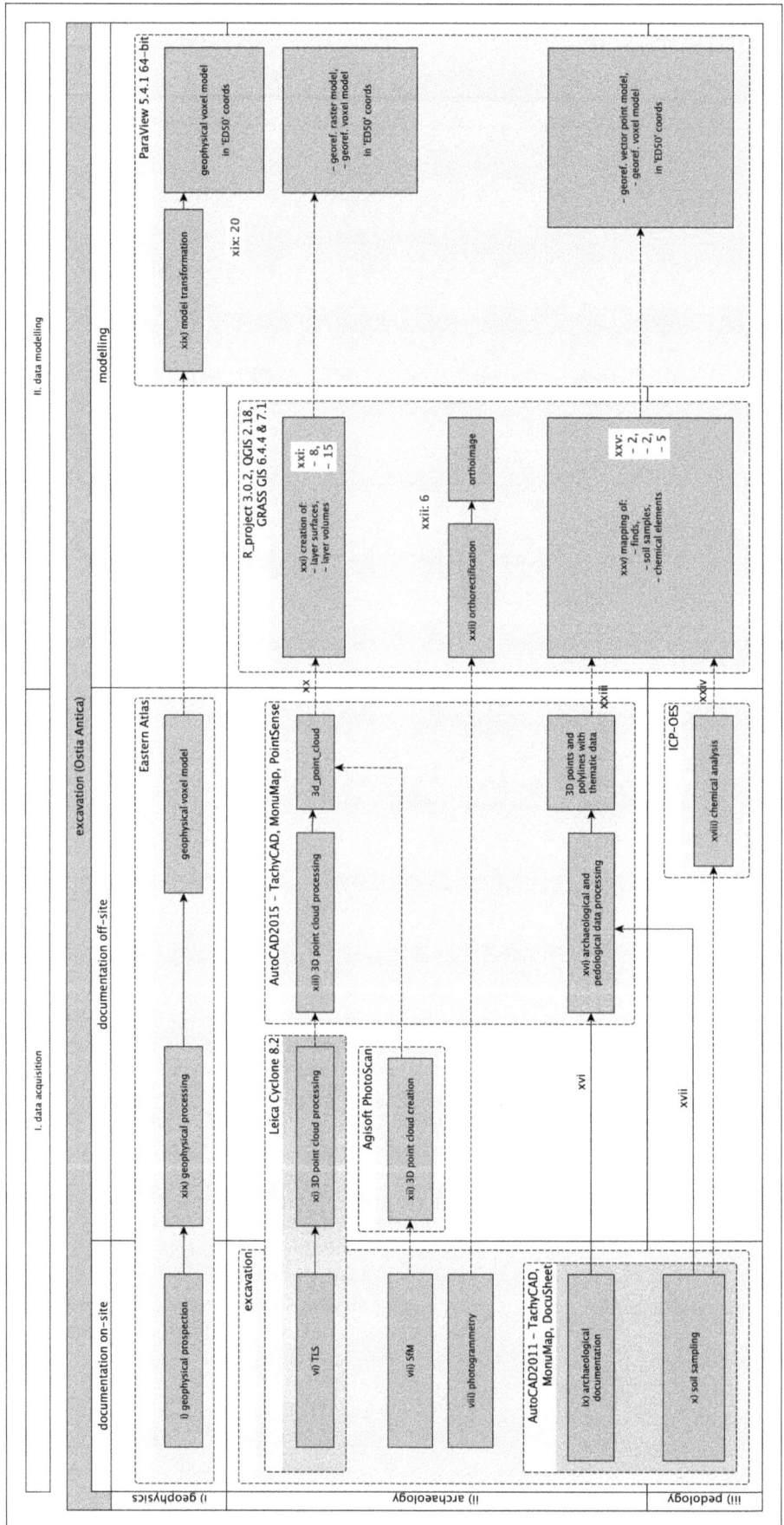

Figure 5.6. Process chain 4-time, copy of fig. 3.12: general workflow of on-site data acquisition, off-site data processing and modelling of *Ostia Antica* excavation data with average processing time for one layer in minutes. With reference to the tables 2.2, 2.3, 2.6, 2.7, 2.8, 3.1, 3.2 and 3.3.

me could be optimised by developing a macro for the vector file manipulation in RStudio©.

5.3.2 Voxel volume versus interpolation, 3D polyline, raster surface – AN iii, iv-vii)

advantages

The generation of a geophysical voxel model as a result of further archaeological analysis was also new for the cooperation company Eastern Atlas®, who took up this challenge for their own improvement. The cooperation worked very well according to the model's 3D extension and resolution.

Since the geophysical model was also generated by interpolation the result is a cuboid '3D block'. Compared with the geochemical model, this result is statistically correct because the whole 3D space was investigated and hence provides legacy data up to the calculation borders (compare with generating the geochemical model2 in sec. 4.2.3). The combination of geophysical and archaeological data clearly showed overlaps in the anomalies and features with a decreasing tendency downwards (decreasing z-values).

disadvantages

With an optimal workflow, the model transformation would not have been necessary.

conclusion

Fortunately, the company Eastern Atlas® was an innovative cooperation partner because creating a 3D model from geophysical data was also new to them. The combination of a complex 3D volume model of geophysical and archaeological results was a complete success in terms of methodology, archaeological interpretation and comparison.

The analysis in ParaView© showed convincing coincidences between the geophysical and the archaeological models. The filtering and selection options give infinitely variable access to continuous data distribution of geophysical anomalies inside the virtual archaeological trench in full 3D. Selections can also be presented and exported for further analysis as descriptive statistics via histogram or table.

outlook

The geophysical model was only roughly interpreted by Eastern Atlas® to show the method's potential. A more precise approach might reveal more anomalies and overlaps.

There is room for improving the geophysical model concerning resolution and precision.

The model transformation process could easily be avoided by optimal excavation preparation. Unfortunately, this can not be done in practice very often.

5.3.3 Voxel volume versus interpolation, 3D polyline, raster surface, DB-link – AN viii-x)

advantages

All archaeological data could be represented in a real 3D digital environment. The examples shown in chapter 4 offer an insight into the potential of the visualisation and analysis options. Even the visualisation of 2.5D raster surfaces (which is also possible in common GIS) in 3D space gives a better overview about the stratigraphical sequence than that in GIS. The same is true for labelling vector, raster and voxel data which represent also the connection to the attached geo-database. Thus, data can be summarised, selected and categorised. Different combinations of features, finds, surfaces and volumes are possible in this complexity for the first time in archaeology.

disadvantages

Spatial queries in terms of topology are not possible. The same is true for spatial statistics common in 2D GIS, like buffer, cluster, neighbourhood analysis and regression analysis.

conclusion

The chosen 3D viewer for this study not only displays the archaeological features and objects but also analyses them. Filter options can be applied for analysing archaeological deposits by clipping, slicing, transparency, selection and labelling.

The generated VTK-files are not yet common data types in archaeological contexts. However, they can be easily converted without loss of information in e.g. PLY or OBJ (formats which are e.g. excepted by the DAI https://www.ianus-fdz.de/it-empfehlungen/archivierung and ARCHES 2013). Therefore the format might be suitable for a standardised approach for a complex archaeological 3D information system.

Compared with the prototype there is a general improvement of performance (e.g. real-time graphic interaction).

outlook

Since spatial analysis in ParaView© is still limited, it could be alternatively outsourced into GRASS or other external programs, like RStudio©.

However, analysis options for voxel volumes are also rare in GRASS (only the modules *r3.stats, r3.univar*). Incorporating 3D spatial statistics and a 3D mask (e.g. a polyhedra) for calculating archaeological voxel volumes or clipping would immensely improve the application towards 3D analysis in GIS in general.

Developing an interface between both programs (GRASS and ParaView©) to omit the working step of VTK-file generation would save time.

5.3.4 Geochemistry: calcium – AN xi-xiv)

advantages

Compared with archaeological voxel objects, the geochemical voxel models are created by interpolation. Hence, each voxel has a different value which can be selected by single threshold values, intervals, isosurfaces and isovolumes. Display options like transparency, clipping and cutting give insight into the spatial distribution of the exemplary element calcium, chosen for this study.

The same is true for displaying a histogram which will change according to the selection (see comparison of model1 and model2 in sec. 4.2.3). Its values can be interpreted and exported for further studies. 'Plot over line' is a spatial filter for generating the distribution of a value through selected 3D space.

Compared with the distribution calculation of geophysical data, geochemical data have the advantage of consistent precision throughout the whole 3D space (the geophysical data lose precision at greater depth because of signal reduction).

disadvantages

See disadvantages for AN viii-x

conclusion

The visualisation of trench 1's calcium distribution turned out to be successful. The results show clear spatial congruence with the archaeological record. Spatial analysis is possible by overlaying the pedological, archaeological and geophysical models and applying filters like thresholds, selections etc. (see above).

Furthermore, the selection by isosurfaces and isovolumes revealed very similar 3D shapes between the three subjects. Relevant structures can be further analysed by clipping, cutting and labelling distribution values.

Applying a histogram can extract the quantified information from the selections.

outlook

See outlook of AN viii-x

5.3.5 Experiment: colour test

advantages

Calculation results of the colour distribution show several clusters in ParaView©, an indication that the method works in general.

disadvantages

Unfortunately, the results of this study are not scientifically proven since their acquisition was not a standardised procedure which required defined excavation conditions, for example constant light conditions, colour matching and a high-grade digital camera inside the TLS for more precise photographs (the internal cameras of TLS are of low quality).

conclusion

Although the results could not be used for scientific interpretations in this study, the procedure works well and was successful from a technical point-of-view.

outlook

Proposals for a standardised colour acquisition could be:

– acquire the data underneath an excavation tent or similar coverage in order to generate constant light condition,
– acquire the data by TLS or SfM under constant light conditions and
– reduce the time to calculate the external RGB-value by applying a macro or script.
– Verifying the results could be done by comparing the colour results with archaeological models because both are described by the same proxy 'colour' but generated by different workflows (human perception for archaeological models and unbiased colour measured by device).

5.3.6 Experiment: SfM processing

advantages

The SfM-test results could be used for further analysis in this study for modelling the curve of the top and bottom surfaces of the archaeological layers. Their models were precise and accurate according to comparisons with models from the same legacy data; compare with Lieberwirth (2015).

disadvantages

The visualisation of the coloured textured maps or 3D point clouds from SfM-calculations resulted in false colours in ParaView©. According to the comparison from 2013, the software Agisoft PhotoScan® made the most of the photographs (Lieberwirth et al., 2015). Its cost for educational licenses is acceptable. However, the software is proprietary which does not match the requirements of the study.

conclusion

Even when the FOSS results from our study in 2013 (Lieberwirth et al., 2015) are only considered, the SfM-method calculates astonishing precise results with high resolution and accuracy. It can be concluded that it is an adequately replacement for 3D laser scanning. When the acquisition costs and processing time are taken into consideration, it can compete with TLS.

outlook

To avoid proprietary SfM-software, SfM-processing FOSS (e.g. VisualSFM) should be improved where the algorithm for point detection is concerned.

Visualisation software like ParaView© should be improved in order to import real colour information (at the moment, only JSON and XML colour files are readable).

5.3.7 Summary of discourse: 3D data analysis

Data analysis in general is inherently topic related. For this reason, the technical discourse questions were seen from an archaeological perspective in this study.

The analysis in this study proved that a georeferenced 3D solid model can be combined with (nearly) unlimited information within a certain 3D region or territory. The 3D volume map can visualise archaeological volumes as well as natural scientific data as continuous 3D variables at various heights, depths and resolutions. Interactive filtering makes it possible to select or combine with other geographic maps. As long as they are transformed into *decimal32-bit* (ISO, 2011) coordinates they can be visualised in ParaView©. 3D maps can display scientific data and make them available for further analysis in a more realistic digital environment than commonly is at hand.

This summary takes up the research questions (RQs) formulated in chapter 1 and 2.

Research Question i - xiii

RQ no. i)	The model should become a true 3D map by fulfilling all the requirements of a cartographic representation.	**Result**
chap. 1, 4	A complete map should contain standardised information about the location, its context and azimuth. According to these requirements and definition (chapter 1), the resulting models are maps *per definitionem*.	✓

RQ no. ii)	The model should be generated from digital excavation data.	**Result**
chap. 1, 4	Digitally documenting all archaeological information proved feasible in this study. For safety reasons, a daily backup was applied without any problems.	✓
	It can be summarised that the model calculation could be created from all acquired digital excavation data. The selected devices for acquisition were well suited to this study. Mainly the high-resolution GPR-antenna and the SfM-method proved very suitable for 3D measurements. This procedure is recommended for similar excavations.	
	In general, the distribution of archaeological material in 3D space can be virtually reconstructed, visualised and analysed more precise and faster than 10 years ago. The approach of 'digging numbers' (Fletcher & Lock, 2005) can be pursued further and even extended by including 'numbers' of geophysics and pedology. With this combination, different and more complex archaeological questions can be answered, which was not possible before.	
	However, at the moment, visualising the model is only possible with a local coordinate system.	*x*

RQ no. iii)	The 3D environment should provide similar spatio-temporal analysis functions as in common 2D GIS.	**Result**
chap. 1, 4	*'The archaeological record [...] is not static. [...] Natural site formation processes must be understood before using the archaeological record for interpretations'* (Morton, 2004, p.1). Hence, the main aim of the model in this study is to support scientific analysis. Understanding an archaeological record is the research task we face at each archaeological site. With the virtual reconstruction a copy of the real world is created. It can be interactively accessed for better understanding at any time. Formations of layers and volumes can be rebuilt, allowing for a virtual re-excavation.	
	The virtual 3D model of trench 1 can be chronologically re-constructed and re-excavated by providing also a fourth dimension.	
	All vector and raster data can be analysed in GRASS GIS in 2D. For voxel data, descriptive statistics are provided.	

In the viewer ParaView© all data can be categorised, classified, selected, filtered and combined according to their quantified information stored in the attached geo-database. Volumes can be filtered (thresholds, isosurfaces, isovolumes), clipped and sliced.	✓
To summarise, common 2D and 2.5D GIS data can be analysed as usual in GIS. 3D statistics is not yet possible neither in GIS nor in the viewer. The latter does also not provide SQL ('Structured Query Language') queries for attributes or location. The same is true for topological questions in general. In contrast, ParaView© offers a different approach to answer these questions by graphical selections or filters of the attached tables for structuring the data.	*x*
3D statistics is an analysis which has not yet been incorporated into FOSS GIS software. 3D statistics could be outsourced into e.g. RStudio©.	

RQ no. iv)	The result of this work should now become an interactive, archaeological, digital 3D volume map.	**Result**
sec. 1.2	The answer here is clearly positive.	✓
	However, according to the artificial coordinate system applied in ParaView©, the map does not belong to the real geographic space.	*x*
	This last of the three main parts of the study (acquisition, modelling, analysis) started with importing all VTK-data generated in GRASS. This step turned out to be the greatest obstacle of the whole study. It took about a year to find the reason for the described visualisation problem and several months to test different solutions. The error tracing started with verifying the GRASS calculation results, followed by testing the -c flag option of all GRASS VTK-export modules (see sec. 4.1), testing several coordinate systems and discussing the matter with the ParaView© developers. The decisive hint finally came from my colleague Irmela Herzog (see Preface) after the presentation of first study results at the CHNT conference Vienna 2016 (https://www.chnt.at/) pointing towards the OpenGL library implementation in ParaView©.	
	The reason why this error did not happen with the first prototype of 2007 (Lieberwirth, 2008a) was the application of a local coordinate system with 'short' numbers – a fortunate coincidence.	

RQ no. v, xi, xii)	It was an aim of this study to minimise platform and system changes in order to save time and money and to avoid exchange errors. The less programs are needed, the fewer working steps have to be executed. This helps to avoid data transformation and conversion.	**Result**
sec. 1.2	The digital excavation turned out to be successful according to the requirements. The documentation software options were strongly limited according to the requirements of the study. The great advantage is that it can also be changed and tailored actively.	✓
	There is still room for improvements in terms of acquisition and visualisation software: - using a true 3D GIS for acquisition and - using a viewer which accepts real coordinates.	*x*

RQ no. vi)	The aim is to create a digital 3D GIS model of the excavation trench. It should not only visualize surfaces, features and finds but also archaeological stratigraphy as real 3D volume objects.	**Result**
sec. 1.2.1	The digital, quantitative visualisation of archaeological trench 1 in a measurable, cartographic 3D space achieves an enormous boost in reality. The scientific viewer environment provides insights into structures that were previously invisible. You can see and investigate compact information above and below the Earth's surface by cutting it or structuring it in any direction.	✓
	The trench's data are visualised as real 3D objects in a local 3D coordinate system.	

RQ no. vii)	From an archaeological point-of-view, I would like to answer the following questions:	**Result**
sec. 1.2.1	- Is it possible to extract archaeological stratigraphical borders out of the geophysical record? Yes, in this study until a depth of approx. 60–80cm.	✓
	- Is it possible to extract archaeological stratigraphical borders out of the geochemical (pedological) record? Yes, the geochemical concentration volumes show a clear overlay with archaeological features. - Are the 3D borders of the archaeological strata, geophysical strata and geochemical strata congruent? Are the concentration centres of the archaeological, geophysical and geochemical anomalies and their statistical outliers congruent? Both questions can be answered positively with slight deviations.	
	Finally, with the combination of data from the three subjects (geophysics, pedology and archaeology) I try to answer the following questions:	
	- Can we recognise the same structures with different methods? Yes.	
	- Can they act as verification for each other? And does this mean we can get reasonable results with just one method? Yes.	
	- Is it possible to extract archaeological stratigraphical borders out of laser scan RGB-values?	
	Not yet; there may be a way to generate volumes out of RGB-values but this has to be verified (see RQ x in this section).	*x*

RQ no. viii)	From a methodological point-of-view, should the analysis of the 3D volume model enable the user to:	**Result**
sec. 1.2.1	- include all quantified information and combine them into thematic multi-scale 3D maps? Yes.	✓
	- analyse information statistically in 3D space? Yes.	
	- get a model as precise as the documentation data? Yes.	
	- extend the analysis into the fourth dimension? Yes.	
	The final model can be analysed in a descriptive, statistical way.	

RQ no. ix)	The archaeological question here is: does the geophysical or geochemical information shows the same course and borders as the archaeological? If this question can be answered positively, there might be a way to predict archaeological remains without a complete excavation by using geophysics and geochemical sampling in 3D.	**Result**
sec. 1.2.2	The first question has already been answered in RQ vii. Hence, this study laid the basis for further hypothesis testing in order to predict archaeological layers out of e.g. bore drills by investigating not only the archaeological content but also by interpolating the geochemical content. Additionally, a geophysical investigation with a high-resolution antenna could support the geochemical results.	✓

RQ no. x)	It is therefore ideal, to use colour values (besides the deposit number) to separate archaeological stratigraphy.	**Result**
sec. 1.2.2	RGB-colour values can be extracted from TLS and from the SfM method. This study demonstrates that these values can be further processed and even modelled and interpolated as 3D volumes. It can therefore be concluded that it might be worth the effort to acquire the colour values in a standardised way. Although it might take more acquisition time, the result could be a third objective model (besides the geophysical and the geochemical) for verifying archaeological stratigraphy.	✓

RQ no. xiii)	Is there also evidence of flooding and earthquakes and can they be dated? Does these dates coincide with others from the site?	Result
sec. 2.1.1	According to a first rough analysis together with the archaeological cooperation partner Prof. Axel Gering:	✓
	The high calcium concentrations of layers 'se101' and 'se104' show traces of two different mortar beds (figs. 4.18 and 4.30). Layer 'se108', the deep central cavern in trench 1, lies in between these layers containing material from the 2nd to 5th century AD. This is a *terminus post quem* for the subsequent layer 'se101' and can hence date the second mortar bed.	
	The inference also answers the question why the cavern was refilled. During excavation, we favoured two possibilities: firstly, it had been part of a repair to build a new paving bed (the calcium would then be evenly distributed all over the surface) or it was a trash pit (less evenly). The archaeological hint came from the marble *spolia* at the lowest point of the cavern ('se108') which belongs to the plaster above layer 'se101'. The *spolia* and its place *in situ* can be interpreted as a hint of a second earthquake repair of the portico plaster putting unusable plaster stones aside and preparing the foundations for a new pavement. The geochemical evidence to support this theory can be seen in e.g. figs. 4.18 and 4.30, layer 'se101' – an evenly distributed surface. The same is true for layer 'se104' which might have been the mortar bed of the first pavement before destruction. The possible earthquake can hence be dated before the 2nd century AD.	
	It can be summarised that the Main Forum of *Ostia Antica* got its last prestigious marble pavement probably in the late 5th or early 6th century AD. This is more than 100 years later than previously thought, indicating that this part of the city centre was in use longer (compare in sec. 2.1.1).	
	Despite its small dimensions, trench 1 provided one of the most interesting archaeological testimonials. These results can be revealed because of the fine selection possibilities due to the previous geophysical investigation, the very detailed 3D cutting units of the archaeological remains and the pedological model. This fully legitimises the study, because a large excavation at this site would not have been feasible according to time and costs (Lieberwirth & Gering, 2016).	

Concerning the **time** needed for the last processing step, it can be levelled at more or less the same time (see fig. 5.7, 5.8). However, I hope this transformation step can be dismissed in the future.

Analysis can be also time relevant because 10 years ago the opening and editing (slicing, etc.) of voxel models took several minutes for each step. This was no longer the case with ParaView© version 5.4.1 and the following hardware: processor: 3.4 GHz Intel Core i5, memory: 32 GB 1600 MHz DDR3, graphics: NVIDIA GeForce GTX 775M 2048 MB.

The analysis options provided in ParaView© and GRASS for 3D volumes focus on a graphical perspective than on spatial statistics. As mentioned above, the latter might be a topic for specialised software like RStudio©. An interface between ParaView© and GRASS could ease this operation.

The graphical perspective is something only a graphical viewer can provide. Hence, using the scientific viewer ParaView© is still the right choice. From this point-of-view many new and highlighting aspects can be revealed through the options of isosurfaces, isovolumes, cuts, slices, selection filters, etc. The simultaneous display of different data can support archaeological theories from an objective perspective.

The topic of objectivity has already been taken up in this chapter (see 5.1.15). In contrast to the archaeological data, the geophysical and geochemical are taken randomly in order to get an objective counterpart. Both showed similar courses that can be interpreted as a verification of the archaeological layers. However, this procedure was applied for the first time in archaeology in full 3D with this study. This means that it needs further verification studies in different situations to prove this result. Further suggestions can be found in the outlook columns of this section.

5.4 Summary: theoretical concepts & practical implementation

This study assumes that a digital 3D GIS model of an excavation site including all acquired data will finally produce a profit to the analysis of excavation documentation.

This assumption is based on experience with GIS systems in archaeology in general. We know that since incorporating this subject into archaeology we have been able to quantitatively analyse large amounts of archaeological data from a spatial perspective by using statistics and mathematics (Conolly & Lake, 2006; Orton, 1980).

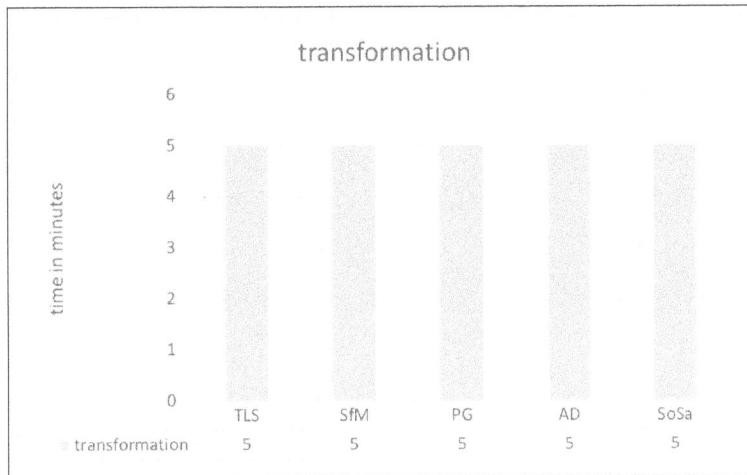

Figure 5.7. Time diagram of WS 'transformation'. Times are average values for one layer (see also process chain 4-time, fig. 5.8). Legend: TLS = terrestrial laser scanner, SfM = *Structure from Motion***, PG = photogrammetry, AD = archaeological documentation, SoSa = soil sampling.**

The use of GIS allows the researcher to incorporate also data from side subjects like geology, topography, climate parameters and anthropogenic preferences. Hence, this environment is a merger of different data into one system. Additionally, GIS is a mapping tool which works in a geographic space. This cartographic option makes it possible to create thematic maps tailored for the purpose of the research question (see e.g. fig. 2.2).

The assumption of extending these 2D GIS options into the third dimension could not be confirmed sufficiently with this study. However, it introduced new 3D analysis options which led to a knowledge discovery of phenomena not considered during the theoretical concept's development. Since the latter not only includes analysis, the complete study needs to be considered for a total judgement.

All parts of this study show that there is not yet an 'all-in-one' system which can execute all steps within one environment. Each software used has its advantages and limitations; for example tables 5.1 and 5.2 show the different depictions and analysis options of all software applications used. Comparisons of hardware properties (fig. 5.1) could show that the new SfM method is very well suited for archaeological purposes. These overviews finally help to decide the appropriate tool for certain research questions.

The **time** diagram (fig. 5.9) summarises the working hours for all WSs in this study. It shows a clear negative bias towards TLS. This result again supports my suggestion to favour SfM as a method, now also from a time perspective.

Although SfM needs most of the time compared to the other entities, mainly in post-processing and modelling, I hope I can convince the reader that it is well worth generating a 3D point cloud of the archaeological layer surfaces in order to calculate layer volumes (and raster surfaces) to obtain a full 3D reconstruction of the destroyed archaeological trench. Additionally, time is taken up incorporation the

geochemical data, which is approximately the same time needed for archaeological documentation (AD) and therefore is best estimated by an experienced excavator.

Geophysical working steps are not integrated in this diagram because they were mainly in the responsibility of the external company. Compared to usual geophysical co-operations, their price did not differ from common geophysical applications.

A surprising result revealed a comparison of the necessary **memory space**. After excavation, the required storage space needed of 18 GB was 6x higher than the final amount for VTK-data with 3.18 GB (fig. 4.32). Even the growing memory demand of voxel resulted in a final, efficient model with high and suitable resolution.

The greatest disappointment of this study was that the viewer cannot yet work with a real coordinate system. This vital aim could not be achieved.

Validation options for the model are rather limited. Hence, information from side subjects were included to verify the archaeological record from a different perspective and to minimize the unknown amount of information E. This incorporation makes it possible to interpret the structures at different levels. However, the modeller should always keep in mind that the model M_n is an incomplete part of the reality. The amount of missing information in the model stays unknown (fig. 1.2). A second suggestion for how 3D models can be verified as long as one has trustworthy data for comparison is described in my teaching movie 'SfM in archaeology' by measuring *Hausdorff distances* (Lieberwirth & Bussilliat, 2017, slide 40-41).

Some might argue that model building is always also a kind of simplification that can be seen as an advantage. Computational simulations of similar complexity like *Agent-based modeling* (ABM) tend to simplify matters for the sake of a clear overview (Romanowska, 2015).

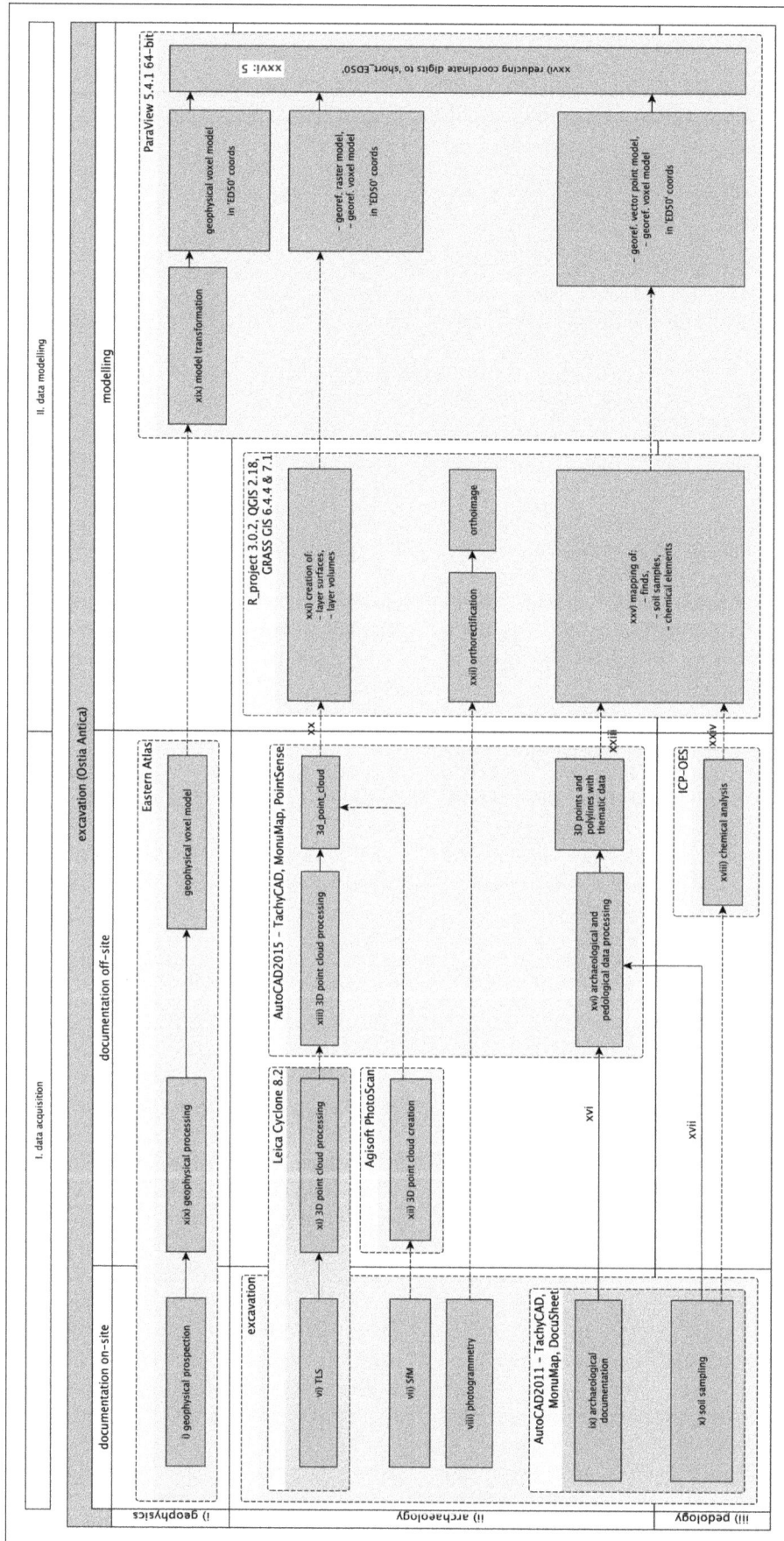

Figure 5.8. Process chain 5-time, copy of fig. 4.5: general workflow of on-site data acquisition, off-site data processing and modelling of Ostia Antica excavation data with average processing time for one layer in minutes. With reference to the tables 2.2, 2.3, 2.6, 2.7, 2.8, 3.1, 3.2 and 3.3.

Table 5.1. Comparison of software properties – depiction options

depiction properties of 3D volumes

	CAD	GRASS	ParaView©
model depiction	- vector - raster (2.5D) - faces (2D) - wireframe	- vector - raster (2.5D) - faces (2D) - wireframe	- vector - raster (2.5D) - faces (2D) - wireframe - volume
ortho photo	- 2D - texture mapping on point cloud* - real color*	- 2D - real color	- 2D - texture mapping on geometry** - false color
coordinate system	- 3D - real	- 2D - real	- 3D - local

*CAD plug-in PointSense®, **geometry: only sphere, cone, cylinder

Table 5.2. Comparison of software properties – 3D analysis options

analysis properties of 3D volumes

	CAD	GRASS	ParaView©
queries	x	x	x
selections	x	x	✓
filters	x	x	✓
spatial analysis	x	x	x
cutting/slicing	✓	x	✓
measuring	✓	x	✓

Since archaeological sites are actually destroyed during the excavation process, this study shows that they can be documented with the most precise tools available for later analysis. Documentation differs slightly from each other because of the research question and focus. This study found a way to present a more objective approach in a digital 3D GIS environment by filling all the 'empty spaces' of an archaeological reconstruction.

It needs to be said, that all new methods described in my study and 'Yes-answers' in this section need to be verified by further studies. Nevertheless, a start has been made. Thus, the introduction question, 'Can we quantify archaeological stratigraphy and so enrich archaeology?', can be answered finally: yes – we can!

Does the use of GIS in archaeology change the perception of archaeological space? This monograph started by describing model-building as needing a concept or theory behind it. These virtual models provide a test-bed for exploratory simulations (Barceló, 2012). On the other hand, the possibility of creating virtual simulations provides a path to more flexible approaches, either deductive or inductive, toward concepts and theories, and their transformation into the digital, quantified world. The results of the case studies should no longer be treated as prediction, but rather as information. This approach allows us to build a plurality of models for experimenting and comparison and opens the way to simulations with hybrid systems (Heppenstall et al., 2012, p.740). GIS in archaeology tries to solve archaeological problems by testing conceptual models. Without theory, the method would be neutral,

which corresponds to the definition of a tool (Wright et al. 1997, Conolly and Lake 2006, p.3). Modelling archaeological data in GIS follows statistical principles of theoretical hypothesis creation -> practical sampling, modelling and testing -> and final theoretical interpretation. Once a research question has been defined (a hypothesis), the research area is described with the means for modelling, to prepare the model for the evaluation techniques planned.

The sampling process ideally follows as a second step, either with a trip out into the field with the purpose already in mind, or with a selection of archived data. Then a suitable method for analysis is selected so that the data can be modelled and tested. Background knowledge about the material is needed for this task, as is an understanding of the system and methods applied to estimate the differences between the model and reality. Finally, decisions must be made about the model's frame, resolution, and scale, as well as about the space of the study area.

As in Romanowska's model development sequence, the stages of the sequence can vary according to the research circumstances (Romanowska, 2015, p.10 fig.2). The sequence itself can also be seen as a circle (Orton, 1980, p.20 fig.1.3). Checking the interpretation against the hypothesis might either be the last step of the analysis or lead to the rejection of the hypothesis, in which case a new circle has to start.

GIS in itself provides the functions and the virtual space to test theories and hypotheses and does not follow a general theory. It is the researcher's decision what to model and

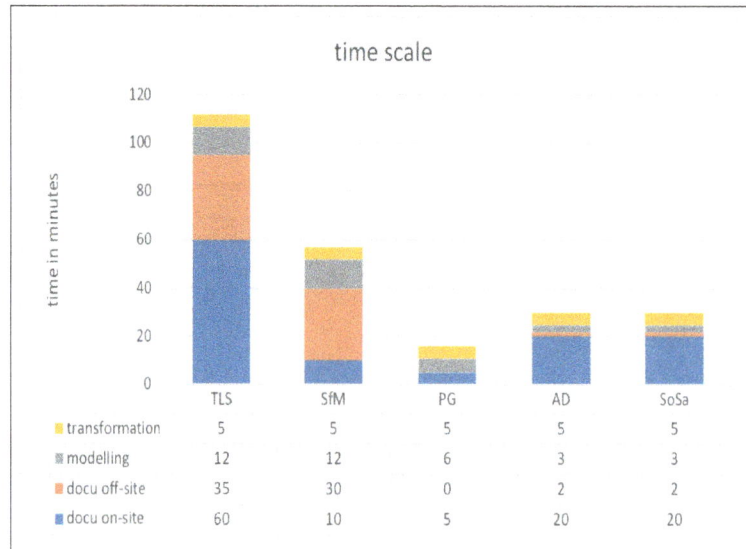

Figure 5.9. Time diagram of all WS. Times are average values for one layer. Legend: TLS = terrestrial laser scanner, SfM = *Structure from Motion*, PG = photogrammetry, AD = archaeological documentation, SoSa = soil sampling.

how. Models do not have to show the truth. They should be treated as the basis for calculating the probability of events in space. For these calculations, certain kinds of data are required (Premo et al., 2005). As stated above, GIS has changed the mode of thinking in archaeology and therefore the mode of thinking on space (Hodder & Orton, 1979). It therefore cannot be regarded as atheoretical (Wheatley, 1993). GIS provides an environment for dealing with the special nature of archaeological information which can be either precise or fuzzy. It is an environment suitable for both the localization of facts and the depiction of ideas. Explorative data analysis and spatial data analysis allow these ideas to be tested against the facts in the predefined space of archaeological periods. Since GIS is a container for data from different disciplines in this study, the results can be either maps or numeric information and should be interpreted by experts in the relevant subject. Like Snow (1855), an expert in medicine who chose the right combination of parameters in space to detect geospatial patterns, archaeological background knowledge is vital for analysing data, whether in a GIS or elsewhere. The challenge in archaeology is to transfer incomplete, blurred and subjectively perceived information into a quantified model. For evaluating specific archaeological issues, a 2D or a 3D GIS remains an ideal medium for managing all digital, spatial information in one system. The system not only facilitates precise and high-quality display (in accordance with the quality of raw data), but also allows the option of statistical analysis. This makes a GIS suited to any project data containing a location (Lock, 2003, p.182). Even in a highly efficient system, results will never meet reality (Ervin & Hasbrouck, 2001, p.4). Archaeological data are always incomplete. A viable and transparent procedure is available to help fill those gaps with results from probability statistics. The lack of information can be balanced with assumptions and probability valucs. For more facts, we should not dismiss working in the field.

The study shows that concepts and scales are universally applicable in 2D GIS and in 3D environments.

Work with 3D models is becoming increasingly popular in other subjects as well: surveying and cartography tend to use virtual 3D globes that are accessible even to amateurs (NASA Ames Research Center, 2016), (Google, 2021), (Cesium GS, Inc., 2016). The subject of cartography may already have reached a turning point where projections (to transform the surface of a 3D object into the surface of a 2D plane) are no longer necessary. Consequently, 2D plane maps might be dismissed in a future disciplinary step. This development would open the way towards a fully established 3D coordinate system. Time could be incorporated as a fourth dimension. Visual impressions are an interpretation of background information that includes all other senses as well: auditory, haptic, olfactory, and gustatory. They all belong to the perceptual system (Gibson 1966, Llobera 1996, p.619). These senses are measurable and can therefore be assigned with location and since these perceptions are spread across a 3D space, a truly 3D analysis environment is required (Lock, 2003, p.182).

The initial developments have now been done. There is a strong need for 3D analysis functionalities. Users are now able to measure in 3D space, perform queries, and execute 3D spatial analyses like pattern analysis and trend or volume calculations.

The real world exists in three dimensions. This is why measurements are generally taken in 3D.

At this point, archaeology is departing from the principles of cartography, which refer only to position (x and y coordinates). GIS provides precisely the 3D environment we need.

References

Agisoft. (2014). *Agisoft PhotoScan, vers. 1.1.0.* Petersburg: Agisoft LLC. Retrieved from http://www.agisoft.com/

Agisoft. (2018). Agisoft PhotoScan User Manual – Professional Edition, vers. 1.1.0 [Computer software manual]. Petersburg: Agisoft LLC. Retrieved from http://www.agisoft.com/

Akahoshi, K., Ishimaru, N., Kurokawa, C., Tanaka, Y., Oishi, T., Kutzner, T., & Kolbe, T. H. (2020). i-Urban Revitalization: Conceptual Modeling, Implementation, and Visualization Towards Sustainable Urban Planning Using CityGML. In N. Paparoditis et al. (Eds.), *Proceedings of the XXIV ISPRS Congress* (Vol. V-4-2020, p. 179–186). Göttingen: Copernicus GmbH.

ArcGIS. (2018). *ArcGIS, vers. 10.6.* Redlands: ESRI, Inc. Retrieved from https://www.esri.com

ArcGIS 3D Analyst. (2018). *ArcGIS 3D Analyst.* Redlands: ESRI, Inc. Retrieved from https://www.esri.com/en-us/arcgis/products/arcgis-3d-analyst

ARCHES. (2013). *The Standard and Guide to Best Practice in Archaeological Archiving in Europe. EAC Guidelines 1.* Namur: ARCHES. Archaeological Resources in Cultural Heritage – a European Standard.

AUTODESK. (2019). *AutoCAD Civil 3d, vers. 23.0.* San Rafael: AUTODESK, Inc. Retrieved from https://www.autodesk.de/products/civil-3d

Ayachit, U. (2018). The ParaView Guide (Full Color Version): A Parallel Visualization Application (5.5 ed.) [Computer software manual]. Los Alamos: Kitware, Inc.

Barceló, J. A. (2012). Computer simulation in archaeology. Art, science or nightmare? *Virtual Archaeology Review (VAR), 3*(5), 8–12.

Barceló, J. A., & Pallarés, M. (1998). Beyond GIS: The archaeology of social spaces. *Archeologia e Calcolatori*(9), 47–80.

Baxter, M. (2003). *Statistics in Archaeology.* London – New York: Oxford University Press.

Bevan, A., & Lake, M. (Eds.). (2013). *Computational approaches to archaeological spaces.* Walnut Creek, California: Routledge.

Bezzi, A., Bezzi, L., Francisci, D., & Gietl, R. (2006). L' utilizzo di voxel in campo archeologico. In M. Brovelli (Ed.), *7th Italian GRASS user meeting proceedings.* Como: Politecnico di Milano – Polo Territoriale di Como.

Biel, J., & Klonk, D. (Eds.). (1994). *Handbuch der Grabungstechnik.* Stuttgart: Verband der Landesarchäologen in der Bundesrepublik Deutschland e.V. Retrieved from https://landesarchaeologen.de/kommissionen/grabungstechnikerhandbuch

Blankholm, H. (1991). *Intrasite Spatial Analysis in Theory and Practice.* Aarhus: Aarhus University Press.

Boardman, C., & Bryan, P. (2018). *3d Laser Scanning for Heritage. Advice and guidance on the use of laser scanning in archaeology and architecture* (3rd ed.). Swindon: Historic England. Retrieved from https://historicengland.org.uk/images-books/publications/3d-laser-scanning-heritage/heag155-3d-laser-scanning/

Brandt, R., Groenewoudt, B., & Kvamme, K. (1992). An experiment in archaeological site location: Modeling in the Netherlands using GIS techniques. *World Archaeology, 24*(2), 268–282.

Breitenecker, F., Bicher, M., & Wurzer, G. (2015). Agent-Based Simulation in Archaeology: A Characterization. In G. Wurzer, K. Kowarik, & H. Reschreiter (Eds.), *Agent-based Modeling and Simulation in Archaeology* (p. 53–76). Cham: Springer International Publishing.

Brughmans, T., Keay, S., & Earl, G. (2014). Introducing exponential random graph models for visibility networks. *Journal of Archaeological Science, 49,* 442–454.

Calza, G., Becatti, G., & Gismondi, I. (1953). *Scavi di Ostia. Topografia generale* (Vol. 1). Roma: Istituto Poligrafico e Zecca dello Stato/Libreria dello Stato.

Cesium GS, Inc. (2016). *Cesium – The Platform for 3D Geospatial.* Retrieved from https://cesiumjs.org

CMake. (2018). *CMake, vers. 3.12.0.* New York: Kitware, Inc. Retrieved from https://cmake.org/

Conolly, J., & Lake, M. (2006). *Geographical Information Systems in Archaeology. Cambridge Manuals in Archaeology.* Cambridge: Cambridge University Press.

DeLaine, J. (2008). Between Concept and Reality: Case Studies in the Development of Roman Cities in the Mediterranean. In J. Macus & J. Sabloff (Eds.), *The Ancient City. New Perspectives on Urbanism in the Old and New World. Conference publication* (p. 97–118). Santa Fe, N.M.: School for Advanced Research Press.

Deng, Y., & Revesz, P. (2001). Spatial and Topological Data Models. In M. Rossi & K. Siau (Eds.), *Information modeling in the new millennium* (p. 345–359). Hershey, PA: IGI Global.

91

Descartes, R. (1637). *Discours de la méthode pour bien conduire sa raison et chercher la verité dans les sciences, La Géométrie.* Leiden: A Leyde de l'imprimerie de Jan Maire.

Doneus, M., & Neubauer, W. (2006). 3D Laser Scanners on Archaeological Excavations. In E. Baltsavias, M. Baltsavias, A. Grün, L. van Gool, & M. Pateraki (Eds.), *Recording, Modeling and Visualization of Cultural Heritage* (p. 193–203). London: Taylor & Francis.

Eckelmann, W., et al. (Eds.). (2005). *Bodenkundliche Kartieranleitung. KA5.* Stuttgart: Schweizerbart Science Publishers.

Einstein, A. (1917). *Über die spezielle und die allgemeine Relativitätstheorie.* Braunschweig: Vieweg.

Ervin, S., & Hasbrouck, H. (2001). *Landscape Modeling: Digital Techniques for Landscape Visualization.* New York – London: McGraw Hill Professional.

Fedorov, A., Beichel, R., Kalpathy-Cramer, J., Finet, J., Fillion-Robin, J.-C., Pujol, S., ... Kikinis, R. (2012). *3D Slicer as an Image Computing Platform for the Quantitative Imaging Network, vers. 4.6.* Nov:30(9). PMID: 22770690. PMCID: PMC3466397: Magn Reson Imaging. Retrieved from https://www.slicer.org/

Fera, M., Neubauer, W., & Doneus, M. (2013). 3d documentation and visualisation of stratigraphic archaeological excavations., *Virtual Archaeology (non destructive methods of prospection, modeling, reconstruction), Proceedings of the first international conference held at the State Hermitage Museum 4–6 June 2012,* 140–142.

Fletcher, M., & Lock, G. (2005). *Digging Numbers: Elementary Statistics for Archaeologists.* Oxford: Oxford University School of Archaeology.

Foucault, M. (1966). *Les mots et les choses.* Paris: Éditions Gallimard.

Gaffney, V., Gaffney, C., Garwood, P., Neubauer, W., Chapman, H., Löcker, K., & Baldwin, E. (2013). Stonehenge Hidden Landscape Project: Geophysical investigation and landscape mapping of Stonehenge World Heritage Site. In W. Neubauer, I. Trinks, R. Salisbury, & C. Einwögerer (Eds.), *Archaeological Prospection: Proceedings of the 10th International Conference – Vienna May 29th – June 2nd 2013* (p. 19–23). Vienna: Austrian Academy of Sciences Press.

Galilei, G. (1632). *Dialogo sopra i due massimi sistemi del mondo.* Florenz: Carlo Caraffa Pacecco.

Gatrell, A. C. (1983). *Distance and Space: A Geographical Perspective.* Oxford – New York: Oxford University Press.

Gering, A. (2011). Krise, Kontinuität, Auflassung und Aufschwung in Ostia seit der Mitte des 3. Jahrhunderts. In R. Schatzmann & S. Martin-Kilcher (Eds.), *Das römische Reich im Umbruch. Auswirkungen auf die Städte in der zweiten Hälfte des 3. Jahrhunderts.*

Internationales Kolloquium Bern/Augst (Schweiz) 3.-5. Dezember 2009 (Vol. 20, p. 301–319). Montagnac: Édition Monique Mergoil.

Gering, A. (2015). *OSTIA FORUM PROJEKT 2010-2022. Forum plans.* Retrieved from http://ostiaforumproject.com/forum-plans/

Gibson, J. (1966). *The senses considered as perceptual systems.* Houghton Mifflin.

Google. (2021). *Google Earth.* Google Ireland Limited Inc. Retrieved from https://www.google.de/earth/

GRASS. (2018a). *GRASS GIS, vers. 7.4.0.* Open Source Geospatial Foundation, GRASS Development Team. Retrieved from http://grass.osgeo.org

GRASS. (2018b). Voxel [Computer software manual]. Beaverton: Open Source Geospatial Foundation, GRASS Development Team. Retrieved from https://grasswiki.osgeo.org/wiki/Voxel

Green, D. (2003). *Stratigraphic Visualisation for Archaeological Investigation* (Doctoral dissertation, Brunel University London of Engineering and Design). Retrieved from http://bura.brunel.ac.uk/handle/2438/2168

gvSIG. (2018). *gvSIG Desktop.* gvSIG Association. Retrieved from http://www.gvsig.org/

Harley, J., & Woodward, D. (Eds.). (1987). *Cartography in prehistoric, ancient, and medieval Europe and the Mediterranean.* Chicago: University of Chicago Press.

Harris, E. (1989). *Principles of archaeological stratigraphy.* London: Academic Press, Inc.

Heinzelmann, M. (2001). Les nécropoles d'Ostie: topographie, développment, architecture, structure sociale. In J.-P. Descoeudres (Ed.), *Ostia: port et porte de la Rome antique.* Genève: Ville de Genève, Département des Affaires Culturelles.

Heinzelmann, M. (2002). Bauboom und urbanistitische Defizite – zur städtebaulichen Entwicklung Ostias im 2. Jh. In C. Bruun & A. Galina-Zevi (Eds.), *Ostia e Portus: Nelle loro Relazioni con Roma,* (p. 103–121). Rome: Institutum Romanum Finlandiae.

Heppenstall, A. J., Crooks, A. T., See, L. M., & Batty, M. (2012). Reflections and Conclusions: Geographical Models to Address Grand Challenges. In A. J. Heppenstall, A. T. Crooks, L. M. See, & M. Batty (Eds.), *Agent-Based Models of Geographical Systems* (p. 739–747). Dordrecht: Springer.

Herzog, I., & Yépez, A. (2015). Least-Cost Kernel Density Estimation and Interpolation-Based Density Analysis Applied to Survey Data. Extended abstract CAA 2010. In E. Melero, P. Cano, & J. Revelles (Eds.), *Across Space and Time. Papers from the 41st Annual Conference of Computer Applications and Quantitative Methods in Archaeology (CAA), Perth, 25–28 March 2013* (p. 447–450). Amsterdam: Amsterdam University Press.

Hietala, H., & Larson, P. (1984). *Intrasite Spatial Analysis in Archaeology*. Cambridge: Cambridge University Press.

Hixon, S., Lipo, C., Hunt, T., & Lee, C. (2018). Using Structure from Motion Mapping to Record and Analyze Details of the Colossal Hats (Pukao) of Monumental Statues on Rapa Nui (Easter Island). *Advances in Archaeological Practice*, 6(1), 42–57.

Hodder, I. (1986). *Reading the past*. London – New York: Cambridge University Press.

Hodder, I., & Orton, C. (1979). *Spatial Analysis in Archaeology. In: New Studies in Archaeology, Volume 1*. Cambridge: Cambridge University Press.

IANUS. (2017). *IT-Empfehlungen für den nachhaltigen Umgang mit digitalen Daten in den Altertumswissenschaften*. Berlin: Deutsches Archäologisches Institut. Retrieved from https://www.ianus-fdz.de/it-empfehlungen/

ICA. (1992). Cartography and Geographical Information Systems. Report of the ICA Executive Committee. *ICA News*, 20(3), 187–195.

ISO. (2011). *ISO/IEC/IEEE Information technology | Microprocessor Systems | Floating-Point arithmetic* (No. 60559). Vernier: International Organization for Standardization. Retrieved from https://www.iso.org/standard/57469.html

ISTI-CNR. (2018). *MeshLab, vers. 1.3.3*. Pisa: Visual Computing Lab ISTI-CNR. Retrieved from http://meshlab.sourceforge.net/

Kaden, R., et al. (Eds.). (2020). *Leitfaden Geodäsie und BIM*. Bühl: DVW – Gesellschaft für Geodäsie, Geoinformation und Landmanagement e. V. and Runder Tisch GIS e.V.

Katsianis, M., Tsipidis, S., Kotsakis, K., & Kousoulakou, A. (2008). A 3d digital workflow for archaeological intra-site research using GIS. *Journal of Archaeological Science, March 2008*, 35(3), 655–667.

Kinne, A. (2009). *Tabellen und Tafeln zur Grabungstechnik – ein Hilfsmittel für die archäologische Geländearbeit* (5th ed.). Dresden: Selbstverlag.

Konsa, M. (2013). Intrasite spatial analysis of the cemeteries with dispersed cremation burials. In T. Sly et al. (Eds.), *Archaeology in the Digital Era* (Vol. II). Amsterdam: Amsterdam University Press.

Kowarik, K., Wurzer, G., & Reschreiter, H. (Eds.). (2015). *Agent-based Modeling and Simulation. Advances in Geographic Information Science*. Cham: Springer International Publishing.

Landeschi, G., Dell'Unto, N., Ferdani, D., Leander Touati, A.-M., & Lindgren, S. (2015). Enhanced 3d-GIS : Documenting Insula V 1 in Pompeii. In F. Giligny, F. Djindjian, L. Costa, M. P., & S. Robert (Eds.), *CAA2014 21st Century Archaeology. Concepts, Methods and Tools. Proceedings of the 42nd Annual Conference on Compter Applications and Quantitative Methods in Archaeology* (p. 349–360). Oxford: Archaeopress Publishing Ltd.

Laurini, R., & Thompson, D. (1992). *Fundamentals of Spatial Information Systems*. SanDiego: Academic Press, Harcourt Brace & Company.

Lauro, M. (1995). Lineamenti di storia degli scavi. In V. Mannucci (Ed.), *Atlante di Ostia Antica. Cartografia. Atlanti* (p. 41–52). Venice: Marsilio Editori. Soprintendenza archeologica di Ostia.

LBI. (2011). *Harris Matrix Composer, vers. 1.0*. Vienna: Ludwig Boltzmann Institute (LBI) for Archaeological Prospection & Virtual Archaeology, Ludwig Boltzmann Gesellschaft GesmbH. Retrieved from http://harrismatrixcomposer.com/

Leica. (2009). *Leica ScanStation 2 – Product Specifications*. Leica Geosystems AG, Heerbrugg. Retrieved from http://w3.leica-geosystems.com/downloads123/hds/hds/ScanStation/brochures-datasheet/Leica_ScanStation%202_datasheet_en.pdf

Leica. (2011). *Leica Geosystems Cyclone, vers. 8.2*. Heerbrugg. Retrieved from https://leica-geosystems.com/products/laser-scanners/software/leica-cyclone

Lieberwirth, U. (2008a). 3d GIS voxel-based model building in archaeology. In A. Posluschny, K. Lambers, & I. Herzog (Eds.), *CAA 2007 – Layers of Perception 35th Conference on Computer Applications and Quantitative Methods in Archaeology, Berlin, Germany, April 2–6, 2007* (pp. 8 ff. + CD-ROM). Dr. Rudolf Habelt GmbH.

Lieberwirth, U. (2008b). Voxel-based 3d GIS: modelling and analysis of archaeological stratigraphy. In B. Frischer & A. Dakouri-Hild (Eds.), *Beyond Illustration: 2d and 3d Digital Technologies as Tools for Discovery in Archaeology* (Vol. 1805, p. 78–86). Oxford: British Archaeological Reports Ltd.

Lieberwirth, U., & Bussilliat, J. (2017). *Structure from Motion in der Archäologie - ein interaktiver Lehrfilm*. TIP AV-PORTAL: Freie Universität Berlin. doi: https://doi.org/10.5446/35260

Lieberwirth, U., Fritsch, B., Metz, M., Neteler, M., & Kühnle, K. (2015). Applying Low Budget Equipment and Open Source Software for High Resolution Documentation of Archaeological Stratigraphy and Features. In A. Traviglia (Ed.), *Across Space and Time* (p. 104–119). Amsterdam: Amsterdam University Press.

Lieberwirth, U., & Gering, A. (2016). *3D GIS in Archaeology – A micro-scale Analysis*. Berlin: DIGITAL CLASSICIST BERLIN. Retrieved from http://de.digitalclassicist.org/berlin/2016/11/01/Lieberwirth#video

Lieberwirth, U., & Herzog, I. (Eds.). (2016). *3D Anwendungen in der Archäologie. Computeranwendungen und Quantitative Methoden in der Archäologie – Workshop der AG CAA 2013* (Vol. 34). Berlin: Edition Topoi.

Llobera, M. (1996). Exploring the topography of mind: GIS, social space and archaeology. *Antiquity*, *70*(269), 612–622. doi: https://doi.org/10.1017/S0003598X00083745

Lloyd, C., & Atkinson, P. (2004). Archaeology and geostatistics. *Journal of Archaeological Science*, *31*(2), 151–165.

Lock, G. (2003). *Using Computers in Archaeology: Towards Virtual Pasts*. London – New York: Routledge.

Mandelbrot, B. B. (1982). *The Fractal Geometry of Nature*. San Francisco: W.H. Freeman.

Mar, R. (1991). La Formazione dello Spazio Urbano nella Città di Ostia. *Mitteilungen Deutsches Archäologisches Institut Römische Abteilung*, *98*, 81–109.

Martin, A. (1996). Un saggio sulle mura del Castrum di Ostia (Reg. I, Ins. x, 3). In A. Gallina-Zevi & A. Claridge (Eds.), *'Roman Ostia' Revisited: Archaeological and Historical Papers in Memory of Russell Meiggs* (p. 19–38). London & Ostia: British School at Rome and the Sorpintendenza Archeologica di Ostia.

Mastrorillo, L., Mazza, R., Tuccimei, P., Rosa, C., & Matteucci, R. (2016). Groundwater monitoring in the archaeological site of Ostia Antica (Rome, Italy): first results. *Acque Sotteerranee – Italian Journal of Groundwater*, *5*(1). doi: https://doi.org/10.7343/as-2016-192

Meiggs, R. (1973). *Roman Ostia*. Oxford: Clarendon Press.

Melichar, P., & Neubauer, W. (Eds.). (2010). *Mitteilungen Der Prähistorischen Kommission. mittelneolithische Kreisgrabenanlagen in Niederösterreich: Geophysikalisch-archäologische Prospektion – ein interdisziplinäres Forschungsprojekt* (Vol. 71). Vienna: Verlag der Österreichischen Akademie der Wissenschaften.

Merlo, S. (2004). The 'contemporary mind'. 3D GIS as a challenge in excavation practice. In K. Ausserer, W. Börner, M. Goriany, & L. Karlhuber-Vöckl (Eds.), *Enter the Past. The E-way into the four Dimensions of Cultural Heritage. CAA 2003, Computer Applications and Quantitative Methods in Archaeology* (p. 276–279). Oxford: British Archaeological Reports Ltd.

Merlo, S. (2016). *Making Visible: Three-dimensional GIS in Archaeological Excavation* (No. 2801). Oxford: British Archaeological Reports Ltd.

Meynen, E. (1984). *Multilingual Dictionary of Technical Terms in Cartography*. Stuttgart: French & European Publications.

Morton, A. (2004). *Archaeological site formation: understanding lake margin contexts*. Oxford: BAR Publishing International Series 1211.

Munsell, A. H. (1975). *Munsell soil color charts*. Baltimore, Md.: Munsell Color Corporation.

NASA Ames Research Center. (2016). *NASA WorldWind*. NASA Ames Research Center. Retrieved from https://worldwind.arc.nasa.gov

Newton, I. (1687). *Philosophiae Naturalis Principia Mathematica*. London: Edmund Halley.

Nibby, A. (1819). *Viaggio antiquario ne' contorni di Roma*. Rome: Presso Vincenzo Poggioli Stampatore Camerale.

Nigro, J., Limp, F., Kvamme, K., de Ruiter, D., & Berger, L. (2002). The Creation and Potential Applications of a 3-Dimensional GIS for the Early Hominin Site of Swartkrans, South Africa. In G. Burenhult & J. Arvidsson (Eds.), *Archaeological Informatics: Pushing The Envelope* (p. 113–124). Oxford: Archaeopress Publishing Ltd.

Orton, C. (1980). *Mathematics in archaeology*. Cambridge – New York: Cambridge University Press.

Orton, C. (2000). *Sampling in archaeology*. Cambridge – New York: Cambridge University Press.

Paliou, E. (2013). Reconsidering the concept of visualscapes: Recent advances in three-dimensional visibility analysis. In A. Bevan & M. Lake (Eds.), *Computational Approaches to Archaeological Spaces* (p. 243–264). Walnut Creek: Left Cost Press.

ParaView. (2016). *ParaView, vers. 5.2*. Albuquerque: National Technology & Engineering Solutions of Sandia, LLC (NTESS), Kitware, Inc. Sandia National Laboratories. Retrieved from https://www.paraview.org/

Parker, D. C., Manson, S., Jansen, M., Hoffmann, M., & Deadman, P. (2003). Multi-Agent Systems for the Simulation of Land-Use and Land-Cover Change: A Review. *Annals of the Association of American Geographers*, *93*(2), 314–337.

Petrie, W. M. F. (1899). Sequences in prehistoric remains. *The Journal of the Anthropological Institute of Great Britain and Ireland*, *29*(3), 295–301.

Peuquet, D. (1984). A conceptual framework and comparison of spatial data models. *Cartographica: The International Journal for Geographic Information and Geovisualization*, *21*(4), 66–113.

Picolli, C. (2018). *Visualizing cityscapes of Classical antiquity: from early modern reconstruction drawings to digital 3D models*. Oxford: Archaeopress Publishing Ltd.

Pointscene. (2018). *Pointscene*. Helsinki: 3point Ltd. Retrieved from https://pointscene.com

PointSense. (2015). *PointSense Pro, vers. 16.0*. Korntal-Münchingen: FARO EUROPE GmbH and Co. KG. Retrieved from https://knowledge.faro.com/Software/Legacy-Software/Legacy-PointSense_and_CAD_Plugins/PointSense/PointSense_Heritage

Premo, L., Murphy, J., Scholnik, J., Gabler, B., & Beaver, J. (2005). Making a Case for Agent-based Modeling, *28*(3), 11–13.

QGIS. (2018). *QGIS, vers. 3.2.* Open Source Geospatial Foundation. Retrieved from http://qgis.osgeo.org

Reindel, M., Zipf, A., von Schwerin, J., Auer, M., Loos, L., Fecher, F., & et al. (2016). *Abschlussbericht des BMBF E-Humanities Verbundprojektes MayaArch3d: Ein webbasiertes 3d-GIS zur Analyse der Archäologie von Copan, Honduras.* Bonn: Deutsches Zentrum für Luft- und Raumfahrt e.V. (DLR). Retrieved from https://mayaarch3d.org/wp-content/uploads/2016/08/MayaArch3D_Abschlussbericht_reduced.pdf

Reinhard, J. (2016). Structure-from-Motion-Photogrammetrie mit Agisoft PhotoScan. Erste Erfahrungen aus der Grabungspraxis. In U. Lieberwirth & I. Herzog (Eds.), *3d-Anwendungen in der Archäologie. Computeranwendungen und Quantitative Methoden in der Archäologie – Workshop der AG CAA und des Exzellenzclusters Topoi 2013* (p. 17–44). Berlin: Edition Topoi.

Ripley, B. (1981). *Spatial Statistics.* New York: John Wiley & Sons.

Ripley, B. (1988). *Statistical Inference for Spatial Point Patterns.* Cambridge: Cambridge University Press.

Romanowska, I. (2015). So You Think You Can Model? A Guide to Building and Evaluating Archaeological Simulation Models of Dispersals. *Human Biology. The Official Publication of the american Association of Anthropological Genetics, 87*(3).

RStudio. (2018). *RStudio, vers. 1.1.414.* Boston, MA: RStudio, PBC. Retrieved from https://www.rstudio.com/

RStudio Team. (2020). RStudio: Integrated Development Environment for R [Computer software manual]. Boston, MA. Retrieved from http://www.rstudio.com/

Salisbury, R. (2013). Integreating archaeo-geochemical methods for intra-site archaeological prospection. In W. Neubauer, I. Trinks, R. Salisbury, & C. Einwögerer (Eds.), *Archaeological Prospection: Proceedings of the 10th International Conference on Archaeological Prospection.* Vienna: Austrian Academy of Sciences.

Sandmeier, K.-J. (2017). *Reflexw, vers. 7.0.* Karlsruhe: Sandmeier geophysical research. Retrieved from https://www.sandmeier-geo.de/reflexw.html

Sarris, A., Kalayci, T., Moffat, I., & Manataki, M. (2018). An Introduction to Geophysical and Geochemical Methods in Digital Geoarchaeology. In C. Siart, M. Forbriger, & O. Bubenzer (Eds.), *Digital Geoarchaeology* (p. 215–236). Cham: Springer International Publishing.

Schwarz, D. (2014). BundlerTools [Computer software manual]. San Fransisco: GitHub, Inc. Retrieved from https://github.com/qwesda/BundlerTools

Scianna, A., & Villa, B. (2011). GIS Applications in archaeology. *Archeologia e Calcolatori, 22*, 337–363.

Segal, M., & Akeley, K. (2010). The OpenGL Graphics System: A Specification (Version 4.0 (Core Profile) - March 11, 2010) [Computer software manual]. The Khronos Group, Inc. Retrieved from https://www.khronos.org/registry/OpenGL/specs/gl/glspec40.core.pdf

Snow, J. (1855). *On the mode of communication of cholera* (2nd ed.). London: John Churchill.

Soler, F., Melero, F., & Luzón, M. (2017). A complete 3d information system for cultural heritage documentation. *Journal of Cultural Heritage, 23*, 49–57.

Soprintendenza. (1984). *Norme per la Redzione della Scheda del Saggio Stratigrafico.* Rome: Soprintendenza Archeologica di Roma, Ministero per i Beni Culturali e Ambientali Istituto Centrale per il Catalogo e la Doumentatzione.

Stachowiak, H. (1973). *Allgemeine Modelltheorie.* Wien – NewYork: Springer Verlag.

Stanilov, K. (2012). Space in Agent-Based Models. In A. J. Heppenstall, A. T. Crooks, L. M. See, & M. Batty (Eds.), *Agent-Based Models of Geographical Systems* (p. 253-270). Dordrecht – Heidelberg – London – New York: Springer.

Stöger, J. (2011). Rethinking Ostia : A Spatial Enquiry into the Urban Society of Rome's Imperial Port-Town. In C. Bakels & H. Kamermans (Eds.), *Archaeological Studies Leiden University* (Vol. 24). Amsterdam: Leiden University Press.

TachyCAD. (2017). TachyCAD Archaeology, vers. 18.5 [Computer software manual]. Korntal-Münchingen: FARO EUROPE GmbH and Co. KG. Retrieved from https://faro.app.box.com/s/s6n96u6ynlhnbw4xalq852n2i4raqg7o/file/249782262778

Taylor, J., Issavi, J., Berggren, A., Lukas, D., Mazzucato, C., Tung, B., & Dell'Unto, N. (2018). 'The Rise of the Machine': the impact of digital tablet recording in the field at Çatalhöyük. *Internet Archaeology*(47).

Traoré, M., Hurter, C., & Telea, A. (2018). Interactive obstruction-free lensing for volumetric data visualization. *IEEE Transactions on Visualization and Computer Graphics, 25, Jan. 2019*, 1029–1039. doi: https://doi.org/10.1109/TVCG.2018.2864690

Traxler, C., & Neubauer, W. (2008). The Harris Matrix Composer - A New Tool to Manage Archaeological Stratigraphy. In M. Ioannides, A. Addison, A. Georgopoulos, & L. Kalisperis (Eds.), *VSMM 2008: Digital Heritage – Proceedings of the 14th International Conference on Virtual Systems and Multimedia, 20–25 October 2008, Limassol, Cyprus* (p. 13–20). Budapest: ARCHAEOLINGUA.

Verhagen, P. (2017). Spatial Analysis in Archaeology: Moving into New Territories. In C. Siart, M. Forbriger, & O. Bubenzer (Eds.), *Digital Geoarchaeology: New Techniques for Interdisciplinary Human-Environmental Research.* Cham: Springer International Publishing.

Wallrodt, J. (2016). Why Paperless: Technology and Changes in Archaeological Practice, 1996—2016. In E. Averett, J. Gordon, & D. Counts (Eds.), *Mobilizing the Past for a Digital Future: The Potential of Digital Archaeology* (p. 33–50). Grand Forks, ND: The Digital Press at the University of North Dakota.

Weisberg, M. (2013). *Simulation and Similarity: Using Models to Understand the World.* Oxford: Oxford University Press.

Wheatley, D. (1993). Going over Old Ground: GIS, Archaeological Theory and the Act of Perception. In J. Andresen, T. Madsen, & I. Scollar (Eds.), *Computing the Past: Computer Applications and Quantitative Methods in Archaeology. CAA92* (p. 133–138). Aarhus: Aarhus University Press.

Wheatley, D. (2004). Making space for an archaeology of place. *Internet Archaeology, 15*.

Wright, D. J., Goodchild, M. F., & Proctor, J. D. (1997). Demystifying the Persistent Ambiguity of GIS as 'Tool' versus 'Science'. *Annals of the Association of American Geographers, 87*(2), 346–362.

Wu, C. (2014). VisualSFM : A Visual Structure from Motion System [Computer software manual]. Retrieved from http://ccwu.me/vsfm/

Abbreviations & Glossary

3D cartography is the extension of 2D cartography in the third dimension within a real national or international coordinate system, see sec. 1.1. 2, 5, 11

3D models in archaeology are mainly used for visualisations in a VR-environment. The term can be understood as a generic term of '3D maps' and '3D volume maps' which are all 3D models. See also sec. 1.1.2. 1, 5, 7, 87, 90

3D volume map Additional to common representation formats, it can be represented in a 3D cartography environment as solid volumes which consist of quantitative information inside 3D space. See also sec. 1. 1, 2, 7, 83

AN *analysis approach* in this monograph. 45, 49, 52, 53, 55, 69, 79, 81, 82

CAD *computer-aided design*. 2, 3, 7, 11, 22, 26, 27, 29, 35, 36, 43, 70, 71, 73–75, 78, 89

DB *database* in this monograph. 14, 17, 22, 23, 26, 29, 49, 50, 53, 70, 71, 73–75, 78, 81

ER *entity relationship* diagram mainly used in connection with relational databases. 14, 23

FOSS *Free and Open Source Software*. 1, 2, 8, 9, 59, 72–74, 78, 79, 82–84

GCP *ground control points*. Reference points whose position is known in a corresponding coordinate system and can be clearly recognized in an image. 22, 23, 29, 35, 36, 59, 69, 70, 72

GIS *Geographic Information System*, a system for storing and manipulating digital geographical information. XV, 1–7, 9–12, 26, 27, 29, 33, 35, 36, 43, 45, 56, 71–74, 78, 79, 81, 83, 84, 86, 87, 89, 90

GPR *Ground Penetrating Radar*. 8, 11, 15, 21, 22, 33, 45, 49, 52, 83

GUI *graphical user interface*, mainly used in the context of software programs. 9, 74, 78

HM *Harris Matrix* in this monograph. 26, 70, 73

ID actually 'UID' for *unique identifier*. In this monograph it is used for identification numbers in context of databases and tables. 23, 26, 27

isosurface is a 2.5D surface in 3D space that represents the same value or value interval. 49, 52, 54, 56, 82, 84, 86

isovolume is a solid object representing a value range where the outer surface is built by the lowest range value. 54, 56, 57, 82, 84, 86

multipoint clouds can be handled as one single object for efficient graphical depiction to optimise the display of large point data sets, e.g. LAS-data ('Log ASCII Standard'. A LAS-file is an industry standard binary format for storing airborne Lidar data. Lidar is the abbreviation for 'light detection and ranging'. It is a radar-related method for optical remote measurement of atmospheric parameters using laser beams.) or TLS-data. 11, 29, 33, 39, 49, 73

polyhedra is the plural of *polyhedron* which is a 3D polygon (convex hull) in geometry. 78, 79, 81

RGB *red-green-blue*. 9, 15, 43, 55–57, 59, 68, 73, 82, 85

RQ *research question* in this monograph. V, 1, 7–13, 43, 45, 56, 69, 83–86

SfM *Structure from Motion*, a methodology for generating 3D point clouds out of digital photographs. 21, 23, 26, 27, 29, 33, 50, 55, 59, 69, 70, 72–75, 77–79, 82, 83, 85, 87, 90

SHP *shapefile*, originally an ESRI® vector file format which has been established GIS-wide (ArcGIS, 2018). 3, 29, 74

TLS *terrestrial laser scanner*. It is used for a stationary, optical measurement method that captures laser-based distance measurements in an automated sequence of quasi-equal sampling steps in the vertical and horizontal directions by extracting geometric information about the object's surface by creating a 3D point cloud. 11, 15, 21, 23, 26, 27, 29, 33, 56, 57, 59, 68, 69–72, 75, 77–79, 82, 83, 85, 87, 90, 97

voxel is a word combination of 'volume' and 'pixel' describing an extruded pixel in the third dimension. 1, 2, 4, 9, 33, 41, 43, 69, 77–79, 81–83, 86, 87

VR *Virtual Reality*. 1, 3, 7

VTK *visual tool kit*, an open source C++ graphics library that is particularly suitable for 3D computer graphics with a focus on scientific visualisation. V, 33, 43, 45–47, 54, 56, 57, 67, 79, 81, 82, 84, 87

WS *working step* in this monograph. 12, 15, 21–23, 27, 29, 31, 33, 35, 36, 43, 45, 49, 69–74, 77–79, 87, 90

www.ingramcontent.com/pod-product-compliance
Lightning Source LLC
Chambersburg PA
CBHW051302270326

41926CB00030B/4699